W9-DAT-390

African-American Children at Church

A Sociocultural Perspective

African-American Children at Church explores African-American socialization beliefs and practices, based on the findings of a unique, four-year study in a Baptist church in Salt Lake City, Utah. By combining the ethnographic approaches of anthropology with the detailed naturalistic observations of developmental psychology, Dr. Haight provides a rich description of actual socialization practices along with an interpretation of what those patterns mean to the participants themselves. Based on extensive interviews with successful African-American adults involved with children, this book begins with the exploration of adults' beliefs about socialization issues focusing on the role of religion in the development of resilience. Drawing from naturalistic observations of adult–child interaction, the book then describes actual socialization contexts and practices that may help to nurture competencies in African-American children. The text focuses on Sunday School and includes narrative practices and patterns of adult–child conflict and play. A final section describes how this research was used in the development of a preventive, educational intervention program for children.

Wendy L. Haight is Associate Professor of Social Work at the University of Illinois, Urbana–Champaign.

AFRICAN-AMERICAN
CHILDREN AT CHURCH

A Sociocultural Perspective

Wendy L. Haight
University of Illinois, Urbana–Champaign

CAMBRIDGE
UNIVERSITY PRESS

#46660854

PUBLISHED BY THE PRESS SYNDICATE OF THE UNIVERSITY OF CAMBRIDGE
The Pitt Building, Trumpington Street, Cambridge, United Kingdom

CAMBRIDGE UNIVERSITY PRESS
The Edinburgh Building, Cambridge CB2 2RU, UK
40 West 20th Street, New York, NY 10011-4211, USA
10 Stamford Road, Oakleigh, VIC 3166, Australia
Ruiz de Alarcón 13, 28014 Madrid, Spain
Dock House, The Waterfront, Cape Town 8001, South Africa

http://www.cambridge.org

First published 2002

Printed in the United States of America

Typeface ITC New Baskerville 10/13 pt.   *System* MagnaType 3.52 [AG]

A catalog record for this book is available from the British Library.

Library of Congress Cataloging in Publication Data
Haight, Wendy L., 1958–
African-American children at church : a sociocultural perspective / Wendy L. Haight.
p. cm.
Includes bibliographical references and index.
ISBN 0-521-79210-X (hb) – ISBN 0-521-00345-8 (pbk.)
1. African-American children – Religious life. I. Title.
BR563.N4 H33 2001
303.3′25′08996073–dc21

2001025952

ISBN   0 521 79210 x hardback
ISBN   0 521 00345 8 paperback

To Jim, Matthew, and Camilla

Contents

PART FOUR. CONCLUSION

Tables

Acknowledgments

I would like to thank a few of the many people who supported me throughout this project. Pastor France Davis, Mrs. Edith Hudley, and the adults and children at First Baptist Church were welcoming, Christian souls who patiently guided me toward a clearer understanding of their lives and perspectives. Peggy Miller, my longtime friend and colleague, generously discussed and advised on this project throughout its 10-year labor. Dean Jill Doner Kagle provided me with support and opportunity at a critical point in my own development. Julia Hough and Darcy Tromanhauser were careful and thoughtful editors. Carl N. Johnson provided a particularly extensive, insightful review of the final manuscript.

This study was generously supported by a National Academy of Education postdoctoral fellowship and by the University of Illinois School of Social Work.

PART ONE

OVERVIEW

CHAPTER ONE

Introduction

Religious beliefs can be central to children's healthy development. In the following narrative fragment, Mrs. Edith Hudley, a 73-year-old African-American, recounted to me her experiences as a 7-year-old child walking to a segregated school.

> The whites would be walking one way, and we'd be walking the other. They'd yell at us, "You dirty, black niggers! We hate you! We hate you!" I'd go to Mama and ask her, "Why do they hate us?" She'd always take me to the Bible. She taught me that God loves us all. God is the judge. She taught me not to take hate inside of myself. (Haight, 1998, p. 213)

Mrs. Hudley went on to explain that when we hate, we destroy that part of God which he left inside each of us when he created us. Thus, from Mrs. Hudley's perspective, she was not the victim of this story; rather, her taunters were (Haight, 1998).

As a scientifically educated developmental psychologist, my interest in African-American children's religious experiences emerged only gradually through repeated exposure to stories such as this one. As Mrs. Hudley spontaneously recounted her own experiences, I often wondered how children of any ethnicity could develop optimally within racist communities. As I listened more closely, it became clear that, for Mrs. Hudley, human development is rooted in spirituality, a perspective in which everyday human events are contextualized by strongly held and deeply felt personal beliefs about the meaning of life including an ultimate love, which all may receive, and an ultimate justice, to which all are accountable.

I first met Mrs. Hudley and the other individuals described in this book in the summer of 1991. My family had just moved from Illinois to Utah. Although my husband and I were very excited about our new jobs,

3

we also had many concerns about moving our biracial family to Salt Lake City. Our main reservation centered around how our children would develop within this relatively homogeneous context. Many miles from extended family and friends, we wondered where we would find a community in which to raise our family. Upon voicing our concerns, we were directed to "First Baptist Church" by a colleague.[1] Here, we were told, we would find acceptance and support, as well as many activities for children and families. Over the next four years, our family benefited greatly from my colleague's advice as we participated at First Baptist Church.

In describing my own involvement at First Baptist Church, I am contextualizing this book within an intellectual tradition that views all research, ultimately, as representing a perspective (e.g., Briggs, 1992; Denzin & Lincoln, 1994; Peshkin, 1991). In this instance, it represents my perspective on adults' socialization beliefs and practices, and children's participation within a complex community. As a parent, developmental psychologist, and professor of social work, I have personal and practical, as well as intellectual and professional, interests in the lives of African-American children. Although my perspective is disciplined by systematic ethnographic and developmental methods, it emerged from the particular questions that I knew to ask, the particular stories that others felt appropriate to tell me, and the ways in which I understood the stories that I heard and the practices in which I participated. It is my hope that this perspective may shed some light on children's development within an African-American community from which researchers, educators, social service providers, and others interested in promoting the development of all children may learn.

GOALS OF THE BOOK

The first goal of this book is to provide a more nuanced description of African-American adults' socialization beliefs and practices. Much of the existing literature describing the socialization practices of African-American adults is limited and negatively biased. For example, although research on teachers has been extensive, relatively little empirical research has highlighted the methods of African-American teachers, and positive portrayals are infrequent. Whether through omission, distortion, or negative portrayals, some researchers have conveyed the idea that African-American teachers are intellectually understimulating, interpersonally harsh, and ineffective (see Foster, 1995, for discussion). In

---

[1] To protect the privacy of the participants in this study, I will use the pseudonym "First Baptist Church" throughout this book, as well as pseudonyms for all individuals.

contrast, limited descriptions of African-American teachers nominated
as effective by other African-Americans present a picture of caring individuals dedicated to the children, families, and communities whom they
serve (Foster, 1994).

One explanation for such contrasting perspectives is the considerable
variation across cultural communities in adults' socialization beliefs and
practices. For example, "child-centered" beliefs and practices that prioritize children's individual needs and interests are typical within many
middle-class, European-American communities (e.g., Chow, 1994; Fung,
1994; Greenfield, 1994). Beliefs and practices more typical of middle-
class, Chinese communities prioritize children's mature and socially sensitive conduct (e.g., Chow, 1994; Fung, 1994; Miller, Wiley, Fung & Liang, 1997). Understanding how such diverse socialization beliefs and
practices relate to children's competence and well-being requires that
they be embedded within their broader sociocultural context (e.g., see
Göncü, 1999). This context includes the challenges and opportunities
encountered by adults in the larger society, for example, in relation to
employment, as well as their beliefs regarding attitudes and behaviors
that facilitate success, for example, showing respect to superiors. In this
book, I will systematically describe the socialization beliefs and practices
of African-American adults from this sociocultural perspective.

The second goal of this book is to contribute to our understanding of
children's development within an African-American community. Overall,
the number of articles in mainstream developmental journals pertaining
to African-American children is very small, and, indeed, decreased from
1970 to 1990 (Fisher, Jackson & Villarruel, 1998). Historically, develop-
mentalists, educators, and social service professionals have paid very little
attention to African-American children except when they pose social
problems such as educational underachievement, poverty, adolescent
pregnancy, drug use, and crime (see Fisher, Jackson & Villarruel, 1998;
Lee & Slaughter-DeFoe, 1995; Slaughter & McWorter, 1985). Hence, we
know relatively little about the contexts in which competencies emerge
in well-developing African-American children. In this book, I will
describe children's stable and changing patterns of participation with
adults and other children at church.

The third goal of this book is to provide a more nuanced description
of children's experiences within a religious community. The existing
empirical literature is also limited with regard to children's participation
within religious contexts, and it is negatively biased. Descriptions of children's participation within a European-American church (Zinsser, 1986)
and within a private, religiously based African-American school (Mehan,

Okamoto, Lintz & Wills, 1995) focus on practices that appear antithetical to children's development. Interactions between adults and children are characterized as highly structured and adult centered with a one-way flow of communication from adult to child. Literal meaning is privileged, and children are discouraged from questioning, speculating, or extending presented material. In this book, I will provide a detailed and contrasting description of the participation of adults and children in a range of activities at church.

The fourth goal of this book is to consider the implications of these patterns of socialization and participation for professionals involved in supporting children and their families. The absence of knowledge about the practices through which competencies emerge in well-developing African-American children, in conjunction with the existence of negative stereotypes, can be highly problematic for helping professionals. For example, speaking from her experience as an educator, Mary Smith Arnold (1995) asserts that too often teachers, social workers, counselors, and others view "at-risk" and "black" as interchangeable terms.

> I am deeply concerned that those who work with Black children be exposed to a range of images that represent the abundant variations of Black experiences in the United States. Too often the stereotypes and one-dimensional portraits paraded before us on society's vast channels of communication (television, print media, movies, schools, etc.) become the defining contours of the children we have been commissioned to serve . . . flat, narrow, negative images . . . impair our ability as professionals to see the strengths . . . (p. 146)

In this book, I hope to contribute to a fuller, more complex, and three-dimensional perspective of African-American adults and children. I will describe how this perspective informed the development of an intervention for African-American children. I also will consider the implications for educators involved in preparing university students to enter the helping professions.

A SOCIOCULTURAL PERSPECTIVE ON THE DEVELOPMENT OF RESILIENCY

This book focuses on religious practices that may promote the development of resiliency in African-American children. Investigators of resiliency use the concepts of risk and protective factors to understand how individuals like Mrs. Hudley have developed well despite profound, ongoing stress (e.g., Fraser, 1997; Masten, Best & Garmezy, 1991). In brief, risk factors such as poverty can increase the probability of onset, digression to a more serious state, or the maintenance of a problem condition. Protective factors such as positive relationships with adults in adolescence can moderate the effects of risk factors so that more positive developmental outcomes may occur (Fraser, 1997).

In this book, the development of psychological resiliency in children is conceived of as occurring through the dialectical processes of socialization and acquisition. In brief, socialization is the process by which adults structure the social environment and display patterned meanings for the child (Haight & Miller, 1993; Miller & Sperry, 1987; Wentworth, 1980). It is this process on which I focus in this book. Socialization may be direct, as when a pastor preaches a special children's sermon; or indirect, as when parents bring their own religiously oriented reading material into the home. Socialization may be intentional, as when a grandmother escorts her grandchild to Sunday School, or unintentional, as when a child observes her godmother engrossed in prayer. Acquisition is the process through which children interpret, respond to, and ultimately embrace, reject, or elaborate upon the social patterns to which they are exposed (Miller & Sperry, 1988; Wentworth, 1980). For example, adults alter the content and structure of their socialization messages in relation to individual children, and children adjust their understanding and behavior in relation to adults' socialization practices. For example, Sunday School teachers described the ways in which they influenced individual children's lives, but they also described how interactions with their young students enhanced their own understanding of the scriptures.

From this dialectical perspective, development occurs within a social context as children actively observe and participate with adults and peers in the routine, everyday practices through which culture is maintained and elaborated (see, e.g., Corsaro, 1996; Lave & Wenger, 1991; Rogoff, 1990). For example, children's spiritual belief systems emerge through their observations of, and increasingly complex participation in, cultural practices such as storytelling and verbal conflict with teachers and peers in Sunday School. This dialectical perspective reflects a movement in the field of human development away from defining developmental trajectories in universal terms, abstracted from the particular practices within which children develop, toward the identification and description of various kinds of expertise that emerge within particular cultural contexts (Rogoff, 1990).

Understanding and promoting resiliency within individuals, then, re-

quires that development be embedded within its sociocultural context.
From this perspective, the nature of risk and protective factors can vary
tremendously depending on the context of development. For example,
racism is a significant risk factor in the development of African-American
children (Garmezy, 1985), limiting opportunities for development and
undermining motivation, confidence, and self-esteem.

Children's spiritual belief systems, on the other hand, can be protective factors (Hill-Lubin, 1991; Werner, 1989). Spiritual belief systems
encompass ideas and feelings pertaining to a nonmaterial higher force
(Boykin, 1994) and address the meaning and purpose in life (Coles,
1995). Belief systems, including spiritual belief systems, are taken-for-
granted ideas about the nature of reality that provide a frame of reference within which individuals interpret experience and formulate goals
and strategies for living within the constraints of culture (Bruner, 1990;
Goodnow, 1988; Harkness & Super, 1996).

Scholars of black history and culture have argued, essentially, that
spiritual belief systems are protective factors for many African-
Americans. Spiritual belief systems have been portrayed as a common
cultural value (e.g., Boykin, 1994; Schiele, 1996), a strategy for coping
with adversity (Hale-Benson, 1987; Potts, 1996), and an agent of socialization (Brown, 1991) for African-Americans from the time of slavery
through the present (e.g., Hill-Harris, 1998; Lincoln, 1999; Riggs, 1997;
Smitherman, 1977; Sobel, 1988; Stewart, 1935). For example, spiritual
beliefs helped enslaved African-Americans find purpose and meaning, as
well as the strength to develop, despite extremely difficult lives. Indeed,
responding to evil and other challenges of life while remaining a moral
person was viewed as an important opportunity for spiritual
development.

> They might remain slaves in body for the rest of their lives, but they
> were free in ways their white masters might or might not be. Theirs was
> a freedom that could not be bought. This conviction provided blacks
> with an internal strength. It was not just an accommodation, a way to
> accept their status as slaves. It was a spiritual wisdom that became the
> core of their lives. External status, external appearances, aspects of
> personality, and the outer me did not share the eternal spirit. (Sobel,
> 1979, p. 117)

In twentieth-century North America, spiritual belief systems also have
been portrayed as a key factor in African-American families' abilities to
cope with and thrive despite stressful lives (Hale-Benson, 1987). For

example, in Maya Angelou's (1969) autobiography, the spirituality of African-American women sustains families. James Comer (1988) begins the biography of his mother, Maggie, at the doorway of a black Baptist church. Robert Coles (1995) describes children and families who call upon their rich spiritual traditions to deal with the trials of their own, everyday lives. For example, spirituality was an important tool on which African-American children relied to survive racial hatred during forced school desegregation. In the words of an 8-year-old North Carolina girl in 1962:

> I was all alone, and those people [segregationists] were screaming, and suddenly I saw God smiling, and I smiled. . . . A woman was standing there (near the school door), and she shouted at me, "Hey, you little nigger, what are you smiling at?" I looked right at her face and I said, "At God." Then she looked up at the sky, and then she looked at me, and she didn't call me any more names. (Coles, 1990, pp. 19–20)

Religious meanings also have been portrayed as a source of great creativity. As African-Americans have come to terms with the negativity of their situation, many have transformed it to create another view of reality (e.g., Angelou, 1969; Hale-Benson, 1987; Long, 1997; Smitherman, 1977). For example, it was the enslaved African who gave religious meaning to the concept of freedom; in other words, that to fully serve God one must have no other master. According to Charles Long (1997),

> The black community in America has confronted the reality of the historical situation as immutable, impenetrable, but this experience has not produced passivity; it has, rather, found expression as forms of the involuntary and transformative nature of the religious consciousness. (p. 28)

With few exceptions, however, social scientists, educators, and social service providers have been silent with respect to the role of children's spirituality in the development of resiliency. Despite a resurgence of interest in spirituality in the field of social work (e.g., Bullis, 1996; Canda & Furman, 1999; Pinderhughes, 1989; Sheridan, Bullis, Adcock, Berlin & Miller, 1992), very little attention has been paid to children's spirituality. Similarly, very little research exists within the fields of developmental psychology and education, although age-related changes in religious reasoning (see Oser, 1991) and faith development (Fowler, 1981) have received some attention. From the perspective of these disciplines, the most deeply meaningful spiritual experiences described by Mrs. Hudley, as well as by scholars of African-American history, are what Jacqueline Goodnow (1990) has called "homeless phenomena." There is literally no place for them within existing theories of human development (Hudley, Haight & Miller, in press).

Thom Moore (1991) offers an explanation for the neglect of religion by many social scientists and social service providers. Focusing on psychology, he points to a value base in which religiosity is equated with irrational thinking. He also describes the competing assumptions and intents of religion and social science.

> The knowledge foundation of the church, based on religious principles, is faith, while the knowledge base of psychology comes from scientific research. . . . The science of psychology studies human behavior, and when it is applied the intent is to change behavior. A church, on the other hand, is established to nurture the spiritual needs of an individual or individuals, and in the process has an impact on the social lives of the people involved. (p. 149)

Fortunately, there are some hints that the situation described above may be changing. For example, during in-depth interviews with mothers of young children, Cindy Clark (1995) explored the connections between children's beliefs in childhood myths, such as Santa Claus, the Easter Bunny, and the Tooth Fairy, and the developmental foundations of religious faith. In their edited volume, Karl Rosengren, Carl Johnson, and Paul Harris (2000) move toward a more complex portrayal of children's cognitive development – one that includes metaphysical and theological as well as rational experience.

THE AFRICAN-AMERICAN CHURCH AS A CONTEXT OF SOCIALIZATION

In this book, I contribute to these recent efforts to bring a fuller appreciation of children's religious experience to the fields of human development, education, and social work by exploring patterns of socialization and participation within an African-American church. Psychologists have characterized churches, in general, as potential contexts for the development of resilience (Garmezy, 1985; Maston, Best & Garmezy, 1991). Given its unique role within black communities, the African-American church may be an especially important context for the development of resilience in children. In many African-American communities the church is the only institution that is owned, managed, and supported by African-Americans (McAdoo & Crawford, 1991). Indeed, the black church has been described as the oldest, the most powerful, and the most influential African-American institution (e.g., Moss, 1988; Smitherman, 1977).

Throughout its history, the African-American church has played a significant role in the provision of social support and services (e.g., Franklin, 1969; Moore, 1991). For decades, scholars have elaborated upon the multifaceted roles of the African-American church in providing concrete aid and refuge in times of need. Historically, strong involvement in churches has been one of the means through which African-American families have coped with adversity (e.g., McAdoo & Crawford, 1991).

Consistent with these characterizations of the African-American church, many blacks consider the church to be second in importance only to the family (Moore, 1991). In a Gallup report on religion, 76% of African-Americans claimed church membership, and 94% said that religion was fairly important to them (as reported in Moore, 1991). Despite the unique significance of the African-American church, its role in the development of children has not been explored. As John Ogbu (1985) noted, "There are hardly any studies of the full role of the church in the transmission of competence [to black youth], but it is likely that the church does indeed play an important role" (p. 61).

Within the African-American church, Sunday School is a particularly significant context for children's socialization. Ella Mitchell (1986) observed that

> many a mature Black still remembers with pride an Easter recitation or a Christmas play which awakened his or her first conscious awareness of personal dignity and worth. . . . Perhaps the crowning contribution of the Sunday schools would have to be the tremendous percentage of Black adult church persons whose sense of identity with and commitment to Jesus Christ was evidenced and symbolized in a conversion experience during childhood or youth. Almost all of these were directly or indirectly the result of the love, concern and influence of teachers in the Sunday schools, and the joyous activities associated with this program. (p. 109)

Although Sunday School is an important part of the lives of many African-American children and youth, it has been virtually ignored in the mainstream developmental, educational, and social service literature. According to Diane Brown and Lawrence Gary (1991), the absence of research examining the role of Sunday School in the development of

African-American children represents "a glaring gap in the existing body of knowledge on African-American social and cultural life" (p. 423).

THE CASE: FIRST BAPTIST CHURCH

By design, the study reported in this book is rooted within one community, First Baptist Church in Salt Lake City, Utah. It attempts to understand, in-depth, the coherence and diversity of adults' socialization beliefs and practices, and children's emerging participation within this specific cultural context. It seeks to characterize, as opposed to simplify, the complexities of everyday life to obtain a more complete, accurate understanding of community members' points of view (Becker, 1996). In the long run, the complex and differentiated portrait emerging from this case-based research strategy can provide a basis for meaningful comparisons with other communities. In the short run, it will highlight and perhaps challenge culturally based assumptions about educational practices and social service interventions with children and families.

First Baptist Church is an important case for at least two reasons. First, the African-American community in Utah shares many similarities with African-American communities in other parts of the United States. For example, many African-American Utahns experience racial discrimination in employment, housing, education, and everyday social interactions (Coleman, 1981). The developmental literature, however, is virtually silent with respect to the impact of racism on children's development (Fisher, Jackson & Villarruel, 1998). This case allows for a close examination of socialization strategies that support adaptive functioning and educational achievement despite racial discrimination.

Second, the African-American Utahn community also has characteristics distinct from many other African-American communities. For example, the overwhelming majority of African-American Utahns find themselves within the religious as well as the racial minority. In contrast to the predominantly Baptist African-American community, most of the population of the state of Utah belong to the Church of the Latter Day Saints (whose members are commonly known as "Mormons"). Despite the diversity present across African-American communities, there remains an unfortunate tendency in some of the developmental, educational, and social service literatures to minimize such complexities. This case provides an important illustration of the adaptation and development of a particular African-American community in relation to a geographically and culturally distinct larger community.

THE ETHNOGRAPHIC–DEVELOPMENTAL STUDY

This book is based upon ethnographic and developmental materials collected over a 4-year period. It focuses on the practices, particularly storytelling, through which African-American Sunday School teachers and their students, aged from 3 to 15 years, construct personal meanings from an important cultural resource, the Bible. These observations are contextualized by multiple, in-depth interviews with the pastor, Sunday School superintendent, and Sunday School teachers. Practices and beliefs associated with Sunday School are further contextualized through description of key events occurring in the larger church community including yearly events such as Vacation Bible School, monthly events such as "youth emphasis" day, weekly events such as the pastor's sermons for children, a variety of other special occasions focusing on children, adult Sunday School classes, and weekly Sunday School teachers' meetings. Observations and interviews are further contextualized through historical and social background information obtained from a variety of local newspaper articles, historical documents, and church publications.

AN OVERVIEW OF THE BOOK

In chapter 2, I examine the significance of children's participation in African-American churches. It integrates a variety of materials from African-American religious and historical studies, literature, autobiographical accounts, clinical case studies, and theoretical and empirical research in the social sciences. This material suggests that Sunday School within the African-American church may be one important context for the development of resiliency in many African-American children and that storytelling may be an important activity in this process. Existing research has not, however, systematically described socialization practices and children's participation in practices such as storytelling within African-American churches.

In chapter 3, I outline a developmental–ethnographic research strategy for studying systematically children's socialization and participation in religious practices at First Baptist Church. This strategy reflects an important movement within the field of human development to combine ethnographic and developmental methodologies, particularly to illuminate the development of vulnerable children (see Jessor, Colby & Shweder, 1996), including vulnerable African-American children (Heath, 1996). A basic tenet of this multimethod strategy is that quantita-

tive and qualitative approaches to human development may be strengthened through their integration. As Linda Sperry and Doug Sperry (1996)
concisely described: "Quantitative and qualitative methods can be inter-
twined to consider both what happens developmentally and why. Specific
microlevel observations permit quantification of the regularity inherent
in everyday life, and ethnographic or qualitative techniques provide a
method for assessing what the regularity may mean" from the participants' perspectives (p. 444). In this study, I describe the regularities of
adult–child participation in religious practices, that is, how children and
adults interact together within Sunday School and other church
contexts – for example, how they tell stories together. I interpret the
meaning of regularities in practices through examination of the broader
cultural context, including adults' beliefs, for example, about the role of
storytelling in children's spiritual development.

In chapter 4, I provide an overview of the social and historical contexts
of the African-American Utahn community necessary to understand fully
adults' socialization practices and beliefs and children's participation at
First Baptist Church. In brief, First Baptist Church emerged in the 1890s
from a small "Baptist Prayer Band" comprised of African-Americans excluded from worshipping in white churches. It continues to be a center
of the local African-American community. Indeed, as one of the few
public institutions run by and for African-Americans, First Baptist
Church is viewed by many as a haven, one of the few contexts in which
they may interact with other African-Americans.

In chapter 5, I provide a fuller description of the individual Sunday
School teachers. It is perhaps with these esteemed members of the community that children have their most extensive, direct contact with adults
at church. An appointment to teach Sunday School is viewed as a great
privilege and responsibility. Sunday School teachers were viewed as spiritually mature and as critical influences on the lives of children. Many
Sunday School teachers held their positions for decades.

Chapter 5 also describes the children and their relationships with
their teachers. Appreciating the impact of culturally distinct socialization
practices on individual children requires exploration of the personal
contexts in which they occur. Throughout their childhoods at First Baptist Church, children repeatedly participate in storytelling, verbal conflict, and other practices with several individual teachers and many classmates. The impact of this participation on an individual child depends,
in part, on the participants' characteristics and relationships. For example, a story may take on significance not only because of the content of its

message, but because it is told by a respected teacher or favorite grandparent.

In chapter 6, I elaborate upon the broader framework of adults' socialization goals. To summarize, all adults placed the development of African-American Utahn children within a social and cultural context that they viewed as negligent toward African-Americans at best, and virulently racist at worst. The church was viewed as a unique context in which children learn about their heritage from other African-Americans who value and nurture them. Through the church, children are exposed to a hopeful, loving, and egalitarian interpretation of the Christian gospels. Children's emerging spirituality is perceived by adults as a lifeline, most importantly to eternal life through belief in Jesus Christ, but also as a healthy way of coping with racial hatred and other trials of everyday life. Accordingly, an important pedagogical goal of Sunday School articulated by adults was to help children to know and then to apply the Bible to their own lives. Storytelling was described as a central and deliberate educational tool in this process.

After this general background, I describe in chapters 7 and 8 the narrative practices in which children and teachers participated during Sunday School classes. The analysis of children's Sunday School classes suggests that storytelling is one important practice through which biblical texts are elaborated and related to children's everyday lives. Teachers and children in all Sunday School classes, from the kindergarten through the intermediate classes, regularly told stories together. The majority of these stories were initiated and led by the teachers. The children, however, were far from passive participants. They actively contributed through call-and-response sequences, responses to teacher questions, and their own spontaneous comments.

Consistent with the adults' emphasis on "knowing" the biblical text, teachers and children retold biblical stories. Consistent with adults' emphasis on relating these events to everyday life, teachers also told stories of personal experiences. These stories related past events from the narrator's life that paralleled the biblical text and typically featured the teacher, as protagonist. Teachers and children also told hypothetical narratives, a genre rarely described in the developmental literature. These narratives extended the biblical material by elaborating hypothetical examples of instances that explicitly suspended the details of the text or of reality as experienced by the participants. Hypothetical narratives allowed the participants to engage in play with the biblical text or concepts, discussing what might be or might have been, given the presented or altered circumstances. For example, in discussing with her 8- to 10-year-old children the miracle in which Jesus walked on water, Sister Justine suggested,

> Imagine . . . if you was just lounging on the beach and all of a sudden you took your shades off, looked up, and there was somebody and they were walking on water! (*Loud laughing from the children followed by a discussion of their own possible responses.*)

Hypothetical narratives typically featured children as the protagonists. These stories seemed to address teachers' concerns both with helping children to relate biblical concepts to their own lives and with doing so in a manner that preserved the privacy of individuals and families.

Cross-sectional data from kindergarten through intermediate classes suggest developmental changes as well as stability in children's participation in storytelling. Remarkably, even children in the kindergarten class participated in hypothetical narratives, but they participated in relatively few retellings of the biblical text. In this context, hypothetical events may be "easier" for young children to insert into an ongoing narrative than specific and sequenced details of complex events presented as historical facts.

When telling stories, teachers used a variety of devices to highlight significant points. Teachers in all classes frequently and explicitly stated that the biblical concepts or stories described in narratives were relevant to children's everyday lives and described with the children how they were relevant. These explicit devices, however, were more frequent in the kindergarten class. Specific narrative events also were highlighted through the use of figurative speech, the historical present, code switching, and role play, but figurative speech and role play were more frequently observed in classes for older children.

In chapter 9, I explore adult–child conflict at First Baptist Church to illuminate further adult–child relationships, and children's unique perspectives and reactions to routine practices in Sunday School. Knowledge of variation in patterns of adult–child conflict, while important in its own right, also has the potential to reduce confusion and misunderstandings when adults interact with children from different cultural communities in educational, social service, and other contexts. Analyses presented in chapter 9 indicate that adult–child conflict was a routine occurrence in Sunday School. Furthermore, serious adult–child conflicts typically were initiated by the children. The conflicts initiated by teachers tended to be playful teasing. A substantial proportion of the topics of conflicts initiated by both teachers and children were facts about the biblical text or lesson. Children, however, frequently initiated conflicts regarding interpretations of the relevance of biblical concepts to their own lives. Remarkably, even children in the kindergarten class occasionally initiated disputes with their teachers over such interpretations of biblical concepts.

In chapter 10, I describe a variety of activities that supported children's socialization through practices complementary to those observed in Sunday School. For example, midway through the Sunday morning worship service, the pastor invited children aged 10 and under to come down to the center of the sanctuary where they sat in a circle on the floor for the "children's sermon." In contrast to Sunday School, where the relationship between the child and biblical concepts typically was made at a personal level, the children's sermons typically linked children to the biblical concept at a cultural/historical level. For example, children's sermons included African folk tales and stories of famous African-Americans, which were then linked to biblical scriptures.

In chapters 11 and 12, I consider the relationship between research and practice. I describe how knowledge generated through this study informed the development of the "Computer Club," an intervention designed to support children's development and educational achievement. Consistent with ethnographic materials generated within other African-American communities (e.g., Williams, 1994), the pastor and other adults at First Baptist Church both prioritized educational achievement and identified school as problematic for many African-American children. In particular, children's computer literacy was identified as a specific area of need and one which the church members and I, in cooperation, could fulfill.

I then describe how experience acquired through my participation in the Computer Club led to empirical research addressing the complex issue of multicultural higher education. As the population of the United States becomes increasingly diverse, recruiting individuals from diverse cultural communities into social work, education, health care, and other helping professions is critical. Also critical is the development of effective multicultural education strategies. This issue is explored in chapter 12 through a short-term, longitudinal study of the varied responses of European-American undergraduate students to their participation as helpers at the Computer Club. Their responses anticipate the challenges faced by educators and social service professionals in incorporating into practice material such as that described in the body of this book.

In chapter 13, I provide an integrative summary, focusing on spiritual socialization as a protective factor and the implications for supporting the development of all children through our public schools and social services institutions. The picture that emerges of socialization and participation at First Baptist Church is both child-sensitive and growth-oriented. Adult–child interactions are growth-oriented in that they typically are adult-led, and they do prioritize knowledge of biblical text and mature conduct. Adults retain their status as respected leaders, setting and enforcing high standards for children's increasingly mature participation in culturally valued practices such as community worship. At the same time, socialization beliefs and practices are child-sensitive in that they consider children's emotional needs and relative immaturity. They also engage children's active participation through a variety of culturally specific communication practices such as call-and-response sequences, assertive questioning, and verbal conflict, and they draw upon a rich tradition of metaphor and story to enrich and relate biblical concepts to the joys and challenges of children's everyday lives.

CHAPTER TWO

The African-American Church and the Socialization of Children's Resiliency

In the following narrative fragment, Sister Justine and her class of 8- to 12-year-old students grapple with the complex question: What is the church?

> sj: Do you see what this lesson [Ephesians 4: 1–16] is all about? . . . The church is, is not just a building. What the church is, is not just comin' and putting in your money and sittin' in and listening to the choir. The church is the whole people. The church is us.
>
> TRANESE: Everybody.
>
> sj: The community. This is *us*. . . . How do you think Jesus wants this church to work? . . . He wants all of us to *do* something! We're not just supposed to come into this church and sit down! And just lo – ok! He wants us to do something. He gave us . . . gifts! . . . We all have certain gifts – and we're supposed to find out what they are . . . [What are we] supposed to use them for . . .
>
> JAVARIUS: [to] build the church.
>
> sj: [to] build the church! This boy is *sha–rp!* He's *o–n* it.

Sister Justine and the children define the church as a living community, as "us." Within this community, children are valued as resources and opportunities are created for their increasing participation. Every individual is treasured, everyone has gifts, and everyone has a responsibility to use those gifts for the common good. Historically, the value of children as resources within the African-American church may be best exemplified in the provision of educational opportunities. Indeed, the African-American church was the only place where children could receive a secular and religious education during and after slavery. Today, the provision of religious education and youth programs remain important services provided by the modern church to the African-American com-

munity (e.g., see McAdoo & Crawford, 1991). The value of children as
active participants is exemplified by children's multiple opportunities for
meaningful involvement, for example, in the children's choir, as ushers,
and as junior deacons and deaconesses (Mitchell, 1986).

In this chapter, I first will consider psychological and ethnographic
data suggesting that the church is an important context of participation
for African-American children. The literature on African-American history and culture provide a perspective on how and why the African-
American church gained its importance. I will discuss the church as a
context in which an oppressed people freely elaborated an alternative
system of beliefs that allowed them to maintain their humanity and
develop their creativity. Then, I will anticipate some of the beliefs that
children may acquire through their participation in church by highlighting some general aspects of African-American theology. Next, I will examine evidence that children generally do benefit from their participation
in the black church. Finally, I will consider specific socialization
practices – focusing in particular on narrative practices – within African-
American churches.

THE CHURCH AS A CONTEXT OF PARTICIPATION FOR AFRICAN-AMERICAN CHILDREN

A small body of evidence from a variety of African-American communities suggests that the contemporary black church remains an important and formative context for children's participation. Of 53 African-
American parents interviewed from North Carolina, 83% reported attending church with their children (Hurd, Moore & Rogers, 1995).
These parents emphasized a need to nurture their children's spirituality
and described how they attained considerable personal comfort and
guidance from participating in church-related activities. Similarly, Arnold (1995) reports from her interviews of 60 inner-city, African-
American mothers that they generally expressed a strong religious
orientation.

> A crucial component of the socialization process for Black families is
> the role of spirituality or the church. In most homes we visited, God was
> a real and present figure. Whether Jehovah's Witness, Muslim, or
> Christian, these homes had well-defined religious and spiritual prac-
> tices. The Bible was read, or attendance at Sunday school and church
> was a weekly occurrence. . . . Children were held accountable for their

participation in religious activities, such as choir practice or youth religious studies. (p. 54)

An emphasis on church and spirituality also is apparent in Kimberley Williams' (1994) ethnographic study of literacy development within a northern, urban, middle-class African-American community. This study included extensive, naturalistic, home observations of young children and their families. Williams noted frequent references to Sunday School activities and displays of Sunday School–related activities. In addition, children memorized and recited Sunday School poems, practiced writing and coloring Sunday School homework, and observed their parents reading the Bible. The children also listened to their parents' discussions about their own church-related activities, for example, writing reports for adult Sunday School and developing speeches to deliver in church.

Ethnographic descriptions of child rearing in rural, southern African-American communities, although not focused on the church and spirituality, also point to the church as a significant context of participation for children. Shirley Brice Heath (1983) documented stories told by very young children involving the church. For example, 2 1/2-year-old Lem recalled,

Way
Far now
It a church bell
Ringin'
Dey singing
ringin'
You hear it?
I hear it
Far now. (p. 170)

Linda Sperry (1991) described a multitude of church buildings, present even in very impoverished rural communities, and religious affiliation as an important part of life. Martha Ward (1971) listed two African-American Baptist churches as among the major elements of a small, southern community, and church services as a main event on Sundays.

THE CHURCH AS A CONTEXT FOR THE DEVELOPMENT OF AN ALTERNATIVE BELIEF SYSTEM

The African-American church may be important for children's development not only because of the social services and other concrete aids it supplies, but because of the unique belief systems elaborated within it. For more than 200 years, the African-American church has been a context in which an oppressed people have maintained and developed a culturally distinct, alternative identity and view of reality (e.g., Becker, 1997; Ellison, 1997; Frazier, 1964; Fulop & Raboteau, 1997; Hill-Lubin, 1991; Lincoln, 1999; Long, 1997; McAdoo & Crawford, 1991; Smitherman, 1977; Sobel, 1979; Wills, 1997). This alternative system of beliefs is not a simple imitation or derivation of European-American Christianity (Long, 1997), but evolved in relation to a distinct, African heritage, shaped by unique experiences in North America (Becker, 1997; Hale-Benson, 1987; Long, 1997; Smitherman, 1977; Sobel, 1979; Wills, 1997). For example, African-American Christian belief systems can trace some roots to Africa. Although often forbidden to practice openly their native religions, many enslaved Africans who were brought to North America were Muslim or practiced some form of traditional African religion. These meaning systems were particularly significant given that Christianity was not formally introduced to significant numbers of enslaved Africans until about 1760, and the conversion of slaves did not peak until after 1830 (Wills, 1997).

Over time, African belief systems were integrated into European-American, Christian spiritual belief systems. For example, this integration process is illustrated by the visionary experiences reported by nineteenth-century blacks and whites during Christian conversions. A content analysis of accounts of white and black visionary experiences reveals a number of common characteristics, likely reflecting a common Christian heritage (Sobel, 1979). For example, the individual begins in a low state, is saved by a cry to God for mercy, and is reborn. Black visionary experiences, however, also had a number of unique aspects that are traceable to West African belief systems. For example, central to West African spiritual belief systems was the concept of the essential being, "the little me" within the "big me." This "little me" was regarded as the true self that had existed before life and would continue after death. In narratives of black visionary experiences, it is the essential being, the "little me," who is brought to the brink of Hell, cries for mercy, is led to Heaven, and is reborn (Sobel, 1979).

The eventual integration and elaboration of African and European-American spiritual belief systems also occurred within a cultural context encompassing the complex and troubled relationships between blacks and whites in North America. To summarize, in the eighteenth and early nineteenth centuries, many blacks and whites shared a church life. At this time, Baptists (along with Quakers and Methodists) held strong antislavery feelings. Indeed, primary among Baptist beliefs is the equality of believers (Fitts, 1985). Belief in the spiritual equality of the races was so intense that these early European-American and African-American Baptists worshipped together as equals, and blacks even served as preachers. From about 1823 to 1844, when thousands of European-Americans joined Baptist churches, white Baptists became increasingly conformist and less concerned with opposition to the racist establishment (Sobel, 1979). Gradually, the rights of black Christians to participate fully and openly with white Christians was reduced; for example, blacks had to sit in the back or balcony, and they were not allowed to preach.

During this time, many African-American and European-American Christians found it increasingly difficult to tell a shared, religiously meaningful story. Although both black and white emancipationists continued to share a common belief that Christianity and slavery were incompatible, one prevalent European-American interpretation of Christianity suggested that slavery benefited Africans. In short, slavery allowed the "sons of Ham" to unlearn their heathenism through continuous labor for morally and spiritually superior white masters and mistresses. This view of Christianity stressed obedience and submission for African-Americans (Sobel, 1979). In contrast, the African-American interpretation of Christianity stressed freedom, the ultimate justice of God, and the equality of believers (Fitts, 1985). The view that religion and slavery were inconsistent and incompatible – that to fully serve God, one must have no other master – was a critical motivation for freedom (Lincoln, 1999). Indeed, much of the strategy for escape via the Underground Railroad was planned during religious gatherings. Black revolutionaries such as Nat Turner and Gabriel Prosser were devout Christians who saw their own enslavement as inconsistent with the freedom they believed a Christian life required.

The conflict between European-American and African-American interpretations of Christianity resulted in the eventual withdrawal of many blacks from white churches and the establishment of large numbers of independent black churches (Lincoln, 1999; Fitts, 1995). By 1865, more than 205 formal, separate black Baptist churches – some numbering thousands of parishioners – and many other less formal plantation congregations had been organized (Sobel, 1979). Although biracial churches continued to exist through the nineteenth century, the norm has remained through today for racially separate Christian churches (see Fitts, 1985; Wills, 1997).

In the eighteenth and nineteenth centuries, African-Americans also worshipped in underground settings, such as forests and remote cabins. These underground settings were particularly significant when the full participation of blacks in European-American churches was restricted and when plantation slave owners were reluctant to permit independent worship with black preachers in all-black settings (Fitts, 1985).

Into the twentieth century, the black church has remained a support for African-Americans' beliefs in freedom, justice, and equality. For example, the Southern Christian Leadership Coalition, led by Dr. Martin Luther King, Jr., and other southern black ministers, organized protests against segregation and voting restrictions in the 1950s and 1960s, using Ebenezer Baptist Church as the primary base of operations.

SOME GENERAL CHARACTERISTICS OF AFRICAN-AMERICAN THEOLOGY

Although it is beyond the scope of this book to describe the complexities of African-American theology, I would like to highlight several general characteristics of this meaning system and related practices that seem particularly relevant to children's resilience. First, African-American religion has been described as a pragmatic intertwining of the sacred and the material (Smitherman, 1977). Consistent both with a traditional African world view and with the experience of racism within the United States, a key to the African-American notion of spirituality is its importance in facilitating survival (Hale-Benson, 1987). African-American religion addresses specific human needs and experiences, and helps individuals to cope with the more traumatic aspects of human existence (Lincoln, 1999). For example, C. Eric Lincoln (1974) states that "it was mainly their dynamic and pragmatic religion which helped the slaves survive in their new environment" (p. 311). A more modern example is the nonviolent resistance of the civil rights movement, which put Christian beliefs such as nonviolence, love, and forgiveness into practice to end segregation and other forms of unequal treatment under United States law (Sobel, 1979). The pragmatic characteristics of African-American theology also are reflected in recent advice from the National Baptist Convention, U.S.A., Inc., to those developing programs of Christian education within black Baptist Churches:

> The concern of Christian education is to bring the gospel to bear upon human lives. . . . Our approach to Christian education . . . [is to] trans-

form the meaning of the message into active Christian service. . . . Of primary concern . . . [is] the day-to-day struggles which impact upon human lives. Such concerns focus in upon the very real issues of our humanity, such as, the family, jobs, politics, economics, sex, drugs, and secular education. (Bernstine, 1989, pp. 7, 34)

A second feature of African-American religion is an emphasis on community. Although numerous scholars have commented upon the centrality of community to African-American culture (e.g., Stack, 1974; Young, 1969), Janice Hale-Benson (1987) has articulated its religious underpinnings. She discusses a preoccupation in spirituals with the threat of loneliness and despair to disrupt the community of faith.

> I couldn't hear nobody pray,
> Oh, I couldn't hear nobody pray.
> Oh, way down yonder by myself,
> And I couldn't hear nobody pray. (p. 15)

According to Hale-Benson:

> The spirituals lamented the loss of community and [African-Americans] felt that this constituted the major burden. They [African-Americans] felt that the suffering was not too much to bear if you had brothers and sisters to go down in the valley and pray with you. (p. 15)

The significance of the community of faith to children's survival is clear. For example, Mitchell (1986) describes the emphasis on relationships extending from the nuclear family throughout the entire slave community:

> Bereft of other treasures, one treasured relationships. . . . The whole [slave] quarter was a collection of extended family kin who loved the young and accepted responsibility for them. (This pattern has not died . . .) . . . children were loved and taught by that same impressive cadre of neighbor/relatives. What these surrogate parents taught was penetrating, because their love made of them significant personages or influences. (p. 102)

A third feature, viewed by some as a cornerstone of contemporary African-American theology (see Mitchell, 1986; Hale-Benson, 1987), is the belief in the inherent dignity and worth of each individual. Each child, each individual, is special because s/he was created by God (Hale-Benson, 1987). In her discussion of the role of faith in the development of self-esteem, Mitchell (1986) notes that this "lesson was learned so well that despite the ravages of dehumanization, very few slaves ever gave up and fully accepted the servile image thrust upon them" (p. 101). According to Leroy Fitts (1985), black Baptist preachers "discovered in the 'Fatherhood of God' and 'brotherhood of man,' a . . . concept of human freedom and dignity" (p. 44). The belief that God recognizes African-Americans as equal to European-Americans – each personally as one of his children – has given many the inner resolve to "keep on keeping on" (Hale-Benson, 1987). In the words of one nineteenth-century African-American woman:

> Many think, because your skins are tinged with a sable hue, that you are an inferior race of beings; but God does not consider you as such. He hath fashioned you in his own glorious image, and hath bestowed upon you reason and strong powers of intellect. . . . It is not the color of the skin that makes the man, but it is the principles formed within the soul. (Stewart, 1935, pp. 4–5)

SPIRITUAL BELIEFS AS A PROTECTIVE FACTOR

The social science literature, although sparse, also suggests that children's spiritual beliefs can be a source of resiliency. During interviews, some children in the fourth and fifth grades reported the use of faith in coping with everyday stressful situations (Britt, 1995). Emmy Werner (1989), who conducted a 32-year longitudinal study of at-risk children on Kauai, Hawaii, observed that many resilient individuals pointed to their religious beliefs and practices as providing stability and meaning in their lives, especially in times of hardship. Such faith can give resilient children a sense of coherence, a conviction that their lives have meaning, and a trust that things will work out in the end. Sarah Moskovitz (1983) concluded from her study of child survivors of the Nazi Holocaust that a sense of hope for the future rooted in religious faith enabled children to love and behave compassionately toward others in spite of the atrocities they had experienced.

Some evidence also exists from a variety of autobiographical, clinical, and social scientific reports that culturally distinct spiritual beliefs, maintained and elaborated within the context of the black church, have provided African-Americans with an alternative world view which can, indeed, be a source of resilience and creativity. In her examination of the grandmother–grandchild relationship as portrayed in autobiography, Mildred Hill-Lubin (1991) identifies spiritual socialization as a central function. The grandmother is portrayed as powerful, determined to endow her offspring with the values that will allow them to develop despite a hostile, racist world. For example, in Maya Angelou's (1969) autobiography, she recounts her observation of a group of impoverished white girls trying to humiliate her grandmother. The girls called the grandmother names, and one even stood on her hands to show that she was not wearing underwear. Although the young Angelou was extremely angry, her grandmother stood, prayed, and sang. In the end, her grandmother was happy: The spirit had possessed her and she had triumphed. Then she bent down and touched her granddaughter, just as the mothers of the church lay hands on the sick and afflicted. As Hill-Lubin interprets the story, it was through this symbolic act that the grandmother passed on to her granddaughter the power, strength, and spirit of her life.

The clinical literature also suggests the importance of religious beliefs as a source of resiliency for African-American children. For example, Robert Coles (1990) talked with African-American children from newly desegregated schools in the South. As they talked and drew pictures about God, the sense of self-worth, comfort, and hope children had from their religious beliefs was clear. For example, an African-American girl with difficulties at school said, "I keep my mouth shut here in school. . . . They're [i.e., teachers are] blind when it comes to us" (p. 176). She then went on to draw a picture of Jesus healing the blind man. She described some individuals within Jesus' lifetime as viewing him as "dumb" and "stupid" but went on to explain that he was both powerful and compassionate. "He'd see someone," she said, "and he's stumbling and he might be blind, and Jesus could feel just the way the man felt, blind Himself, and He'd get right in there, try to get the man back to seeing" (p. 179).

The comments of another African-American girl with whom Coles (1990) talked highlight the capacity for comfort through spirituality. This child, recently made parapalegic in a car accident that killed her father, noted: "I hums to the Lord, and I sings to Him. There'll be a day, I just tells him of my 'down-and-out blues'" (p. 200).

Empirical studies focusing on African-American communities suggest that adults view the church and spirituality as significant factors in their own abilities to cope with stressful life events. In a national survey of

African-Americans, prayer was most frequently reported as the coping response of greatest efficacy in dealing with serious personal problems (Neighbors et al., 1983, as cited in Potts, 1996). During interviews, African-American cancer survivors spontaneously referred to spiritual beliefs and practices as central to their abilities to cope with cancer (Potts, 1996). Diane Brown and Lawrence Gary (1991) found in a survey of 532 urban African-Americans adults that more than half answered "often" or "very often" to the statements: "Ideas I have learned from religion sometimes help me understand my life" (66%), "I feel that the church or religion helps me in getting ahead in life" (56%), and "The religious beliefs I learned when I was young still help me" (74%).

There also is some empirical evidence of a relationship between African-Americans' involvement in church and positive functioning. A variety of studies have linked African-American adults' religious beliefs and involvement with an array of positive psychosocial outcomes, including self-esteem, and with the ability to cope successfully with a wide variety of stressful conditions (Ellison, 1997). In addition, church involvement is associated with relatively good educational achievement. Self-reports of church involvement were positively related to educational attainment among African-American adults (Brown and Gary, 1991). Brown and Gary's survey of the urban African-American adults revealed a positive relationship between educational attainment (number of years completed in school) and religiosity. This positive relationship between educational attainment and religiosity has since been replicated in a sample of 215 adults who attended African-American churches (Hill-Harris, 1998). In an interview study of 218 African-American, urban, male adolescents, youths who left high school before graduation and were not employed but who attended church had relatively low levels of alcohol and drug abuse (Zimmerman & Maton, 1992).

There is some evidence that children may indirectly enjoy the positive effects of religious involvement through the enhanced functioning of their parents. A central part of religious affiliation often involves commitment to a set of beliefs and values about how children should be reared (Clayton, 1988; Heath, 1983). In her study of middle-class, European-American mothers, Angela Wiley (1997) documented a relationship between mothers' religious beliefs and the extent and ways in which they regulated the behavior of their 2- to 3-year-old children at home. Within a low-income community, mothers' frequent church attendence was positively associated with their positive parenting behavior (Slesinger, 1981). Within an urban, African-American neighborhood, the psychological well-being of mothers was positively related to church attendence (Thompson & Ensminger, 1989).

SPIRITUAL DEVELOPMENT THROUGH STORY TELLING

Empirical researchers have not yet considered the culturally specific practices through which children develop spiritual beliefs within African-American churches. The oral tradition, however, is a highly valued component of African-American, Christian education that is thought to be central to the development of an adequate belief system (Mitchell, 1986). The oral tradition, including stories, proverbs, and songs, was brought by Africans to North America and then elaborated within the independent, African-based culture of the slave quarters and its underground church (Smitherman, 1977). Even when literate, slaves preferred the songs and prayers from their oral tradition over those from hymn and prayer books (Levine, 1997). After emancipation, the new emphasis on formal education, including reading and writing, did not take the place of the oral tradition in deeper matters, such as the development of an adequate belief system and coping with oppression (Hale-Benson, 1987). Today, the oral tradition remains an important vehicle for socialization (Smitherman, 1977).

Within the African-American oral tradition, storytelling has been described as particularly significant to the development of children. Hill-Lubin (1991) describes the use of stories by African-American grandmothers to teach their grandchildren strategies for survival and living fully. Williams (1994) characterizes narratives as an antidote, a corrective tool for socialization within African-American families. According to Kathryn Morgan (1989):

> This was our folklore and it was functional. It was the antidote used by our parents and grandparents and our greats to help counteract the poison of self-hate stirred up by contradictions found in the home of the brave and the land of the free. . . . They served the purpose of diminishing feelings of racial inferiority imposed on us as children. (pp. 296, 298)

According to Henry Louis Gates (1989):

> Of the cultural forms that emerged from their complicated historical process, only black music-making was as important to the culture of African-Americans as has been the fine art of storytelling. . . . Telling

ourselves our own stories – interpreting the nature of our world to
ourselves, asking and answering epistemological and ontological questions in our own voices and on our own terms – has as much as any
single factor been responsible for the survival of African-Americans and
their culture. . . . The values that we cherish and wish to preserve, the
behavior that we wish to censure, the fears and dread that we can barely
confess in ordinary language, the aspirations and goals that we most
dearly prize – all of these things are encoded in the stories that each
culture invents and preserves for the next generation, stories that, in
effect, we live by and through. (p. 17)

Despite the significance of storytelling to African-American culture,
the empirical literature is sparse with regard to the occurrence of narration between African-American adults and children. Several ethnographic studies have described the emergence of narrative skills in very
young African-American children (Heath, 1983; Sperry & Sperry, 1996;
Williams, 1994). These studies indicate that young African-American
children participate in storytelling with adults and that sociocultural factors influence the form and function of this participation. However, very
little research has described narration with school-aged African-
American children, or within the context of the black church.

CONCLUSION

In summary, the church can be an important context for the socialization
of resiliency in African-American children through the development of
an alternative system of spiritual beliefs and practices. The oral tradition,
particularly storytelling, has remained a central practice within the
church and the larger African-American community. With respect to the
socialization of African-American children, storytelling has been characterized as an antidote to the self-hate stirred up by racism.

Despite the centrality of the church in the lives of many African-
Americans, little empirical research exists describing adults' spiritual
beliefs and socialization practices, and children's participation within the
church. Such research, however, is highly significant to social service
providers and educators seeking to enhance the development of African-
American children. From the perspective of resiliency research, intervention strategies should be based on naturally occurring processes that
facilitate development. Effective prevention strategies focus on strengthening protective factors and lessening risk factors. According to Werner
(1989), intervention can be conceived of as an attempt to shift the bal-

ance from vulnerability to resiliency by decreasing exposure to risk factors, or by increasing the number of available protective factors in the lives of vulnerable children. From this perspective, effective prevention and intervention includes the identification and enhancement of protective factors within particular communities.

CHAPTER THREE

Research Strategy

> As everyone knows, in science, as in life, two hands (measuring and interpreting, abstracting and exemplifying) are usually better than one.
>
> Shweder, 1996

The research strategy employed in this study reflects an emerging interest in the integration of developmental and ethnographic methods. The intent of such methodological pluralism is to strengthen both developmental and ethnographic approaches in order to better understand development in a variety of sociocultural contexts (see Jessor, Colby & Shweder, 1996), including African-American communities (e.g., Heath, 1996). Developmental methods include the systematic, often microscopic, description of children's participation in everyday activities and changes in participation over time. Ethnographic methods include the interpretation of the meanings of social behavior from participants' perspectives through analyses of a broader context of beliefs and practices. Thus, the intertwining of developmental and ethnographic methods allows both the identification of the regularities inherent in everyday life and an interpretation of what such regularities may mean to the participants themselves (Gaskins, Miller & Corsaro, 1992; Sperry & Sperry, 1996).

A developmental–ethnographic strategy increasingly is recognized as critical for understanding children from diverse cultural communities (e.g., Heath, 1996, 1983; Miller, 1982; Ogbu, 1974; Philips, 1983), including children who grow up in contexts that place them at risk (e.g., Jessor, Colby & Shweder, 1996). Moore (1991) argues that an ethnographic approach is particularly important when those involved – the children, the researchers, and the professionals – come from different communities. The ethnographic approach is a "dialectical, or feed-back (or interactive–adaptive) method" (Hymes, 1982) in which data, research questions, and analytical categories interact as the study evolves. Incorporating such ethnographic methods into more traditional developmental approaches forces professionals and researchers to understand the meaning of observed behavior from categories emerging from the community being studied, not the culture of the professional or the researcher.

For example, in this study, ethnographic analyses of adult participants' beliefs about the centrality of storytelling as a pedagogical tool inspired a developmental analysis of regularities in the ways in which adults actually told stories with children ranging in age from 3 to 15 years. Existing research from other contexts suggested that stories of personal experience would be critical. Our developmental analysis, however, revealed that "hypothetical narratives," a much less studied type of story, were as prevalent as stories of personal experience in adult–child interactions. These observations, in turn, motivated a more detailed analysis of adult beliefs about the functions of particular types of stories in the context of Sunday School.

More generally, a developmental–ethnographic approach is *necessary* to context-specific conceptualizations of development. Recently, scholars have characterized development as a process of children's increasing participation with adults and peers in the routines and communicative events through which culture is maintained and elaborated (e.g., Corsaro, 1996; Lave & Wenger, 1991; Rogoff, 1990). There has been a movement away from defining developmental sequences or trajectories in universal terms, abstracted from the particular practices within which children develop, toward the identification of various kinds of expertise that emerge within particular cultural contexts, and charting developmental progress in relation to these locally defined goals or types of expertise (Rogoff, 1990).

For example, at First Baptist Church, active participation in the communal worship of God is an important socialization goal. Over time, children increasingly participate in, and even shape, worship services. As toddlers, they may sit through worship services with adults for up to 2½ hours with encouragement to clap their hands, sing, or pray when appropriate. As preschoolers, they also may participate in special events, such as Christmas programs, and in groups, such as the children's choir. During middle childhood and adolescence, children are given increasing

responsibilities as ushers and through leading devotions as junior deacons and deaconesses.

METHOD

In this chapter, I will introduce my developmental–ethnographic study
of children's religious socialization. Additional details will be provided in
subsequent chapters.

Research Site

From 1991 to 1995, I engaged in ethnographic and developmental research within First Baptist Church, a community of approximately 374
members, and among the largest African American churches in the state
of Utah. First Baptist Church is located in a downtown neighborhood
which is relatively diverse for Salt Lake City (31% ethnic minorities).
Since 1966, the church has been housed in a simple, brick, A-frame
building surrounded by a parking lot and small, carefully tended lawns
and gardens. The upstairs consists of a sanctuary where Sunday services
are held, the pastor's office and adjacent church office, and a small
meeting room. In the basement are a large meeting room used for social
events, Vacation Bible School, and other large gatherings; a kitchen and
serving area; and a variety of smaller rooms primarily used for Sunday
School classrooms. In chapter 4, I will elaborate upon the social and
historical contexts of First Baptist Church.

The Sunday School Staff

The Sunday School staff at First Baptist Church included the pastor, the
superintendent, and four teachers.

The Pastor

There has been little, if any, question about the central role of the
African-American preacher in the black church and community (Becker,
1997; Du Bois, 1961; Johnson, 1955; Moss, 1988). For generations, the
pastor has been a primary source of hope and inspiration for African-
Americans. Pastor Daniels, an articulate man in his mid-forties at the
time of the study, fits the picture of a charismatic, energetic leader. He
has served as full-time pastor of First Baptist Church since 1974, longer
than any other Baptist pastor in the history of Utah (Davis, 1997). Pastor
Daniels was raised in a large family in a rural Alabama county populated

mostly by sharecroppers. He came to Salt Lake City to attend graduate school at a local university where he earned a master's degree in communications. He currently serves as an adjunct professor of ethnic studies.

Pastor Daniels and his wife have three grown children and a young grandson. His commitment to every child in the church was noted in the church history (Church Historical Committee, 1976), which indicated that under his leadership, "a Young People's Department was initiated, along with a Youth Church, which served to activate and attract the Youth in greater numbers." His interest in children also was reflected in his everyday interactions as he greeted each child by name and with a handshake or hug. He also routinely led the closing discussions of Sunday School; conducted the "Children's Service," a story or discussion for children aged 10 and under during the regular Sunday morning worship services; and "blessed" the new babies. He often was on hand during church activities focusing on children, such as field trips to the local water park, group meetings, and choir rehearsal. He also visited regularly the schools of children within his congregation to teach African-American culture and history. Indeed, family members of children experiencing difficulties at school sometimes contacted Pastor Daniels to act as an advocate for their child.

The following fragment is from a poem dedication written by 12-year-old Mamie and reproduced in the program for Pastor Daniels's 20th anniversary as pastor. This young girl, dying from lung disease, captured the encouragement and kindness many children associate with Pastor Daniels:

> Rev. [Daniels] once said that he was glad that people really couldn't see him. He said that people only see the outside, the skin, the clothes, the earthly vessel. Don't judge what you can not see! The inside, the real deal, the person, the heavenly treasure! Rev. [Daniels] shares his heavenly treasures: his being born again. With his caring heart he shows that he knows Jesus. Rev. [Daniels] also said that if you have found the light, let it shine. God only knows how many dark places Rev. [Daniels] has lightened up. . . . So to my friend . . . for 12 years of . . . kindness and support, I dedicate this poem to you.

The Superintendent

Brother Brown was a native of rural Tennessee who had served as the superintendent of Sunday School at First Baptist Church for more than 20 years. As superintendent, he called Sunday School to order every Sunday promptly at 9:30 with devotions. He frequently functioned to keep order in the Sunday School and instructed the children on proper church behavior. He worked as a librarian at a local university. Although he had no children of his own, Brother Brown helped to raise a nephew who lived with him for several years.

The Teachers

Sister Katherine taught the kindergarten class of 3- to 6-year-olds. She is a native of Alabama, in her mid-thirties, who relocated to Salt Lake City approximately 15 years prior to this study because of her husband's employment. A homemaker and mother of three children, Sister Katherine had a quiet, loving, and slightly humorous manner of interacting with young children. Young children in her Sunday School class clearly were comfortable: they talked, sang, and sat on or next to Sister Katherine. After class, Sister Katherine always provided candy treats.

Sister Patrice taught the primary class of 6- to 8-year-olds. She was in her early sixties and the mother of two grown children. She worked with the elderly as a practical nurse. The great-granddaughter of a Pullman porter working out of Salt Lake City, Sister Patrice had been a member of First Baptist Church all of her life and a Sunday School teacher for 45 years. She had a serious and respectful manner of interacting with children. She allowed the beginning readers painstakingly to read aloud their Sunday School lessons and helped them to complete their written assignments. She described her students as "sensitive," with "tender minds," and showed enormous patience when conducting her classes.

Sister Justine taught the junior class of 8- to 12-year-olds. She was in her late thirties, a descendant of Utah pioneers who also grew up attending First Baptist Church. She had a teenage daughter and two step children, and had always worked in some volunteer capacity with children. At the time of the study, she was the director of the Salt Lake City African American Dance Company, an amateur group of approximately 30 children from First Baptist Church who performed at the arts festival and other local events and aspired to tour Africa. Sister Justine had been teaching Sunday School "on and off" for about 7 years. Her manner of interaction with the children was engaged and humorous. Children responded to her with careful attention and frequent laughter.

Sister Ima taught the intermediate class of 12- to 15-year-olds. She was a native of rural North Carolina who moved to Salt Lake City approximately 20 years prior to the start of the study. In her mid-forties, Sister Ima was the mother of a teenage daughter. She had been teaching Sunday School for 14 years and junior high in the public schools for 23 years.

She was particularly insightful in dealing with issues facing her students at school, such as developing appropriate study habits and dealing with peer pressure. Sister Ima's manner with the children was serious and accepting.

I will provide additional information about the teachers in chapter 5.

The Children

In describing children's responses to biblical texts, Sister Katherine stressed the children's diversity:

> Each child relates to everything different because of what that child is going through. . . . It's the same thing with me. OK. That [Bible] story is important to me, but it may not be that significant to my sister or brothers.

Aside from their common African-American heritage, the children of First Baptist Church varied greatly in their life experience and personalities. During the time of my observations, a total of 75 children, ranging in age from 3 to 15 years, participated in Sunday School classes. Children attended different schools, including a variety of public and parochial schools in the Salt Lake valley. Some children were excellent students at the top of their classes, others were failing. Children's family structures also varied: some were raised by single grandmothers, others had traditional two-parent families. Guardians' income and educational levels ranged from working class to professional. Despite their differences, most children interacted freely and enthusiastically with one another during church activities.

Other Community Members

To help place First Baptist Church within a larger community context, an abbreviated interview also was conducted with a principal of a local elementary school and former member of the state board of education. Although she was not involved directly with the children in Sunday School, she was a member of First Baptist Church. She was interviewed regarding the problem of underachievement in African-American youths.

Sunday School Classes

On any given Sunday during my observations, there were anywhere from 8 to 13 children attending the kindergarten class, from 2 to 8 attending the primary class, from 7 to 18 attending the junior class, and from 3 to 8 attending the intermediate class. Typically, attendance was lowest in the intermediate class. The pastor and teachers viewed the drop-off in children's attendance during adolescence as an issue faced by most churches. The pastor explained that children in early and middle childhood are brought to Sunday School by relatives. As they get older and can begin to exercise some choice in the matter of Sunday School attendance – as well as experience competing social and cultural opportunities – attendance drops off. As young adults, attendance once again increases as individuals begin to form their own families and gain perspective on the value of Sunday School.

Kindergarten and Primary Classes

Due to space constraints, children in the kindergarten and primary classes shared a single room, and the noise levels sometimes were high. Initially, children in the two classes assembled at separate tables with separate teachers. During this time, children typically began with a group reading of a formal, written lesson from their Sunday School booklets, published by the Sunday School Board of the National Baptist Convention, U.S.A., Inc. During and following this reading, teachers posed questions to the children regarding the text and its application to everyday life. Following this group reading and discussion, the children worked individually on the weekly assignment from their booklets. For kindergarten children, the assignment usually involved cutting, pasting, and coloring. For the primary children, the assignment typically involved traditional, school-type worksheet activities, such as "fill-in-the-blanks." After this formal lesson, the kindergarten and primary children assembled together on a rug to participate in active, enthusiastic group singing and movement games.

The singing and movement games were a unique feature of the younger children's classes. They were not part of the older children's classes. By the age of 8 years, children were expected to sit through Sunday School and the following 2-hour worship service without the benefit of such physically active play.

Junior Class

The junior class occupied a small basement classroom. The walls were covered with various religious murals, as well as children's artwork. Children assembled with their teacher around a table. Classes began with an orientation to the lesson in which Sister Justine asked the children to identify the book in the Bible from which the lesson was derived, and the scripture chapter and verses. Following this orientation, classes continued with a scriptural reading. Children took turns reading the formal, written lesson from their Sunday School booklets with Sister Justine providing corrections. These lesson booklets were also published by the Sunday School Board of the National Baptist Convention, U.S.A., Inc. Bible passages were printed in the King James translation. Because this translation is difficult to understand, Sister Justine procured "Good News" Bibles, which she and the children read along with the King James translation. As Sister Justine explained to the children, "The Good News Bible is translated into modern words. Words that we are used to using. . . . So we get a better understanding."

Following the scriptural readings, classes continued with a discussion of the passage. Then the students participated in a variety of activities, including visiting the home of a sick member, or providing some service to the church. Occasionally, children completed written assignments formatted like those of traditional elementary school classrooms, such as fill-in-the-blanks.

Children in the junior class enjoyed relatively more games and competitions than did the children in the other classes. For example, the children participated in a competition involving naming, in order, the books of the old and new testaments. Sister Justine explained to the children that this game would help them to find scripture passages quickly. The game quickly became a favorite, as illustrated by 10-year-old Javon's performance below. Sister Justine had announced that first through third places were "out" for the new testament, and suggested that the class members could continue with the game if "anyone else feels brave enough to try it." Javon announced, "I want to come in fourth." She then stood with her back to the blackboard on which were listed the books of the new testament. She looked out at her classmates and recited from memory:

> JAVON: "Matthew, Mark, Luke, John, Romans, Acts, first and second Corinthians, Galatians, Ephesians, Philippians, Colossians, first and second Thessalonians, first and second Timothy, Titus, Philemon, Hebrews, James, first and second Peter, first, second, and third John, Jude, Revelation."
> SISTER J: "Go girl!!" (*clapping*)
> YOUNGER CHILD: Wow!
> SISTER J: OK. Javon is number 4!

Sister Justine responded to Javon's feat of memory with clear and enthusiastic approval.

Intermediate Class

The intermediate class also occupied a small, basement classroom. The students and Sister Ima assembled around a table facing a chalkboard. The class typically began with an opening prayer during which the members stood around the table, holding hands, as Sister Ima prayed aloud. Before class, Sister Ima outlined on the chalkboard the key points of the lesson, which were taken from the Sunday School booklet. The formal lesson began as Sister Ima went over the outline, noting the lesson objectives, the scriptures to be studied, and the main points of each section of scripture. Her objective, as explained to the children, was to help them learn to study so that they could pursue their Bible studies independently. Typically, the children then took turns standing to read the lesson scriptures. During and after the reading, the scriptures were explained, discussed, and related to everyday experiences familiar to the children. Following the lesson was an activity, often involving writing or drawing in pairs or small groups.

Children in the intermediate class did relatively more drawing than did the children in the other classes. Sister Ima frequently asked them to "visualize" an action as it occurred within the biblical stories, sometimes following this up by asking children to actually draw the story. For example, during their study from the book of Genesis, the children drew "God's creations," adding elements (e.g., water, land, plants, animals, people) each week over a period of several weeks.

Procedures

Entering and Sampling the Sunday School Classes

After participating with my family at First Baptist Church for approximately one year, I approached Pastor Daniels about conducting a systematic research project. We discussed a project that would describe the adults' socialization beliefs and practices and children's participation at church. We also outlined a research strategy and identified a number of key informants and contexts for children's spiritual socialization. Then Pastor Daniels introduced the project to the teachers during the weekly Sunday School teachers' meeting. He explained to the teachers our interest in describing Sunday School for professionals and researchers involved with children. Teachers generally embraced the plan and welcomed me into their classrooms.

During the first several Sunday School classes in which I participated, I explained to the children that I wanted to learn more about their Sunday School and about their thoughts about God and Jesus. This particular learning objective was not unique to me, but shared by a number of adults at First Baptist Church. Indeed, children in the junior and intermediate classes were aware of the weekly Sunday School teachers' meeting in which teaching children was a central focus. On a number of occasions during the juniors' Sunday School class, Sister Justine explicitly referred to the weekly teachers' meeting, which she and I both attended.

I also explained that, as part of my learning, I wanted their permission to tape record the classes. Tape recording was not an unusual occurrence at the church. Recordings of church services and other gatherings regularly were made for those who could not attend in person, such as the elderly or ill "shut-ins." I received from the children their permission to record the classes, as well as a number of enthusiastic offers to sing, recite, or comment directly into the tape recorder. During the first several sessions, I allowed children to perform into the tape recorder prior to and following Sunday School class. Interest in the tape recorder then faded fairly rapidly.

I obtained written permission from the pastor and the teachers to visit and audio tape Sunday School classes. In addition, the project was described in the church bulletin circulated on Sundays, and any adults with questions, suggestions, or concerns were invited to contact the pastor or me.

Sunday School Observations

I was a participant observer in Sunday School classes over a 3-year period. Sunday School classes were held immediately prior to regular church services, and lasted for approximately 1 hour. Ten Sunday School classes each were audiotaped in the kindergarten class for 3- to 6-year-olds, the primary class for 6- to 8-year-olds, the junior class of 8- to 12-year-olds, and the intermediate class of 12- to 15-year-olds. I also took detailed notes during the classes. At the time of the observations, I was a regular participant at First Baptist Church and familiar to the teachers and children. During the Sunday School classes, I participated as appropriate, for example, occasionally reading scripture or helping the teacher with projects, but did not attempt to influence the unfolding of the activities and interactions.

Audiorecordings of all classes were transcribed verbatim by me soon
after each class and integrated with my notes taken during the class. The
notes helped to interpret the text. They described the physical setting
(e.g., "participants are sitting at a table with the teacher at the head"),
objects manipulated (e.g., "teacher holds up a magazine photo of a
football player in full gear"), nonverbal behaviors (e.g., "child leans
against Sister Katherine"), and affect (e.g., "child and teacher are smiling
during verbal conflict"). More details will be provided in subsequent
chapters.

Interviews

Prior to my observations of children's Sunday School, I interviewed the
pastor. Subsequent to my observations of children's Sunday School
classes, the pastor, Sunday School superintendent, and Sunday School
teachers were formally interviewed. Each adult was formally interviewed
on at least two occasions and by at least two independent interviewers. I
interviewed all adults at least once, and one of three African-American,
undergraduate women from Spelman College, who studied with me for a
summer, interviewed at another time. These interviews yielded approximately 2 hours of audiotaped recordings for each adult.

In the tradition of topic-focused ethnography, the interviews included
both open-ended and more focused questions on religious experience.
Within general content areas, the sequencing of questions moved from
open-ended to focused to open-ended. For example: "What were some of
the religious practices that were important to you as child?" "What about
Sunday School?" "Is there anything more you can tell me about your own
Christian upbringing?" The interviews employed a flexible format; that is,
certain questions were always addressed, but the order in which focused
questions were posed varied somewhat, depending on the informant's
response to open-ended questions.

The first general content area dealt with the importance of Sunday
School for children, the teacher's goals, methods for accomplishing
those goals, and characteristics of a good Sunday School teacher. The
second general content area focused on childhood experiences significant in the adult's own spiritual development, including religious practices in the family of origin, people, practices, stories, and songs. This
content area also included a discussion of the informant's own child-
rearing practices. The third content area focused on the role of religion
in coping with everyday problems, including racial hatred. The fourth
content area dealt with the problem of educational underachievement in

African-American children. Individuals were asked to explain the high drop-out rate among African-American youths, describe any unique characteristics of African-American teachers, and advise teachers of African-American children. (See chapter 6 for details.)

From these interviews, I reconstructed verbatim transcripts. Analysis of these transcripts yielded a description of major themes. I also had the opportunity to go back and check out these themes with our informants – to ask whether or not what I understood them to say was what they really meant. The methodology and analyses for this portion of the study are somewhat parallel to those employed in studies of parental ethnotheories (e.g., Haight, Parke & Black, 1997). (More details will be presented in chapter 6.)

Notice that in this study, children were not interviewed individually. Their voices are represented primarily as they participate in storytelling, discussion, and conflict with their teachers during Sunday School classes. I was not able to obtain the permission of legal guardians to individually interview every child. Children's legal guardians sometimes resided outside of the Salt Lake area, and new children often entered classes. I decided not to engage in activities that excluded some children. However, future research ideally would include interviews with children.

Observations of Other Contexts

To understand the ways in which practices and beliefs associated with Sunday School fit into the larger context of the church, I took detailed field notes in a variety of other contexts in the church: (1) key yearly events such as Vacation Bible School, an intensive program lasting 3 hours each night for seven consecutive nights in August, and Easter and Christmas programs in which each child performed a speech, or participated in a group role play; (2) monthly "youth emphasis" days in which the children ushered the regular Sunday morning worship services and conducted the devotions; (3) other special occasions focusing on children, particularly "blessings" in which the pastor asked that each new baby be blessed and introduced him/her to the community; (4) adult Sunday School classes; (5) classes to orient new members to church doctrine and activities; (6) weekly Sunday School teachers' meetings when the pastor and teachers discussed the objectives of the lessons; and (7) a variety of social occasions (e.g., the annual Easter egg hunt, Christmas day parties, and Labor Day picnic). In addition, four "children's sermons," discussions conducted during the regular Sunday worship service with the pastor or other church leader were audio taped.

Key Characteristics of the Data Set

The developmental–ethnographic methods employed to study children's spiritual socialization combined several features designed to maximize the cultural validity, as well as the accuracy and objectivity, of the findings.

Naturalistic Observational Approach

First, I examined adults' socialization beliefs and practices, and children's participation within routine contexts familiar and emotionally meaningful to them (see Dunn, 1988; Tizard and Hughes, 1984; Bronfenbrenner, 1979; Gaskins, Miller & Corsaro, 1992). Adults' socialization practices and children's participation were observed within the contexts in which they ordinarily occurred – during Sunday School, church services, other regularly scheduled church activities, and informal church gatherings. I did not attempt to elicit particular behaviors or to structure the situations in any way.

Sustained Community Involvement

Next, I detailed the complexities of socialization practices through in-depth, sustained involvement in the church community, spanning a four year period and totaling more than 1,000 hours of direct contact. Gaining access to, and understanding, the perspective of others is time intensive. For example, multiple interviews were conducted with each major informant, allowing him/her time to think over and elaborate upon topics, as well as to develop rapport. This strategy was designed to avoid "superficialism." As Richard Shweder (1996) pointed out, it is fallacious to assume that "upon demand and 'off the tops of their heads' the natives [can] tell what they know, know what they are talking about, and keep their answers short" (p. 21).

In addition, repeated observations (10 each) were made in four different classes. These observations allowed the identification of stable patterns of practice both within and across classrooms, in contrast to temporary fluctuations caused by special events (e.g., Black History Month), variations in mood, class composition, and so on. Also, by observing repeatedly several different teachers of different aged children, the data suggest developmental and individual differences in adults' socialization practices and children's participation.

Multiple Informants

This study draws upon the diverse perspectives of a variety of individuals central to Sunday School, such as the pastor, the superintendent, and the Sunday School teachers. The diverse perspectives and experiences of individuals serving complementary roles provides a more complete account of beliefs and practices relevant to children's religious development.

Multiple Contexts of Observation

This study also draws upon data collected in multiple contexts, for example, Vacation Bible School, Children's Sermons, the Easter program, and Sunday School. These observations allow for a more complete account of religious practices. They contextualize Sunday School practices within the larger community and suggest the unique, as well as the redundant, socialization functions of Sunday School. Thus, these observations within the larger context of the church served as critical checks to discipline my emerging interpretations of observational and interview data. In some instances, observations in other church contexts provided counterexamples that motivated reanalyses; in other instances, they helped to identify some of the ways in which major cultural themes are redundantly conveyed. For example, adults as well as children participated in spiritual storytelling in their Sunday School classes and also during regular worship services.

Multiple Methods

The data also reflect a variety of research methods, clustered under the categories of interviews and direct observations. The use of multiple methods balances the strengths and weaknesses of various strategies and provides multiple checks on interpretation. In-depth interviews with key adults contextualized the observational data by suggesting key cultural themes and provided checks on interpretations of behavioral interactions. The observations allowed for the identification of patterns of routine interactions of which the informants were not explicitly aware or able to articulate, and they provided checks on interpretations of the interview data.

Multiple Data Collectors

Characteristics of the investigator influence informants' behavior, and so multiple data collectors were used. Both an African-American, Spel-

man College student and I interviewed adults. Using multiple interviewers has the advantage of expanding the audience to which adults
addressed themselves and, presumably, the range of topics on which they
comfortably elaborated.

Rapport Building

It was essential that community members felt comfortable with me
and my students. Establishing a trusting relationship was a prerequisite to
receiving permission to conduct the study. Community leaders were well
aware of past abuses of African-Americans by researchers. For example,
the pastor and others discussed the Tuskegee syphilis experiment in
which the progression of syphilis was observed by the U.S. Public Health
Service in 400 black, male sharecroppers over a 40-year period (see, for
example, Jones, 1993). During my fieldwork, colleagues from my academic department who did not have ongoing relationships with the
community repeatedly were denied permission by church members to
conduct research within the community.

Good rapport also was essential to obtaining ecologically valid observations. Participants obviously were aware that they were being observed. It
was therefore extremely important that the participants felt comfortable
with the observer. Both adults and children were familiar with me
through my participation in church activities the year prior to the formal
data collection. In addition, adults were familiar with me through my
participation in Sunday School teachers' meetings, and children were
familiar with me through my organization and participation in a computer club (discussed in chapter 9). Establishing and maintaining good
rapport also facilitated the interpretation of observational data. Because
community members generally felt comfortable with me, I could ask if
my evolving interpretations were consistent with their understanding.

Reliability Checks

In order to enhance the accuracy and consistency of our analyses,
extensive interrater reliability checks were conducted on the behavioral
coding of socialization practices. These procedures are elaborated in
subsequent chapters in which the corresponding data are presented.

CONCLUSION

This study employs developmental and ethnographic methods to yield
both microscopic descriptions of adults' socialization beliefs and prac-

tices and children's participation, and holistic descriptions of the broader contexts in which these practices and beliefs are embedded. Over a 4-year period, Sunday School classes were observed and audiotaped, key adults in charge of Sunday School were interviewed, and fieldnotes were taken in a variety of church contexts relevant to children. Throughout, accuracy and consistency were prioritized through, for example, reliability checks on individual coding categories. Also prioritized were issues of cultural validity (see Corsaro, 1985; Harding, 1992), for example, through the triangulation of data, as multiple levels of data from multiple sources were related, including interviews with Sunday School teachers concerning their beliefs regarding spiritual socialization, and direct observations of adult–child interactions during Sunday School. Thus, the interpretations presented in this book are grounded both in detailed examinations of the specifics of everyday life and participants' reflections on those events (see Gaskins et al., 1992).

PART TWO

PATTERNS OF SOCIALIZATION
AND PARTICIPATION

CHAPTER FOUR

African-Americans in Salt Lake City: A Historical and Social Overview

In this chapter, I place children's religious experiences at First Baptist Church within the broader historical and social context of Salt Lake City, Utah. As Ronald Coleman (1981) observed:

> For Black Utahns, the African-American church has historically been the single most important institution in the state. It has served as a place of refuge in the most difficult times and many of the Black religious leaders have been ambassadors of good will for the African-American, and larger, community. (p. 2)

A BRIEF HISTORY OF AFRICAN-AMERICANS IN UTAH

African-Americans have played a role in the development of Utah since the early nineteenth century.[1] James Beckwourth, for example, trapped, hunted, and explored in Utah in the early nineteenth century (1824–26). He fought in the Seminole and Mexican wars, joined the California gold rush, and lived with the Crow Indians. His published dramatic accounts of his experiences have provided valuable historical information (Coleman, 1981).

Permanent African-American settlements were established in Utah with the immigration of the first Mormon pioneers in the mid-nineteenth century. Indeed, three African-American men accompanied Brigham Young on his journey to Utah in 1847. Both enslaved and free blacks continued to accompany the Mormon pioneers to Utah. The 1860 census counted 59 African-Americans in Utah, 29 of whom were enslaved (Mathews & Wright, 1994). Yet, relatively little is known about the

[1] This section draws heavily upon the original historical research of Dr. Ronald Coleman (1981).

African-Americans who helped to settle and develop Utah. In describing the lives of black pioneers, an 1899 editorial in a Salt Lake City African-American newspaper, the *Broad Ax,* notes,

> Their lives in the then new wilderness, was [*sic*] far from happy, and many of them were subjected to the same treatment that was accorded the plantation negroes of the South. (p. 122, as cited by Coleman, 1981)

In 1862, Congress passed legislation abolishing slavery in the territories. After the Civil War, many former slaves left the area, but others remained in Utah. Together with new arrivals and early free African-American pioneers, they struggled to improve their conditions while continuing to experience oppression, including lynchings and, into the 1960s, Jim Crow and antimiscegenation laws. Approximately 150 descendants of the early black pioneers still live in Utah (Coleman, 1981), including two of the Sunday School teachers at First Baptist Church.

The majority of black Utahns have lived in and around Salt Lake City and Ogden (immediately north of Salt Lake City), where employment opportunities have been best. Beginning in the last quarter of the nineteenth century, many African-Americans came to Utah to serve in the military. In 1869, two black military units patrolled Utah (Mathews & Wright, 1994; Coleman, 1981). They were referred to as the "Buffalo soldiers" by Native Americans because of their short, thick hair and their bravery. Shortly after the outbreak of the Spanish-American War in 1898, an additional African-American unit of 450 servicemen was stationed in Utah. These soldiers, however, were not necessarily welcomed by European-Americans. For example, an editorial in the *Salt Lake Tribune* questioned the character of African-American servicemen and suggested that under the influence of alcohol they might become aggressive in the presence of white women. Nevertheless, many soldiers did develop ties to the Salt Lake community and chose to make their permanent homes there. Military-related activities during World War II further influenced the growth of Utah's African-American community (Coleman, 1981; Mathews & Wright, 1994).

The building of the railroad also brought many African-Americans into Utah. The completion of the transcontinental railroad (1869) during the post-Reconstruction period improved the employment opportunities of African-Americans who, along with Greek, Italian, Chinese, Japanese, and, eventually, Latino laborers came to lay tracks (Coleman,

1981; Mathews & Wright, 1994; Wright, 1994). Ogden became a railroad center for the Union Pacific, Southern Pacific, and other railroads. From approximately 1890 to 1940, the railroad companies were the largest employers of African-Americans in Utah (Coleman, 1981; Wright, 1994).

Many blacks also were employed in African-American clubs, restaurants, and hotels. African-American railroad workers required hotel and restaurant facilities because white-owned services were barred to them. Similarly, because blacks were excluded from participating in the general social and cultural life, they developed their own social organizations, a literary press, and a community center. By the 1890s there were several black newspapers (Coleman, 1981). In 1891 a branch of the National Association for the Advancement of Colored People (NAACP) was established in Salt Lake City.

It was about this time that the first African-American churches emerged in Salt Lake City. In the 1890s, Trinity African Methodist Episcopal Church was the first black church to be established, and First Baptist Church was founded shortly thereafter (Coleman, 1981). First Baptist Church emerged from a "Baptist Prayer Band" – a group of African-Americans who, excluded from worshiping in white churches, began meeting for prayer and fellowship in one another's homes in approximately 1892. The Baptist Prayer Band would assemble on a regular basis to worship, pray, and read the Bible (Davis, 1997).

In 1896, black Baptists were allowed to worship in a building located in the rear of a white church. The first pastor of First Baptist Church was retained in 1900. By 1902, the congregation moved to its own chapel. By 1907, numerous auxiliaries were functioning, including the Sunday School and the church choir. According to Reverend France Davis (1997):

> From its inception, . . . [First] Baptist Church saw itself as a beacon in the Salt Lake valley. Her goal was to provide spiritual guidance for Black Baptists in Utah. Beginning as the near flickering efforts of a handful of women, she eventually grew into a glowing congregation by the second decade of this century. (p. 29)

Characterized as the "mother church" of black Baptists in Utah, many other black congregations trace their roots directly to First Baptist Church (Davis, 1997). While serving primarily spiritual needs, First Baptist Church and these other congregations have taken the lead in civil rights, political issues, cultural development, and economic cooperation (Davis, 1997). For example, in 1989 the First Baptist congregation dedicated a low-income, senior citizen housing complex adjacent to the church. Pastor Daniels notes:

> From her earliest years . . . [First] Baptist Church has continued to be instrumental in making better the lives of people, especially those of African heritage. . . . While our purpose is primarily religious and spiritual, we seek to insure that the needs of the whole person are met. We strive as the words of a familiar song declare to live the life we sing about in our songs. (Pastor Daniels as cited in the Church Historical Committee report, 1976)

For more than 100 years, a strong sense of community has emerged around First Baptist Church – and this community embraces children and youth. In approximately 1913, First Baptist Church became the community center for "colored" youth. According to an elderly member of First Baptist Church, "I went to the Baptist Church, because all the kids went to the Baptist Church. You know, that's where you got to see everybody on Sunday. I was the only colored girl in the (public) school" (Davis, 1997, p. 29). At the time of this study, the basement of First Baptist Church served as a children's Computer Club, Saturday School, and African dance troupe rehearsal hall. Here, youth socialized with one another and with caring adults, developed skills, and explored their African-American heritage.

THE AFRICAN-AMERICAN UTAHN COMMUNITY TODAY

Today, African-Americans continue to contribute to all aspects of development in Utah, ranging from education to arts, politics, law, and business (Wright, 1994). African-Americans also continue to experience discrimination. Even with the protection of the Civil Rights Act of 1964, African-Americans still report problems renting or purchasing homes (Coleman, 1981; Mathews & Wright, 1994). Employment opportunities, while improved, continue to be limited for African-Americans, and tokenism is common (Coleman, 1981). The average unemployment for blacks in Utah is 11%, twice the state average. The number of blacks living below the poverty line (31%) is well above the state average for all Utahns (11%). Average income of blacks is $25,000 while the state average is $35,000 (Wright, 1994). Many African-Americans also struggle with the educational system. Only 77% of African-Americans Utahns have a high school degree, in contrast to 85% for all Utahns. Only 16% of African-Americans have a college degree, in contrast to 25% for all Utahns (Coleman, 1981; Mathews & Wright, 1994).

To some extent, these statistics are reflective of the challenges faced by African-Americans throughout the United States. In addition, they may reflect the unique set of challenges to African-Americans living in Salt Lake City. A primary challenge for African-American Utahns is isolation. In the state of Utah, African-Americans are a small minority numbering approximately 11,079, or 0.7% of the total population. In 1990, Utah ranked as the 11th "whitest" state in the nation, with 95.2% of the population classified as white (Nakoryakov, 1994). Although 97% of the people of color reside on the west side of racially segregated Salt Lake City, there are no predominantly black neighborhoods. Even in the most diverse west side neighborhoods, people of color – including Asians, Pacific Islanders, and Hispanics, as well as African-Americans – comprise only 36% of the population.

The latest population statistics, however, indicate that Utah, like the rest of the United States, is becoming more ethnically diverse. More ethnic minority members arrived in Salt Lake City from 1991 to 1994, many fleeing the violence and weak economy of the West Coast. Projections from the Census Bureau indicate that by the year 2020, approximately 9% of the Utah population will be classified as nonwhite and that approximately 6,000 more African-Americans will arrive (Mathews & Wright, 1994).

THE MORMON CHURCH AND THE AFRICAN-AMERICAN COMMUNITY

Another challenge to African-Americans in Utah involves functioning as part of a religious minority in a place where religious affiliation is significant to participation in the larger social and political community.[2] Approximately 70% of the population of the state of Utah are members of the Church of Jesus Christ of Latter-day Saints (popularly known as "LDS," or "Mormon") (Coleman, 1981). In contrast to the European-American majority, relatively few African-Americans are Mormon. Indeed, 10 of the 20 predominantly African-American churches in the

---

[2] This section draws heavily upon the original historical work of Dr. C. Eric Lincoln (1974, 1999).

state of Utah today are Baptist and none are Mormon (Scarlet, Stack & Sullivan, 1994).

In the state of Utah, membership in the religious minority can have social, economic, and political ramifications for non-Mormons, regardless of racial heritage. The Mormon community is close knit, and members typically enjoy a variety of social and cultural programs. My informants, as well as European-Americans who are not Mormon, sometimes commented upon feelings of isolation. For example, some informants reported that as children they felt left out when their classmates participated in after-school, church-related activities. Similarly, the Mormon church has extensive business ventures in Salt Lake City. Some European-American adults who are not Mormon have reported difficulties in establishing themselves professionally.

Membership in a religious minority may be especially challenging for African-Americans because of a complex and sometimes troubled relationship with the LDS church. When Joseph Smith founded the Mormon religion in 1829 in Palmyria, New York, African-Americans were welcomed. One of Smith's closest friends, an African-American man named Elijah Abel, was admitted into the priesthood and latter traveled on to Salt Lake City, where he continued to serve the church actively for many years. When Mormons settled in Missouri in the 1830s, their early pro-black position generated considerable hostility among established settlers. Perhaps in response to these tensions, Mormons subsequently adopted a proslavery position formulated primarily in terms of the "curse of Canaan" (Lincoln, 1999). In brief, this interpretation of the Old Testament asserts that the African race descended from Cain. In punishment for slaying his brother, Abel, a "mark" was put on Cain (White, 1972). Although the Bible does not say what the mark of Cain was, Mormon theology teaches that the "mark" was black skin (Lincoln, 1999). In addition, Mormon theology teaches that the spiritual ancestors of blacks failed to perform properly in their pre-existent state. In what Mormons call the "War of Heaven," some groups took a neutral position during the conflict between Lucifer and God. Those despised neutrals are the spirits who have inherited the bodies of black people now living on earth (Lincoln, 1999).

Initially, the curse of Canaan and the War of Heaven were used to explain the origin of blacks and to justify slavery. Later, however, they became the theological basis for denying the priesthood and prerogatives of the temple to black members. The priesthood is an important key to status in the Mormon community. The LDS church does not have a professional ministry, and "divining for hire" is viewed with some contempt. Instead, at the age of 12 all males are ordained deacons, the first of six orders of priesthood. Only members of the priesthood may hold even the most minor offices in the church. No one ineligible for the priesthood may assist with the sacrament, or bless or perform baptisms. Only those who have achieved the priesthood may enter the Temple and may have their wives and children sealed to them forever in a Temple ceremony (Lincoln, 1999).

Racially exclusive Mormon policies were vigorously protested from within as well as outside of the church. For example, Mormons running for public offices found themselves vulnerable to popular opinion, black athletes rebelled against competing with teams associated with Mormon universities, the NAACP filed suits against the Boy Scouts of America for alleged Mormon manipulation of Scout offices, and marches and disruptions threatened Mormon-sponsored activities.

Over time, racially exclusive policies within the LDS church have lessened. Most notably, in 1978 the president of the Mormon church, Spencer Kimball, described a revelation that allowed African-Americans to hold the priesthood. With the lifting of this ban, membership in the Mormon church among African-Americans began to rise, but most integrated into European-American congregations (Lincoln, 1999). At the time of this study, there were no predominantly African-American LDS churches in Utah.

MEETING THE CHALLENGES

Meeting the challenge of living in Salt Lake City has meant not only that African-Americans draw together within the local community, but also that they develop strategies for connecting with the larger African-American community. For example, in 1913, Booker T. Washington, the African-American educator, spoke at First Baptist Church. Beginning in 1916, First Baptist Church began an active program of outreach and fellowship with Baptists in Utah, Idaho, and Wyoming, as well as with national Baptist organizations. Several members of First Baptist Church currently serve in leadership roles in the National Baptist Congress of Christian Education. In 1995, Pastor Daniels participated in the Foreign Mission Preaching Team of the National Baptist Convention, U.S.A., Inc., traveling with 12 other ministers throughout Africa. At the time of this study, Pastor Daniels served as state vice-president to the Intermountain General Baptist Association at the National Baptist Convention, U.S.A., Inc.

Active efforts also are made to keep youth connected with a larger African-American Christian community. For example, in 1996, First Baptist Church hosted between 2,000 and 2,500 delegates to the National Baptist Western Regional Youth Conference.

CONCLUSION

To summarize, African-American Utahns, like blacks in other parts of the country, have experienced racial discrimination in employment, housing, education, and everyday social interactions. A unique challenge to African-American Utahns in coping with these conditions, however, is the extent to which they are isolated from one another on their jobs, at school, and in their neighborhoods. A second challenge is that the overwhelming majority of African-American Utahns also find themselves within the religious minority in a larger community for which religion is highly significant. Despite these challenges, African-American Utahns, like blacks elsewhere in the United States, have made and continue to make substantial contributions both within the African-American community and within the larger community. When describing his vision for the future, Pastor Daniels projected that:

> [First Baptist Church] will be very active in all facets of life as it affects the daily existence of our people. She will keep spiritual matters first and foremost, while doing everything possible to meet any needs where people hurt. In other words, [First Baptist Church] will take seriously the mission of saving souls while caring for the least, the lost, and the last. (Davis, 1997, p. 89)

CHAPTER FIVE

The Teachers

When asked how her granddad made Sunday School so enjoyable and meaningful to her, Sister Katherine emphasized his distinct personal qualities and her love for him:

> By basically talking, the expression on his face – and just sitting there, I guess, because I was crazy about my granddad . . . he just had this glow about him whenever he would talk. He just glowed, he'd just light up like a light bulb.

In chapter 4, I described the particular historical and sociocultural contexts of First Baptist Church. Sister Katherine's comments, however, remind us of the importance of the *personal* contexts in which socialization occurs. The impact of a Sunday School lesson, a story, or a reprimand can vary widely depending on the distinct personalities, life histories, and relationships of the participants. For example, the impact of a Sunday School teacher's reprimand on a given child may well be influenced by the fact that the Sunday School teacher knows the child's immediate and extended family, has taught her sibling or cousin, and has been taught by her grandmother. In this chapter, I will elaborate the description of individual teachers begun in chapter 3, and their styles of interacting with the children.

An emphasis on positive interpersonal relationships is a characteristic of many African-American communities (e.g., Mitchell, 1986) and extends to modern, African-centered pedagogy (see Lomotey, 1990). Many successful African-American teachers work to establish close personal ties with students, emphasizing both cognitive and affective development (see Lee & Slaughter-Defoe, 1995). Such teachers describe "caring" rather than "professional" relationships and emphasize cultural solidarity and strong attachments to the African-American community (Foster, 1994, 1995). In their daily interactions with students, teachers balance the toughness required for discipline with the tenderness required for personal support (Foster, 1995). For example, they use kinship terms such as "Little Sister" to express an alliance between themselves and their students. Similarly, all teachers nominated as effective by African-American parents were perceived as strict or stern, and were observed to engage in a lot of touching, including putting their arms around the children, hugging them, and holding their hands (Ladson-Billings, 1990). These teachers also worked to develop a bond with students through relationships that extended beyond the classroom and into the community.

Supportive relationships also are emphasized within the African-American churches. Indeed, Christopher Ellison (1993) characterized the quality of fellowship as a distinctive characteristic of African-American religious institutions. In his research, adults gave their congregations particularly high marks for emotional supportiveness. Ellison concluded that African-American churches provide an interpersonal context in which members are appreciated as unique individuals, valued for their sociability and service to others and for spiritual qualities of wisdom and morality.

THE TEACHERS

As described in chapter 3, the four Sunday School teachers were highly respected members of the congregation who were dedicated Christians with a deep love of children. It is perhaps with these highly esteemed members of the community that children have their most extensive, direct contact. An appointment to teach Sunday School is viewed as a great privilege and responsibility. When the teacher of the junior class moved to Texas, church leaders contemplated her replacement from among several interested individuals for several months. Sunday School teachers were viewed as spiritually mature and as critical influences on the lives of children. They typically held their positions for decades. When discussing her own childhood, Sister Justine described that the "mothers of this church" represented to her

> the true value of loving and caring and generosity and – charitable
> spirits. . . . If they saw me outside of this church and there was some-
> thing wrong, you can believe I heard. If my behavior seemed wrong to

them, in public, I would hear from them. And it was never anything brash and abrupt, or, you know, ridicule. It was, you know, with love . . . Christian-love. That's why they were extremely important to me.

This general characterization also applies to the current teachers at First Baptist Church.

Sister Katherine

Sister Katherine was the teacher of the kindergarten class for 3- to 6-year-old children. A devoted wife and mother of two adolescent sons and a 10-year-old daughter, she identified herself as a "homemaker." At the time of the study, Sister Katherine was in her mid-thirties. She had lived in Salt Lake City for approximately 15 years, but still spoke of Birmingham, Alabama, as home. She drew upon this identity in dealing with the challenges of living and raising her children in a primarily European-American community:

> We're from Birmingham, Alabama, so I take them [children] home. *(laughter)* So, they get to see a lot. I take them back to Birmingham, Alabama, so they can get to know that we are not bad. I raise them – we can achieve goals and a lot of [public school] teachers [in Salt Lake City] have that stereotype that blacks are bad. First thing when you walk in the classroom you always have to prove yourself, that I can do something. I can learn. I can. They [children] need more role models.

She also believes that many African-Americans who have grown up in Salt Lake City have internalized negative stereotypes:

> I look at them [African-Americans raised in Salt Lake City], "We can do the same thing they [whites] can. . . . Give us the chance, we can do the same thing. Hey, we can go up to the university and take classes. We can be the mom and raise the kids, and do everything that they're doing – teach." . . . If you look at the news, all they get on the news is what? We're killing each other, you see us in handcuffs thrown in the back of a police car . . . doing drugs, and . . . not going to school. . . . Hey, black people went to college, blacks are achieving, doin' things. I have a little girl. *(laughter)* "You goin' back to Alabama to get married."

At the time of this study, Sister Katherine had been teaching Sunday School for 5 years. Her manner of interacting with the young children was quiet, loving, and playful. During the time in which I knew her, I never heard Sister Katherine raise her voice to a child or speak unkindly. She seemed to enjoy a warm and accepting relationship with the children. She held children who were fearful of leaving their families and sat with children who were having problems behaving. Young children in her Sunday School class clearly were comfortable: they talked, sang, and sat on or next to Sister Katherine. After class, Sister Katherine always supplied each child with a small treat, usually candy.

Although Sister Katherine completed two years of college, she had no formal training in education. Her Sunday School lessons were simple and straightforward, and often injected with verbal play, gentle teasing, and storytelling. Her "teacher training" came entirely through the church and her own childhood socialization. When asked about how she prepared for Sunday School, she discussed the instruction she received at weekly teachers' meetings from Pastor Daniels. She also discussed the model provided to her by her deceased maternal grandfather:

> I think my model was my granddad. . . . My granddad, he was a deacon in the church and made it a point to always come to the house to teach us a Sunday School lesson, and I don't care how late. . . . "Hey, it's Sunday and we know granddad's coming. Do everything and play if we want to – do you know – because when granddad comes . . . you're going to be sitting here two or three hours for a Sunday School lesson." OK! But he didn't – it wasn't boring . . . we didn't have paper, we didn't cut [and paste] or anything, but he just sat there and he talked to us. . . . So you know how a kid gets, "Oh, it's getting late eight o'clock. Granddad ain't gonna come, we can go play," you know, and the next thing you know, here come Granddad knocking on the door, nine o' clock at night . . . *(laughs)*. Next thing you know the room, the house, is totally quiet. Now Mom was in the room listening and Dad was somewhere else, but the kids – all four of us – was sitting there listening to Granddad. Because Granddad . . . you know, he's a deacon in the church and he's going around to everybody else who cannot go to church, but our house is the last house he's gonna hit before he goes home, and if that's at nine or ten o'clock at night, that's OK. But it was fun, he made it fun and enjoyable – and he didn't cut, he didn't paste. So I would like to be like him. To make it fun even if you don't cut and paste, to be like him, that's my goal.

Other of Sister Katherine's role models included African-American teachers in her all-black elementary school in Alabama. When describing characteristics of excellent African-American teachers, Sister Katherine elaborated:

They'll reach out to that kid, they'll take that time. I even remember in my second grade, a teacher. A girl came to school with her hair all messed up – kids just started laughing at her. And, teacher would not teach the class. She said, "Everybody's gonna sit here and put your head down on the desk and wait until I finish combing her hair." She didn't just make her go through that whole day with her hair sticking up on her head. She understood that Mom had to go to work. Mom got to meet the Man. . . . I think that was so great for her [the teacher] to take that time . . . for the rest of the day, that girl could smile, and not, "Hey, I look so funny." So, I think they took their time, and go that extra mile, and not quick to say, "You're handicapped."

When asked why she thought that Sunday School was important for children, Sister Katherine repeatedly stressed that it gives children "a great sense of value." Through participation in Sunday School, children come to value themselves and others as children of God. They also come to have pride in their community. In elaborating upon how her own children have developed in the church, she noted:

They're more positive. They're not as quick to put other people down. Especially my older son. He thinks more. If someone is feeling down or feeling low, he can go over there, and he will try to talk to them and try to make them feel better. . . . He will invite them to come to church. . . . He's a deacon now, he's not shy. He's in praise, and I'm surprised you know, thirteen-year-old . . . But they [her children] have grown in that sense of more positive, working in the church. He [older son] doesn't feel ashamed to say – oh, "I'm a deacon. I live with this in church. I will participate in the Sunday School program." So, he's been growing. He's been growing in that sense that – oh, "This is good, this is good."

Sister Patrice

Sister Patrice was the teacher of the primary class for children aged 6–8 years. At the time of the study she was in her mid-sixties, had raised two children in Salt Lake City, and worked with the elderly as a practical nurse. The great-granddaughter of a minister who also was a Pullman porter working out of Salt Lake City, Sister Patrice was "born into" First Baptist Church. She and her three siblings were raised by her grandmother and lived next door to their great-grandparents.

They [grandparents] were very strict. . . . They always cooked their dinner on Saturday, which I do still, and you didn't do anything on Sunday. You were not allowed to run and play. You didn't play ball, you didn't shoot marbles, you didn't – the only thing that my sister and I did was sit on the front porch . . . or else we could lay on . . . the grass and look up at the clouds and say we see a man or whatever. . . . Back then when I was growing up here in Salt Lake, as you know, . . . there was a lot of places we couldn't go, but the church . . . was the center of our activities . . . we didn't get too far from home, or if you were away from home you were at church. . . . Bible reading and learning Bible verses by memory was [required in the family]. . . . Everybody [went to Sunday School] . . . we always had to tell my grandmother what we learned in Sunday School. . . . Because, see, my grandmother she worked . . . there were some people here who were very, very wealthy. . . . And my grandmother was the cook, and so she would go early [on Sunday]. She cooked the breakfast, the lunch, and the dinner. And then when she got home in the evening, . . . we'd have to tell her what we learned.

Sister Patrice "passed into service" at 17 years of age when she began helping an older woman to teach Sunday School, and she continued as a teacher until her death more than 50 years later. Her style of teaching seemed reserved and formal in relation to the other teachers. There was less verbal play and storytelling in her class, and relatively more time was spent on the written text. Sister Patrice was respectful and patient with children. She always allowed beginning readers – painstakingly, but often with great pride and excitement – to read aloud their Sunday School lessons.

Sister Patrice mentioned a number of sources when asked about how she prepares to teach Sunday School, including a children's Bible with simplified wording, the Bible, the Sunday School booklets, and the Sunday School teachers' meeting. Most importantly, however, she discussed her participation in classes for Sunday School teachers taught at the "Nationals," a yearly meeting sponsored by the National Baptist Convention, U.S.A., Inc., and held at different cities throughout the country. As a model of good teaching, Sister Patrice stated that "Jesus was a great teacher, and I want to be more like him and teach the way he did. Because he taught very simple . . ." Sister Patrice went on to emphasize the importance of focusing on the essential points and doing so in a concrete manner that children can understand. In addition, Sister Patrice emphasized the importance of listening to children.

You draw them [children] out, and . . . you'd be surprised at the answers they give you. . . . You have to make it a two-way street. . . . We do a lot of talking, but we listen too. . . . A good teacher is a good listener too. So the good teacher doesn't try to dominate all the time.

Sister Patrice stated that Sunday School is very important for children because:

We have these lessons to teach them at an early age that Jesus is and was and still is, and that to be a good Christian . . . is very good for one's character. . . . We teach character, [that one should be] helpful, kind and loving. . . . And I believe that all children should have some religious training at an early age. I don't believe in when he gets older let him choose because . . . look at all the stuff that he's missed. . . . [The most important goal of Sunday School is] to bring that child to Christ. . . . You hear people say, "When I was little I went to church." They have a foundation that they usually come back to.

In discussing the role of spirituality in her own life, Sister Patrice reflected, "It helps because I'm able to . . . hold (my) peace . . . to be Christlike and not get upset."

Sister Justine

Sister Justine was the teacher of the junior class for 8- to 12-year-old children. In her late thirties at the time of the study, Sister Justine was the mother of a teenage daughter and two stepchildren. She was an artist involved in a variety of community dance and music productions. She also worked as an aid in the public schools for children with behavioral disorders.

A descendant of Utah pioneers, Sister Justine grew up attending First Baptist Church. As a college student, Sister Justine had spent time in other western cities including Portland, Oregon. In describing her own upbringing in Salt Lake City, Sister Justine noted:

We did a lot of singing in our household . . . lots of singing. Lots of listening to old gospel music too. [And] deep prayers at meals, you know. There were seven of us [children]. . . . Sometimes we had some serious, bad prayers . . . because my five little brothers were characters. . . . My mother would tell us stories about our family a lot – and on her side of the family is just religious people – you know – preachers

and quartets. . . . She tells us about what the churches were like – she's
from the South.

At the time of the study, Sister Justine had been teaching Sunday
School "on and off" for about seven years and had just been appointed as
the regular teacher of the junior class. Her style of teaching was very
lively, engaged, and humorous. Her classes were noisy: filled with verbal
play, teasing, and frequent laughter.

Sister Justine views Sunday School as important for children because it
provides "moral and spiritual strength." She prepares for Sunday School
primarily through literature obtained from a number of local Christian
bookstores. Key characteristics of a good Sunday School teacher for Sister
Justine are "patience and love." She mentioned a number of models she
uses for good teaching, including a local, European-American dancer:

> She's the director of the Children's Dance Theater at the University of
> Utah. And the way this woman handles [children] – I mean she just
> *radiates* love. You know! *(laughs)* And she talks like this, "all right peo-
> ple" *(very soft, high-pitched voice).* And they listen to her! . . . She teaches a
> lot of love. And she's a prayerful woman.

Pastor Daniels also serves as a role model.

> The thing about Rev [Daniels] is he reminds me of being . . . in col-
> lege. He let's you be debative. You know. He let's you ask the questions
> that seem not to have an answer to them.

Sister Justine also indicated a local, African-American educator as an
important role model:

> She's just into children. African-American children knowing every-
> thing there is to know about themselves. . . . She's really into our his-
> tory as African-Americans. And she really cares that kids know this
> because she was fortunate to grow up like that.

Sister Ima

Sister Ima was the teacher of the intermediate class of 12- to 15-year-old
children. In her mid-forties at the time of the study, Sister Ima had one
daughter who had recently started college. Sister Ima had earned a master's degree in education and had been teaching junior high within the

public schools for more than 20 years. The "product of sharecroppers," and one of nine children, Sister Ima was born and raised in rural North Carolina by her mother and father. Throughout her lifetime, Sister Ima has been faced with a variety of challenges, including her father's alcoholism, forced school desegregation as a young adolescent, and a difficult marriage. Throughout these challenges, Sister Ima has relied on spiritual beliefs, practices, and the conviction that "God loves all people."

> My father used to sing . . . "There will be Peace in the Valley." The lion will lay down with the lamb, and the children will be there. Everybody will be getting along. And I can visualize that. . . . "Amazing Grace," "His Eye is on the Sparrow," . . . All those songs we sing. And they go from generation to generation. . . . I asked my daughter . . . "What is your favorite song? Do you have a song?" . . . mine is "Jesus Keep Me Near the Cross." Hers [daughter's] was "Through It All." I learned to trust in Jesus, I've learned to trust in God. There was a lady that used to sing that song here. And she was going through a lot of changes, and the more she sang it the more you could see that she was being freed from whatever her stress was. . . . Most of the songs we sing [at First Baptist Church] are songs that we sang years and years ago. And listening to them as you grow older, you'll understand them better.

More generally, the "Christian atmosphere" in her home and community was a source of strength and comfort throughout her upbringing.

> My father, like I said, might not have been there, but my mother taught us that we were to love him in spite of [that]. . . . I did see him drunk a lot, and we were taught that he is your father and regardless of that you ought to always respect him. . . . He died in 1984 . . . and I can't remember anything that I said or did that I have to feel sorry for as far as he's concerned. I'm from a Christian upbringing, I really am. It was in the house. It was in the atmosphere. . . . I was raised in a Christian home, and what was in that Christian home was coming from every other home in the area, and what was in the area was coming from the church as we congregated. Everybody owned everybody's child, and that was a form of Christian growth, or moral growth. . . . It's called "doing something wrong," even if you were in somebody else's house. Forget it – if you were wrong, you were wrong.

Sister Ima was the only Sunday School teacher with formal instruction in education. To prepare for Sunday School, she studied from the Bible throughout the week and noted everyday examples of the concepts she would be presenting to the children. Her primary resource was the Bible, accompanied by the lesson commentary supplied by the National Baptist Convention, U.S.A., Inc. The Sunday School teachers' meeting also was an important resource. Her model for teaching is Pastor Daniels because of his thoroughness and caring. Her overarching goal is to help children to realize that "Jesus Christ died for us so that we might live."

Sister Ima's manner of teaching was structured and serious. She taught from a lesson plan, outlined on the board, and previewed for the students. Before reading the biblical text, children were always told the purpose of the lesson. Although Sister Ima was an engaging and fascinating storyteller, she rarely engaged in spontaneous verbal play. As she described her teaching:

> I used to be concerned that I wasn't as lively a person as other people are like [Junie, teacher of the "Young Adult" Sunday School class] down the hall there. She's lively! But, I'm just calm *(laughing)*. Like my daughter says, I'm solemn. And she teases me, "Mom your whole family is solemn. You go to your house and everybody sits around looking at each other and smiling. . . . We're always apprehensive what's going to happen next."

CONCLUSION

The teachers at First Baptist Church were distinct individuals varying widely in personality and teaching styles. They shared, however, an emphasis on interpersonal relationships. As will become apparent in the chapters that follow, teachers actively negotiated their relationships with their equally diverse students. For example, a teacher might introduce a playful element into her verbal conflict with a child, transforming a potentially alienating experience for the child into mutual play. Relationships also were maintained and developed when teachers referred to children using kinship terms, such as "Little Sister," or explicitly mentioned their relationship to a child outside of the context of Sunday School. For example, in challenging the claim of an adolescent boy reluctant to complete his assignment, Sister Justine explicitly referred to their common cousin, "the child of my deceased brother," in support of her argument that she knew him and that he could complete the assignment. Teachers also frequently praised or complemented good behavior and made positive comments about children's individual attributes.

CHAPTER SIX

Adults' Perspectives on Spiritual Socialization

In describing to me her own spiritual socialization as a child, Sister Ima stressed the central role of adult church members:

> I gathered my spirit from them. I saw what they did. I saw them pray. I saw what they were going through. I saw them read the Bible. I saw them sing, and they would sing joyously!

In this chapter, African-American adults reflect, in their own words, upon the meaning of spiritual socialization in their own lives and in the lives of their children and students. Their reflections provide an important context for interpreting adults' socialization practices at First Baptist Church. Indeed, a growing body of literature in cultural psychology describes the complex ways in which individuals' belief systems provide a frame of reference within which they interpret experience, and formulate goals and strategies for socialization (e.g., Goncu, 1999; Goodnow & Collins, 1990; Harkness & Super, 1996; Haight, Parke & Black, 1997). As we will see in this chapter, adults' beliefs may be described as child-sensitive and growth-oriented. Adults were sensitive to children's emotional needs and relative immaturity. For example, they valued positive adult–child relationships as a prerequisite for effective socialization. Adults also expressed the importance for African-American children and youth to behave in a mature and highly competent fashion in order to survive and develop in neighborhoods and schools that they perceived to be racist. In this broader context, an African-American boy, for example, may not be given many "second chances" when it comes to responsible behavior and scholarship. Adults viewed the church as a haven in which children form relationships with adults who value them, and in which

they develop the protective spiritual beliefs and competence necessary to
survive and flourish in the larger community.

THE INTERVIEWS

As described in chapter 3, there were six primary adult informants for
this study: the pastor, the Sunday School superintendent, and the four
Sunday School teachers of children and youth. Each adult was interviewed on two or three occasions, and by at least two interviewers – myself
and an African-American student research assistant from Spelman College. During these open-ended interviews, adults described their own
spiritual development, their experiences in Sunday School, and the role
of religion in coping with life's challenges. An effort was made to keep
the interviews conversation-like, allowing adults to tell their own stories in
their own way. Requests for clarification, specific information, or elaboration were inserted, as appropriate, into the flow of the adult's narrative.

The first interview began with the request to "tell me about your own
Christian upbringing." In general, adults talked about the people, religious practices, music, and scriptures significant to them when they
were growing up. During the second interview, adults were asked to "tell
me about your experiences teaching (supervising) Sunday School." In
general, they discussed the importance for children of attending Sunday
School, some of the important goals of Sunday School, and strategies for
accomplishing these goals. During the second or third interview, informants were asked to "describe the role of religion in coping with life's
challenges." In general, they talked about how spirituality helped them as
children and how it helps them now, as adults. They also talked about
how they were taught to handle prejudice and about the role of spirituality in coping with racial hatred.

Interviews yielded approximately 14 hours of audiotaped conversations which were transcribed verbatim, yielding approximately 264 pages
of transcript. In this chapter, I focus on several related themes regarding
children's socialization. These particular themes were chosen for inclusion here as "key cultural concepts" because they were elaborated upon
spontaneously by all six adults. In addition, adults confirmed that these
themes captured "what they were saying."

KEY CULTURAL CONCEPTS

African-American Children Develop within a Racist Society

Consistent with discussions of other African-American communities, racism was viewed as a risk factor to children's development. Indeed, all six adults placed the development of African-American children within a social and cultural context that they viewed as racist; that is, a context in which they are viewed as inherently inferior, excluded from activities, denied opportunities, and sometimes treated with disdain based on their racial heritage. Although adults varied in the extent to which they viewed racism as a formative factor in their own lives and the lives of their children, all six spontaneously related specific, personal incidences involving racism. For example, Brother Brown, the Sunday School superintendent, reported the following behavior by a colleague at a professional conference held at the local public university the previous week:

> This lady had sat beside me all through this conference. . . . they had had an explosion out in Grantsville, and they never found the people . . . it was a bomb or something that blew up. . . . And, as we were concluding, she said, "Oh, that was just like a nigger." And she looked over at me. And, I totally ignored her. I felt sorry for her. I say, "Anybody can be a 'nigger.'"

Although active forms of hostile racism were described, the main forms of racism discussed by adults in reference to children growing up in Salt Lake City today were European-American public school educators' lack of cultural sensitivity and their negative expectations for African-American children. Adults felt that such attitudes contributed to children's feelings of inferiority and not belonging, which adversely affected children's motivation to cooperate and to succeed. For example, in discussing the source of educational problems among African-American children in Salt Lake City, Brother Brown elaborated:

> The lack of cultural awareness leads to negative stereotyping. . . . The first thing they [public school teachers and administrators] do when they see a minority, whether it's Hispanic or black . . . the first opinion, is that we're troublemakers. That you don't pay attention, that you don't want to learn, and that you goof off and all those kinds of things. . . . And then the child is told he or she . . . can't learn. . . .

They [children] get to the point where, "I'm not gonna try because I'm already labeled as the clown of the class."

Adults also commented on the negative effects on all children generated by a lack of positive interest by European-American professionals in African-American children and black history and culture in general. For example, Pastor Daniels elaborated:

Let me give you an example of a personal experience I had. I went to my son's school. He was the only African-American in the school at the time. And I said to the principal, "What are you going to do this year about black history?" And, he said to me, frankly, quickly, without thought, "Nothing." And, I asked him, "Why not?" And he said, "Because we only have one African-American student." And then I reminded him that it wasn't my son who needed that, because he had gotten that at the church and at our home, but that it was the other students who needed it.

Interestingly, a few informants also discussed the detrimental effects of prejudice by blacks toward whites. Sister Justine, for example, related her own experiences as a high school student dating a white classmate.

When I was coming up . . . I basically took the black community for a loop by starting to . . . date white. . . . It wasn't until I became an adult that I realized how my mom was prejudiced. It wasn't until I became an adult. And she's a very, extremely [prejudiced against whites]. I listen to some of the things that she said, I guess you listen more carefully when you're an adult – and I listen. And I think it's just bitterness. . . . We went to high school together. That's where I started dating him and brought him into the black community with me. And it made me realize about, you know, double standards within Christianity. And, you know, I can't, I can't deal with that. I won't. And, it's a shame to have to say it, but that's extremely shallow to me. You know. The mind-set that comes with that, to just group a group of people together like that. That's like saying all black women are prostitutes.

In creating a more hospitable context for the development of African-American children within the public schools, all adults emphasized the need for multicultural education for white teachers and administrators. For example, Pastor Daniels noted that it's only been this . . . past school year that the University of Utah, for example, in its teacher preparation . . . program, will be requiring a multicultural, multiethnic kind of course. And they are still only requiring one course. So we got a long way to go in terms of preparation of teachers.

While recognizing the detrimental effects of racism, adults also discussed the responsibility of African-Americans to intervene proactively to protect their children by instilling in them a strong sense of self-worth, that they are as "good" and as capable as anyone else. They also recognized the difficulty of this task given the relatively few positive African-American role models outside of the church for children in Salt Lake City. In discussing the detrimental effects of racism on African-American children, Brother Brown emphasized,

> But we, as Afro-Americans, got to instill in our youngster that *(lowered,
> intense voice)* "You are as *good* as anyone else. You are as *capable* as anyone
> else. . . ." I used to tell my nephew . . . remind him, "Don't let anyone
> tell you that you are any less than they, given the same opportunity."

Similarly, Sister Ima emphasized that in raising her daughter, Therese:

> I made [Therese] aware of the fact that she is no better than anybody
> else, and nobody's any better than she is. And whatever is out there to
> be gained, go out and get it. You are just as equipped and qualified to
> apply for anything as anybody else. . . . I always dealt with prejudice
> with [Therese] as far as going to school like this – and I had incidences
> happen. . . . [Therese] does not have the thought that she's inferior or
> better than anybody else because we've taught her that what's eligible
> for other people is eligible for you. You're just as good as anybody, and
> get out there and go for it. And people are gonna make statements, call
> you names every once in awhile. You have to get beyond the point of
> rebelling or retaliating, learning ways in which you can cope with
> things in a nonviolent way.

The realities of racism and its meaning for young people at First Baptist Church were discussed in many contexts. Within the context of Sunday School, children were taught basic literacy skills such as decoding, phonics, and study skills. In the words of one deaconess, "When they [the children] get to school, the teachers will know they can learn!" In another example, Pastor Daniels admonished during his Dr. Martin

Luther King, Jr., Day sermon, "Be careful young people because it [racism] is alive and well in Salt Lake City. . . . Pray that we can get justice to mean more than 'just us.' " He went on to describe several recent incidents of racism in which church members were physically abused or threatened. He concluded that "we've come a long way, but we've still got a lot to do, young folks."

Interpersonal Relationships Are Key to Effective Socialization

Consistent with discussions of other African-American communities (e.g., see Mitchell, 1986), adults at First Baptist Church spontaneously stressed the importance of positive relationships between African-American adults and children. Indeed, positive adult–child relationships were viewed as prerequisite to effective socialization. This emphasis on relationships may be particularly strong, given adults' perceptions that educators and other helping professionals in Salt Lake City, who are predominantly European-American, generally are hostile or indifferent to African-American children. Indeed, the underachievement of African-American children in the public schools was attributed by our informants in part to children's inadequate motivation, resulting from inadequate relationships with public school educators. Adults viewed children's feelings of belonging, of being valued and accepted, as a prerequisite to socialization, both in the church and in the public schools. For example, in discussing the qualities of a good teacher, no informant discussed pedagogical theory, higher education, or intellectual characteristics. Good teachers love their children. They are sensitive to students' emotional needs, and they are concerned about their well-being within and outside of school. For example, in discussing effective African-American teachers, and why many African-American children in Utah fail in the public schools, Pastor Daniels elaborated:

> My own high school and elementary school experience [in segregated schools in Alabama] demonstrated that African-American teachers tend to be more concerned about every individual student, . . . about every student and whether that student does their best. . . . There are only a minimal number of African-American teachers in our [public] schools, and so that caring and that special kind of relationship that is unique to the African-American teacher is not always present.

Along the same lines, Sister Ima stated:

African-American teachers seem to have a more nurturing nature. . . .
I'm that kind of [public school] teacher. . . . I can see if something is
wrong with my kids by their looks. . . . I listen to kids. . . . Family exten-
sion is important. I monitor students through years. I just ran into a
parent in the mall, I remembered her after eight years.

Adults also stressed the importance of a positive relationship between
teacher and student in Sunday School. When discussing the goals of
Sunday School, Sister Justine was very explicit:

Love. I know there's a lot of kids that . . . this is another form for them
to obtain love in their life. I know Sunday School can be . . . a means [to
obtain love] for a lot of African-American kids especially. The only
means for them to interact . . . – even on a social level – with their own
people. It's like in the past. People send their children to Sunday
School whether they come or not. You know? . . . It's a situation [Sun-
day School] almost of bonding.

In discussing the qualities of a good Sunday School teacher, Sister Ima
elaborated:

I think the most important thing for any Sunday School teacher is to
know the students – to know them and to call them by name. . . . I have
a little kid who hasn't been here in a couple of weeks – I need to call
him. . . . I need to make an effort to see what happened to him. We
have one Sunday School member who's sick and I need to see her. But
knowing the kids, knowing about them, calling them by name and not
ridiculing . . . knowing something about their background, making
sure they're comfortable. . . . Being conscious of their feelings . . . they
have to know, actually, that you really love them. Yeah – and I have a
love for each of those students. . . . We actually fellowship in there
[Sunday School]. We have grown to love one another.

Sister Patrice elaborated upon the importance of listening to each
child in forming a positive relationship:

listening to your students. You have to listen to them. . . . You find that
when my students come they have a lot to tell me *(laughs)*. They do.
They just have a lot to say, and it's good to listen. I feel like a good
teacher is a good listener too. So the good teacher doesn't try to dominate all the time. You have to draw your students out. And a lot – some
of your students are not outgoing . . . you find some that are talkative

and outgoing, but a lot of them are quiet and very sensitive so you've got to be able to be . . . something to this one and this one and this one.

The Church Is a Haven

Consistent with discussions of other African-American churches (see chapter 2), adults viewed the African-American church as a center of community. The theme of the church as a haven of social and cultural support was especially strong during reminiscences of childhood. For example, Sister Patrice described her own upbringing in Salt Lake City when Jim Crow laws still were in effect:

> Back then when I was growing up here in Salt Lake, . . . there was a lot of places we couldn't go, but the church . . . was the center of our activities. . . . All the parties were sponsored by the church. . . . everything was church oriented for us. . . . There's places where you knew you couldn't go so you didn't go, but we were sheltered, we didn't venture out a lot. You remained in your little area, and you . . . just didn't venture out and you stayed with your friends and that was that . . . . Now my sister and I were the only two black kids in Whitier Elementary and I had white friends. They were my friends for the week. We didn't pal around on Saturday and Sunday. I came to church to meet my black friends. . . . We went to a movie and . . . we just went upstairs. You didn't cause, you know, any disturbance. We just went along. We went to school, we did our homework, and whatnot, and we came to the church for all the interacting. . . . Within the confines of the black church you just immerse yourself . . . you know, you run into it [racism], but you don't dwell on it. I mean there's no sense in dwelling on it.

The church as a center of community also was reflected in discussions of the interrelationships of church, home, and, ideally, the school. In discussing his own upbringing in rural Tennessee, Brother Brown expounded:

> So many of the schools that were rural schools, . . . the classes were held in church, and then on Sundays the service was held there . . . our teachers not only lived in the communities, they went to church. So if you hadn't behaved during the week, they saw your parents at church . . . family-like things were community-type things . . . they were community-based, . . . it was family too, but extended family. . . . School and church was so intertwined and so closely related . . . the teacher knew your parents and the parents knew the teacher.

In describing her own spiritual development as a child in Salt Lake City, Sister Ima also mentioned her relationship with women in the church: "They were like surrogate mothers. . . . Those . . . women were looking out for your social, spiritual growth."

Today, in Salt Lake City, the church still is viewed by adults as a center of community in which children interact with, and are taught by, other African-Americans who value and nurture them. In discussing her daughter's spiritual development, Sister Ima emphasized the importance of children's relationships with African-American adults within a loving, accepting atmosphere:

> She likes the idea that Reverend [Daniels] is there, and the older men and women in the church, and they're examples. I noticed that a couple of years ago when brother Vance's wife died, she had actually gotten attached to her. We had fallen in love with her and just from being around the people fellowshipping with the people in the church, the Christians in the church. [Therese] sang in the choir, she ushered, and she did all kinds of things. She was involved in the programs and everything. She was raised in this church and that's where her background is. And when she left here [last year] to go to school [college], she looked for a church . . . and she has not found it yet. It's the atmosphere in the church. The Word is staying. . . . God's word will be what it is forever, but . . . the atmosphere, the fellowship, makes a difference.

In discussing purely educational issues, Pastor Daniels observed that

> for many of our kids, it's [Sunday School] an opportunity for them to interact with teachers who are from their own heritage and background, and to learn reading and writing, in one sense, from people who come from the same kind of backgrounds.

Spirituality Is Protective

Although adults clearly value the multiple functions of the black church as a social and cultural institution, they emphasized its spiritual role. The main purpose of church is to provide a context for the community to praise God. In the words of a popular spiritual sung during Sunday services, "I don't know what you come to do, but I come to praise the Lord." Community worship nurtures the spiritual development of individuals. When asked to state the most important goal of Sunday School, all adults emphasized children's development as Christians. In the words of Sister Patrice, "The [most] important goal is to bring that child to Christ."

Consistent with the earlier discussion of African-American theology, religion was viewed by those interviewed as protective. Spiritual development is seen as a lifeline, most importantly to eternal life through belief in Jesus Christ, but also as a healthy way of coping with the trials of everyday life. Sister Patrice's statement that "the reason that most blacks survive is because of religion" was echoed by other adults in more than one sense. "Christian" beliefs were seen as spiritually, psychologically, and physically protective, particularly in social contexts hostile to blacks. The physical protection of Christian beliefs arises, in part, from the ability to remain calm and to not respond in kind to hatred. For example, in discussing racial prejudice, Sister Ima elaborated on the importance of "Christian" conduct during potentially volatile situations:

> Let me tell you the story. That's probably how I got through a lot of the things that I got through coming from that Christian background and everything because it could've been just the opposite. . . . It was in the late sixties when they first started integrating schools. . . . They called it my junior year, "forced integration." "You're going to this school . . . and you're just not going to go back to your all-black school next year." . . . I went to an integrated school and it actually wasn't integrated. It was sixty of us among about seven hundred and it was a living nightmare. I shall never forget when I got off the bus that morning. I was walking with my sister and I was crying, tears were falling, I said, "I don't know if I can do this deal." She said, "We'll be all right – it will be all right." The prejudice was deep even to the point in some cases where teachers would talk with their backs to you. They would say things in the classroom . . . that were just not appropriate. The kids would pick on us, and it would always be our fault. We would always be the instigators. We had to deal with teachers who were prejudiced and the students as well. I will never forget my sister telling me about a time that she had been called down to the office because this girl whose name was Horse – they called her "Horse" because she was as big as a horse – she had threatened my sister and then, when [she] got down to the office, she [Horse] was so angry, she was so filled up with hatred that my sister didn't even pursue it. She just looked at her and felt sorry for her, and she went back to class. She said if anybody had that much hate in them, they didn't need to be dealt with. She said it was just beyond her means, so she went on back to class and didn't even mess with it. . . . But, dealing with prejudice – had it not been for my Christian upbringing I probably would be dead now. Because I've been called names . . .

and I've been deprived of things that could have been entitled to me
. . . I've seen a lot of things. . . . When I went to this [integrated]
school, we would get on the bus and the kids would jump back as we
walked on the bus, and our seats were on the back of the bus. But, just
to show you how things turn around, the school that I went to – I went
on to college, went back to my high-school that last year and graduated
from a predominantly black school, but when I came out of school, I
did my student teaching in the area that I had gone to school that one
year. I went back and did my student teaching in the same [integrated]
school . . . so I had some of the kids in my classroom who jumped away
from me as I got on the bus. And I thought, "Here I am in a position to
flunk every last one of them" *(lots of laughing)*. But, I had to go back to
my upbringing – that wasn't right. So I enjoyed my student teaching
there, and didn't remind them of what they had done or anything like
that – I just went on and did my student teaching.

Adults also discussed the grace of God and literal protection from following Christian practices. Sister Justine brought up the issue in a discussion
of Sunday School:

> When I'm teaching, I . . . really point out to the kids about holding on
> to your spirituality. Do not ever make the assumption that because you
> said it with your mouth that your life will be this way, you know. You do
> have to follow the rules and regulations that are set down in the Bible
> . . . and getting off track can lead to some dangerous, dangerous,
> dangerous situations in life. Like they say in [alcoholism] treatment,
> "But for the grace of God, go I." And every time I see someone dying of
> AIDS or doing, then "But for the grace of God!" *(laughs)*. You know, it
> could have been me. And I relate that to the kids on a daily basis,
> because of some of the ills that are out there.

The psychological and spiritual "protection" of Christian beliefs arises,
in part, from the beliefs that God loves everyone, good and bad, and that
there is a higher justice to which all, eventually, are accountable. When
asked how her Christian upbringing helped her to deal with racial prejudice, Sister Ima emphasized that God loves everyone and that, eventually,
all are accountable to God:

> The [Sunday School] lesson this morning tells us God loves everybody.
> We don't hold any exclusive on the love that God gives to people. Even
> the bad ones, even the good ones, everybody. So if we remember that
> and nothing else – that's biblically based. . . . He's [Pastor Daniels]
> always talking about us being together, and us being as one, and no-

body's any better than anybody else. He constantly says that . . . but he does not come right out and say racial prejudice, but you know that he's trying to get the people to think on one accord. That's actually what his bottom line is . . . unity. . . . My mother would always say, "You treat people like you want to be treated, regardless of what they say and do . . . don't be beat up physically without doing something about it, but don't hold a grudge all day. . . . If it was wrong you are going to pay for it whether you admit to it or not . . ." It's like now, that's one of the things that's rooted in me right now. If you mistreat me, you'll answer to it. But I'm going to treat you the way that I've been taught to treat [people].

Christian beliefs learned in childhood also were viewed as protective throughout life. For example, Sister Justine explained:

It [spirituality] helps me . . . now that I'm an adult. It helps me to, I guess, be more humanitarian in my thought process, less judgmental . . . I understand now that everything has a purpose. Everything has a purpose, but, I can be more empathetic . . . with some of the things that I used to be, you know, just militant about. . . . I think I've developed a more wholistic view of people, in general. . . . That's not to say I don't still look at issues and wonder, you know, why this exists.

The Role of Sunday School Is to Help Children to Learn and Then to Apply Biblical Texts

Helping children to understand and then to apply biblical concepts to their everyday lives was also articulated by all adults as a central goal of Sunday School at First Baptist Church. Adults considered knowledge of Sunday School texts to be the foundation upon which children's spirituality develops. For example, in describing how children grew in the kindergarten and primary classes, Sister Katherine noted:

When they're five they sort of . . . know what's going on and why they're coming to Sunday School . . . other than, you know, this is a good time for me to get together with my friends and cut and paste. And when they leave . . . when they're eight, then they know some Bible stories and that way they've grown spiritually.

Although knowledge of Sunday School texts was viewed as necessary in all classes, it was never viewed as sufficient. An important goal even for very young children (3- to 5-year-olds) was to apply that knowledge to their own lives. Indeed, when asked to articulate her most important goal during Sunday School with 3- to 5-year-olds, Sister Katherine stressed the importance of helping children to understand how the biblical text applies to their own lives, and then encouraging them to act upon this knowledge:

> If they can remember one little thing and say, "Oh, I remember my teacher said," and go home and actually do it with Mom or Dad or Sister or Brother – anybody. That is my purpose. If I can actually see them do it.

Similarly, Sister Ima elaborated upon her goals:

> Just learning as much about Christ so that they can apply that in their lives. How Christ lived. What would Christ do if a situation arose . . . if, if He was in this situation that I'm in right now? What would he do, what would he say? . . . If you're feeling anxious, if you're feeling sad, if you're feeling insecure . . . there's a scripture that you can refer to in order to know . . . how to deal with it.

During an interview Sister Justine provided examples of how she worked toward her goal of helping children apply biblical concepts to their own lives:

> We constantly use parallels to what's actually happening in our lives in regards to the story that we're reading about. . . . When Paul was writing to the Romans, well, trying to tell them to stay in there and be encouraged. . . . And in [light] of what was going on with the Romans and in that particular part of the Bible, we're writing to a church in Compton – in our age group, to tell them to hang in there, we're hanging in there. So, it's like – that's how I explain to them, that's what Paul was doing. Encouraging them, yes. And I says, "You guys encourage then." Yes. We know that they got drive-by shooting. And, yes we know that there's crack everywhere you turn, and so on and so forth. But, we're writing to tell them to "hang in there from Salt Lake City!" (*laughs*)

Sister Justine also provided examples of how she tries to help the children to apply biblical concepts to conflicts in everyday life:

> They've [the children in Sunday School] got a lot to say. They've got a lot to say, and we, we use their lives. We use situations in their lives. You

know, we troubleshoot. We troubleshoot through the Bible. "OK, I'll tell you why your reaction shouldn't have been this. Here – here – let's look this up and find out the real solution, the spiritual solution. Instead of the secular, everyday life solution. . . ." And, usually it has to do with violence. I have one student, he's just – I call him my little militant. Cause he's having a hard time dealing with the anglo side of life, and I guess there was just one particular little anglo boy that just would not leave him alone. And I says, "You've got to start fighting." I says, "Well, here's some ammunition. Have you ever asked him to come to church?" You know. "Have you ever told him that you pray?" I said. He's says, "I think I will." And seriously, he went and tried this. He seriously went and tried this. And the boy left him alone. Geoffrey said though *(laughs)*, that he thinks the guy thought he was weird. That's why he left him alone! *(laughter)* And, I said, "Well, we are supposed to be a peculiar people, now!" . . . I said, "That was the unexpected. When you approached him in the name of Jesus Christ . . . you know, you're nine. You talked to a ten-year-old that's a bully, and it's like – you probably blew him away, yes. He probably does think you're weird." . . . [But] it resolved his problem.

This goal of applying biblical concepts to everyday life repeatedly was made explicit to children. For example, Sister Ima informed the children in the intermediate class:

I want you to read from your Bibles . . . because everytime you read scriptures from the Bible, something comes from it that we had not seen before. Hopefully, something that we can apply to our own lives.

Storytelling Is an Effective Context for Socialization

When asked how they accomplished their goals, adults consistently discussed stories as one important activity. They viewed storytelling as an important mechanism through which children are helped to find a personal meaning in the scriptures. For example, Pastor Daniels explained how personal experiences may be used to illuminate biblical concepts:

One of the differences, we believe, in what we try to do here at this church and what happens in some other church settings is the use of . . . stories. We are convinced that it is out of life that the best applications of any kind of principles can be found. And, certainly, if you're going to make sense of it, you have to relate it to life. And, when we tell our own personal stories, there's almost an immediate connection with the youngsters. . . . My own children have been good examples of the use of stories. I have a daughter, for example, who talked about the moon [on a trip to California]. And as we were driving [back to Utah], you could see the moon. And then when we got to Utah she saw the moon. . . . She had been asleep, and we had traveled for the whole day and there was the moon again. . . . So she raised the issue: "I thought we left the moon in California." And so that kind of personal experience allowed us to have the opportunity . . . to talk to her about God being everywhere, and the moon being everywhere, not just in California, but in Utah too.

Sister Justine also elaborated upon how biblical stories may be illuminated through personal experiences:

I tell stories of my own personal experiences. . . . There are kids in my class coming from homes where there are alcoholics and some are coming from split-ups and things. . . . I know that just from observing, and I let them know that I experienced them. . . . Just knowing that somebody has experienced something that you have – it makes you know that maybe you can go talk to them or they know how you feel that makes a difference.

In describing African-American teachers, Sister Justine elaborated,

Oh – I think the African-American teachers have a gift for almost adding a storytelling amongst the teaching, you know? They can give examples throughout.

The importance of stories also was apparent in adults' discussions of their own development. Sister Justine described:

My mother – oh! My mother would tell us stories about our family a lot – and on her side of the family is just religious people – you know – preachers and quartets . . . She tells us about what the churches were like – she's from the South – so that was always fun for us to sit around and listen to her talk about North Carolina. . . . Being brought up here in Salt Lake City – the prevalent religion was the LDS. . . . And, so, stories like that just made you . . . [think about] that old bond that our communities used to have. . . . You know, but we were just a handful when I was coming up here, a handful in the community.

In discussing her own spiritual development as a child, Sister Ima elaborated:

> My daddy used to tell stories all the time. He'd make up stories. . . .
> You'd be sitting there and all of a sudden he'd start making up some-
> thing on two people he saw outside. And you know you could laugh
> about what he was saying, [but] he said a lot of things that made you
> actually think. . . . Now when my brother came home – this is an exam-
> ple, OK? My brother, I think he died from a sad heart. He was married
> and they broke up or something. He moved back and she was in New
> Jersey. And evidently he was seeing a lady, and somebody else was
> seeing a lady. This was just typical of my family, and my mother was
> sitting there after they got back. . . . He was crying and she said, "You
> crying because you want Mary, and so and so is crying cause he got
> Mary." You know *(laughing)*. That made you think now, wait a minute,
> Mary ain't no good for nobody. You need to rethink what you're
> doing. . . . The Bible stories . . . make him start thinking along the
> lines – hey you need to direct your thoughts and maybe you need to
> refer to Proverbs 3, verse five and six. "Lean not to your own under-
> standing." . . . She [mother] kind of steered you in the direction you
> needed to be thinking. "Trust in the Lord you'll be all right – you'll be
> just fine, I'll be praying for you." . . . They [stories] were important
> because, now that I think about it, they were just a source of strength.
> You know?

That storytelling is a deliberate educational device at First Baptist Church is suggested by a recent topic in adult Sunday School, "Teaching through examples," in which Jesus' use of stories as a pedagogical tool was discussed. Similarly, in discussing her own use of stories, Sister Justine reported:

> I went to a workshop that Reverend [Daniels] sent me to last year. . . .
> They brought in this convention of people, and they said that that
> [storytelling] was one of the items of dealing with young Christian
> minds. . . . Stop talking to them in all these big theoretical-type termi-
> nology and stuff that they couldn't even grasp.

CONCLUSION

In summary, I've characterized socialization beliefs as child-sensitive and growth-oriented. All of the adults we interviewed were concerned about African-American children's experience of racism. This concern may, in part, underlie the "growth-oriented" aspect of socialization beliefs. In other words, in a broader sociocultural context perceived to be hostile or indifferent to African-American children, immature behavior may be hazardous. Although the concern about racism may be shared by African-Americans in communities throughout the United States, this concern takes on special significance in a context in which African-Americans are both a racial and religious minority, and are isolated on a daily basis from sources of support within the larger African-American community. Adults discussed the negative effects of racism on children's self-esteem and motivation. They viewed racism as a significant factor in children's underachievement in school, delinquency, and other self-destructive behaviors. Solutions offered by adults included the multicultural education of European-American professionals.

Adults' sensitivity to children's emotional well-being and immaturity also was clear in their discussions of the importance of the involvement of African-American adults with children. The church was presented as a context in which children can learn to cope with the challenges of growing up black in Salt Lake City from adults who love, value, and respect them. Adults characterized the African-American church as a haven within which children develop an alternative, spiritual belief system. This belief system is socialized, in large part, through the nurturing relationships that adults establish with children and that children establish with one another. Within the church, children's relationships with African-American adults, including Sunday School teachers, were viewed as critical for strengthening and developing self-esteem, providing positive role models for healthy coping, and, most importantly, for strengthening spirituality.

Throughout the interviews, spiritual beliefs were characterized as protective factors. Spiritual beliefs were presented as neither remote nor abstract, but as intimate, personal, and immediate. Consistent with the literature discussed in chapter 2 on the pragmatic intertwining of the sacred and the everyday in African-American theology, adults articulated the primary goals of Sunday School as helping children to understand biblical concepts and then to apply those concepts to their everyday lives. Consistent with the literature discussed in chapter 2 on the importance of storytelling to African-American communities, adults described storytelling as an effective context for socialization.

CHAPTER SEVEN

Narratives Related during Sunday School

During one of our early conversations, Pastor Daniels emphasized the importance of helping children to understand and then to apply biblical concepts to their own everyday lives. He went on to identify storytelling as central to this socialization process:

> The most important goal is to teach them [children] Bible principles and to make that applicable in terms of their daily lives. To somehow talk to them about the higher principles like love and faith and patience . . . and also tell them how they can, practically, from examples, apply that in their own lives. . . . And, when we tell our own personal stories, there's almost an immediate connection with the . . . children.

Pastor Daniels's reflections are consistent not just with the observations of other adults presented in chapter 6, but with a large body of literature in African-American studies. From slavery times through the present, African-Americans have derived strength and resilience from culturally distinct, spiritual belief systems developed within the African-American church. Through sustained participation over a lifetime in cultural practices such as storytelling, spiritual beliefs are elaborated and linked to the trials and joys of individuals' everyday lives.

The goal of the next two chapters is to describe children's participation in storytelling at First Baptist Church. Storytelling is a cultural universal (e.g., Bruner, 1986, 1990) basic to socializing children into the meaning systems of their cultures (e.g., Bruner, 1990; Engel, 1995; Fivush, 1993; Miller & Moore, 1989; Miller, Wiley, Fung & Liang, 1997; Nelson, 1989; Sperry & Smiley, 1995). Children from a wide variety of cultural communities participate in storytelling during routine conversations with adults beginning very early in development (e.g., Eisenberg, 1985;

Fivush, 1991; Heath, 1983; Miller & Sperry, 1987; Miller, Wiley, Fung & Liang, 1997; Sperry & Sperry, 1996; Wiley, Rose, Burger & Miller, 1998).

Much has been written about the significance, creativity, and power of storytelling in African-American communities (e.g., Gates, 1989). Indeed, storytelling has been identified as an effective tool for many African-American teachers (M. Foster, 1994; Mitchell, 1986). Systematic study of children's participation with adults in storytelling within African-American communities, however, is only just beginning (see Heath, 1983; Potts, 1989; Sperry, 1991; Sperry & Sperry, 1996; Ward, 1971; Williams, 1994). In this chapter, I will describe the frequency with which children and adults tell stories together during Sunday School, the types of events they relate, and stability and changes over time in children's participation.

DATA SET AND RELIABILITY

The analyses of narrative reported in the next two chapters are based upon lessons taught in 33 Sunday School classes observed from November 1992 through May 1994: 6 kindergarten, 9 primary, 9 junior, and 9 intermediate classes. Although all classes were audiotaped on at least 10 different Sundays, only those classes taught by the regular teachers are included here. In addition, the kindergarten and primary classes sometimes were combined, and these classes are not included in this analysis.

The analyses reported in the next two chapters are based upon the "lesson" portion of the Sunday School class. During this time, children and teachers studied from and discussed their assigned Sunday School papers and related biblical passages. For the kindergarten and primary classes the lesson was taught in the first 30 minutes of the class. The remaining time was spent singing, playing games, doing arts and crafts projects, or filling out Sunday School worksheets. In the junior and intermediate classes, the lesson occurred approximately in the first 60 minutes of class. Time permitting, the older children engaged in small projects, plays, and other expressive activities (e.g., drawing, writing poetry). Thus, analyses are based on approximately 3 hours of kindergarten lessons, 4 1/2 hours of primary lessons, 9 hours of junior lessons, and 9 hours of intermediate lessons.

Narrative talk is displaced speech on one topic in which at least two events are temporally sequenced (Sperry & Sperry, 1996). During Sunday School at First Baptist Church, topics were sometimes outlined on the chalk board, or verbally marked by the teacher, such as, "Now we're gonna talk about your gifts." Narrative talk was displaced temporally (referred to past or future events) and fictionally (referred to imaginary or hypothetical events) (Sperry & Sperry, 1996). To identify the occurrence of narrative in the transcribed texts, two coders independently coded all narratives in eight randomly selected classes: two classes each from kindergarten, primary, junior, and intermediate classes. Percentage agreement for identifying the occurrence of narrative was 91%. Disagreements were resolved through discussion.

For all other analyses reported in the next two chapters, two coders independently coded 20% of all identified narratives, each randomly selected from kindergarten, primary, junior, and intermediate classes. (Percentage agreement for these reliability checks will be reported within the text.)

STORIES WERE A FREQUENT OCCURRENCE DURING SUNDAY SCHOOL

Stories were an important part of Sunday School at First Baptist Church in all classes from kindergarten through intermediate. A total of 299 narratives were observed: 27 in kindergarten class, 25 in the primary class, 86 in the junior class, and 161 in the intermediate class. As summarized in Table 7.1, the mean hourly rate of narratives was 11, ranging from a mean and standard error of the mean (SEM) of 6 ± 1 in the primary class to 17 ± 2 in the intermediate class.

EVENTS NARRATED

The next issue explored in this chapter concerns the types of events highlighted through stories told during Sunday School, and changes in children's participation over time. Sociocultural contexts vary in the types of events that are acceptable or preferred topics for narratives. Such preferences may even relate to children's developmental trajectories. For example, developmental analysis of everyday talk revealed that young boys and their rural, working-class, African-American caregivers preferred producing narratives about the self involving fictional events rather than literal past events (Sperry & Sperry, 1996), as was preferred, for example, by young girls and their white, urban, working-class mothers (Miller & Moore, 1989). In the African-American community, both caregivers and children frequently enjoyed telling thrilling fantasy stories of escaping from "Nicoudini," the "Boogabear," and "Werewolf"; and of

TABLE 7.1. *Frequency of Narratives and Events Narrated by the Class*

	Katherine's Kindergarten Class (3–6 years)	Patrice's Primary Class (6–8 years)	Justine's Junior Class (8–12 years)	Ima's Intermediate Class (12–15 years)
Mean hourly rate and SEM				
Narratives	9 ± 1	6 ± 1	10 ± 2	17 ± 2
Mean percentage and SEM of narratives containing				
Recounting	29 ± 9	67 ± 10	63 ± 8	72 ± 5
Personal				
experience	21 ± 16	1 ± 1	14 ± 5	24 ± 4
Hypothetical	21 ± 14	4 ± 3	34 ± 7	13 ± 3

locking up troublesome family members in closets or refrigerators (Sperry & Sperry, 1996). In this African-American community, young boys' participation in fantasy stories preceded, developmentally, stories of actual personal experience. Sperry and Sperry (1996) argue that, in a context in which fictional storytelling was supported, these events were "easier" for young children to narrate.

Socialization contexts – for example, home or school – also may vary in the types of events that are preferred or acceptable topics for narratives. For example, although stories recounting personal experiences are common in middle-class European-American families, within the contexts of most North American classrooms, telling stories about personal experiences is devalued and restricted, decreasing in frequency with grade level (Michaels, 1985, 1991).

Analysis of Sunday School classes at First Baptist Church revealed several types of events related by teachers and children. For the purposes of this analysis, the events portrayed within narratives will be presented sequentially. Note, however, that a single narrative could contain a variety of types of events. For example, a narrative could begin with talk about personal experiences and conclude with talk about hypothetical events.

Biblical Stories Were Frequently Recounted

Background

Teachers within a European-American religious community have been observed to retell Bible stories to children (Zinsser, 1986). One of

the functions of such recounting may be to support children's comprehension of the literal meaning of the text, a primary socialization goal
of teachers at First Baptist Church. In addition, when biblical texts are
retold using familiar everyday speech patterns such as black English,
children may identify more closely with characters in the story. Such
identification could aid a second socialization goal of teachers at First
Baptist Church, that is, children's recognition that biblical concepts have
relevance to them.

First Baptist Church

We defined "recounting" as the oral, temporally ordered retelling of
all or some of the written biblical stories, or other stories presented in the
Sunday School text. (Interrater reliability for identifying "recounting"
was 92%.) Consistent with adults' emphasis on children's acquisition of
knowledge of the Sunday School text, a substantial percentage of narratives in all Sunday School classes, kindergarten through intermediate,
recounted biblical text. Within the kindergarten class, however, a relatively smaller percentage of stories involved such retellings. (See Table
7.1.)

In the kindergarten class, a mean and SEM of $29\% \pm 9\%$ of narratives
contained some recounting of the text. Some of these recountings occurred after the text was read and seemed to function as paraphrases to
aid children's understanding, or as checks of their comprehension.
Other recountings appeared before biblical texts were read and appeared to function as reviews of earlier discussions. In the following
narrative fragment, Sister Katherine refers to the previous Sunday's lesson when introducing to the kindergarten children a new text pertaining
to Isaac's birth:

> OK, we're gonna talk about, "Isaac is born." Remember the last les-
> son. . . . [We were] talking about who? Abraham and? *(pause)* Sarah.
> Can you say Abraham and Sarah? *(Children repeat.)* Alright! And they
> had a little baby! God promised them that they were gonna have a baby,
> OK? And now the baby's been born! OK! . . . Whose been born? . . .

The emphasis on knowledge of the Sunday School text also was apparent
in classes for older children. Indeed, a mean and SEM of $67\% \pm 10\%$ of
narratives in the primary class, $63\% \pm 8\%$ of narratives in the junior class,
and $72\% \pm 5\%$ of narratives in the intermediate class contained recountings. As in the kindergarten classes, this talk appeared to function as
reviews and as checks on children's knowledge. In the following narrative

fragment, Sister Justine prompted the children in the junior class to help her to recount John the Baptist's conception and birth:

> You know who his [John the Baptist's] parents were? . . . Now there was something real weird about his parents. What was it? . . . Tell me how it happened . . . do you know what else happened?

The next example is the opening of an extended narrative in which Sister Ima explicitly marked the recounting for children in the intermediate class ("back track"), and stated its purpose:

> SI: OK! First of all we're going to do a little back track here . . . see who can remember what's been discussed up to this point. And let's not all speak at one time, OK? *(Teasing. Several young teenagers are sitting with their heads laying on their arms.)* You all need to get some life in ya now. . . . First of all, the subject we're studying from is what?
>
> Children, in chorus: Who unites.
>
> SI: Who unites. And, of course, we know who unites. Paul is trying to get us to remember that, and he's trying to get that across to Philemon. And, if uniting is to be done it must be done by the grace of God, and it must be done in Christian-like principles. That's why Paul wrote this – this letter, so that this man would know that.

Personal Experience Stories Were Told in Sunday School

Background

Stories of personal experience have been widely studied by language socialization researchers. These stories, which report events personally experienced by the narrator, have been observed in the language of children and adults from a wide variety of cultures, including African-American communities (e.g., McCabe, 1997; Sperry & Sperry, 1996). They are viewed by many as integral to the development of concepts of self (e.g., Bruner, 1986, 1990; Engel, 1995; Fivush, 1991; Hermans, 1997; Miller & Moore, 1989; Neisser & Fivush, 1994; Ochs & Capps, 1996; Sperry & Smiley, 1995; Sperry & Sperry, 1996; Wiley, Rose, Burger & Miller, 1998). Through stories of personal experience, people create, interpret, and publicly project images of the self. Within the context of the family, adults and children together routinely apply culture-specific interpretations to their past experiences, allowing children to construct a sense of self in conjunction with significant others (e.g., Miller et al., 1997; Wiley et al., 1998). Such constructions may provide children at First Baptist Church with positive counterexamples to negative stereotypes of African-Americans they may encounter, for example, at school, in the media, or through personal encounters with racism.

A small body of literature points to the significance of stories of personal experience to the socialization of African-American children at home. Within middle-class African-American families, stories of personal experience emerged spontaneously as part of the routine interactions between parents and their preschool-age children. These stories included parents' personal experiences with reading and writing, and may support children's literacy socialization (Williams 1991, 1994). Similarly, spontaneous stories of personal experience jointly constructed with parents and children living in a public housing project in Chicago (Potts, 1989) and in a rural community in Alabama (Sperry, 1991) have been identified as basic to children's socialization.

Within educational contexts, stories of personal experience also may function to help students link new concepts to everyday experiences – another primary socialization goal for teachers at First Baptist Church. African-American teachers identified as excellent by African-American community members emphasized that instructional strategies must relate school materials to students' personal experiences (Foster, 1994). Their pedagogical techniques included the use of first-person narratives linking the content of instruction to children's everyday experiences (Foster, 1995). The use of storytelling by African-American teachers even has been reported in college-level classes. For example, successful African-American community college teachers requested descriptions of students' personal experiences (Foster, 1989). Interestingly, Heath (1983) helped European-American elementary school teachers to enhance their effectiveness with African-American children by including in their lessons questions about children's personal experiences, such as "Have you ever been there?"

Stories of personal experience also have been observed within European-American religious communities. During children's Sunday School and Vacation Bible School in two European-American fundamentalist churches, Caroline Zinsser (1988) observed that teachers emphasized the application of the text to life. As a regularly scheduled follow-up to Bible stories, teachers read "application stories," which related Bible stories to everyday situations familiar to children. One teacher also used personal stories to relate biblical concepts to everyday experiences. Similarly, during adult Sunday School within an European-American, Wesleyan church, the teacher offered examples from his own life as illustrations of how biblical texts apply to everyday situations familiar to students (Martinson, 1994).

First Baptist Church

Stories involving personal experiences also were observed in Sunday School at First Baptist Church. There, personal experience talk within narratives related biblical concepts to the teller's own life through elaboration of a past event actually experienced by the narrator. (Interrater reliability for identifying talk of personal experience within narratives was 100%.) As summarized in Table 7.1, the mean percentage and SEM of narratives including discussions of personal experiences during Sunday School at First Baptist Church ranged up to 24% ± 4%.

Table 7.2 summarizes several important characteristics of stories involving personal experiences. First, discussion of personal experiences always followed discussion of biblical texts. There were no instances of personal stories preceding biblical text. These stories always came after the reading of the biblical text and were used to illustrate and elaborate key points from that text. In addition, children generally did not play key roles in these narratives. Typically, adults related their own experiences to children. Very rarely, except in kindergarten classes, did children initiate discussions of their own personal experiences. Through stories of personal experiences, adults seemed to communicate to children that biblical principles are important in their own lives and exactly how they are important. For example, after discussing with her class several examples of storms at sea from the New Testament, Sister Justine challenged the children in the junior class to understand the metaphorical meaning of "storm." Embedded within this discussion is Sister Justine's personal, spiritual story of recovery from alcoholism.

> sj: What are storms – what are storms in our everyday life? I'm not talking about: it's starting to rain. There's another meaning for the word storm, in a spiritual sense.
> *(Children provide several examples.)*
> sj: Let's get some more serious storms. . . . Now, let's broaden these storms out . . . is there anything really rocky goin' – like a wave goin' on in somebody's life right now? (pause) What?
> bess: Um – someone takes drugs.
> sj: Ohhh!!! Now we're gettin' some real serious storms in people's lives.
> children: Ouuuuuuu! *(Storm sound effect.)*

TABLE 7.2. *Contexts and Protagonists in Sunday School Narratives (percentage across classes)*

	Personal Experience (%)	Hypothetical (%)
Preceded by biblical text	100	100
Protagonist:		
Teacher	80	21
Child	35	83

sj: OK.

BESS: Like when that wave comes!

(Children provide more examples.)

sj: That's a storm in a person's life. *(Asks child to close the door.)* Yeah – OK. I meant to tell you guys a hundred, a million times about a problem that I had in my life that was a storm. Do you remember what I told you?

EDNA: Ahha.

sj: What?

EDNA: When you said that you had taken too many drugs . . .

sj: I think I told you about my miracle. I told you about God comin' straight by me. My drug of choice as they say in the recovery world was – you know what they call me? I'm a recovering alcoholic. That was one of the major storms in my life. That was one of the major storms in my life, but guess who calmed me?

Several children call out: Jesus! . . .

sj: That's how I got calm. Say it again.

JOSH: Jesus calms.

sj: Not men. Man didn't comfort me.

DANIELLE: A friend?

sj: No, Jesus did it. . . . Jesus Christ comforted me. . . . So when you have a storm . . . who are you gonna turn to for your comfort?

CHILDREN, IN CHORUS: Jesus.

In the next example, intermediate class members were discussing keeping God at the head of their lives. Sister Ima articulated to these young teenagers how the biblical concepts under study had guided her through difficult times in her own life:

si: I can remember many instances where I had opportunities, and I was reminded, God will be my strength in this situation. He will never leave me, and he won't forsake me. He'll provide me with everything that I need. OK. I just witnessed one as I was visiting North Carolina. And, ah, this is in line with the lesson, today, and I'll share it because it actually happened to me. When we got ready to take Terese [daughter] to her college dorm room, the roommate that she had was an only child, and she obviously has had her way about things, and, you know, there were certain things that she just did not want Terese to do. The rooms are very small, and it's very hard for you not to touch something that, you know, is in the room. . . . So, Terese happened to touch the answering machine that happened to be on the other side of the room. And the girl got upset and had left Terese a very nasty note, she really had. And it concerned us, and I'll be honest with you, I got all upset. I got all upset because I was leaving my child there. I was coming back across country. And, the girl evidently called her mother. And within a matter of minutes the mother was there, and she came in yelling and doing all kinds of things, "What did you do to my daughter, what did you say to my daughter!" And I remained calm, and I said, "I don't recall saying anything that was offensive. I do remember that she was very obnoxious and disrespectful to me as an adult."

MICHELLE: Well, she's spoiled.

SI: Well, I don't know. It might not be fair for me to say that because to a certain extent my child is. But, there's never an excuse to be nasty to anybody. Never. Never. Like Paul always said, "I'm in jail, but I'm still doing what I know I'm supposed to do," OK? But this is what happened, and this is how I can give you this experience knowing that God is my strength. The woman came in with her husband. And we were all sitting there in the dorm room. And, we all finally came to the point where we said, "This is no way for us to be actin', you know? Let's pray." And that's what happened. The parents joined hands and prayed there in the dorm room, and it was quite beneficial. And no matter what happens, whether the girls stay together or whatever, that will be a decision that they will make, but I within myself, I feel much better. I am at peace with the situation because we, the three parents, did not allow the devil to take control. And, that's what he wanted to do, separate us. And all three of us prayed, "The devil wants to separate us. These are the kinds of things that he wants to see us do." . . . You know? They'll work it out. I mean, if they're gonna live together they gonna live together.

MICHELLE: I won't put up with that. If somebody did that to me, and started getting mad at me because I touched the answering machine, I'd go all wild.

SI: You see, that's what the lesson is about, Michelle. Maybe you could suggest to her that she puts on the whole armor of God, or allow him in in a situation like that. That really could have been a nasty scene because the parents could have ended up fightin', and we could have been hauled off to jail, or whatever. Or, it could have put the girls in a position where they would really be bad off for the rest of the time. But, I haven't thought about it that much anymore, because we did what needed to be done right there. We actually joined hands in the room, sat down, and prayed. And, I haven't – it hasn't concerned me no matter which way it goes. And the girls went into another room and did the same thing. So – that's what counts that the parents were all together. We went out the door and started over again. Literally walked out the dorm door and started over again. And, I just share that with you, not that you need to be worried about it, or anything like that, but that's something that happened to me that's in line with today's lesson. Had none of us had any exposure, or had God in our hearts, we wouldn't have even thought about praying. That's my story *(laughs)*.

It is important to emphasize that both of these stories, like other stories of personal experience told by teachers in Sunday School, were used to elucidate key points, not to elicit personal, emotional support. At the end of her story, Sister Justine makes explicit the significance of her story, "So when you have a storm . . . who are you gonna turn to for your comfort?" Similarly, Sister Ima notes, "And, I just share that with you, not that you need to be worried about it, or anything like that, but that's something that happened to me that's in line with today's lesson."

Stories of personal experience were less central within the kindergarten and primary classes. Although a mean and SEM of 21% ± 16% of narratives within the kindergarten class contained some reference to a specific past event experienced by the narrator, this talk always was initiated by a child and typically was fairly brief. Sister Katherine tended to acknowledge the child's contribution and then move on without requesting further elaboration. In the primary class only a mean and SEM of 1% ± 1% of narratives contained any talk of personal experiences.

Hypothetical Events Were Frequently Narrated

Background
Although stories of personal experience are among the most widely studied narrative form by language socialization researchers, several authors have argued that the study of socialization through narrative should

be expanded to include more than just personal perspectives and past events (e.g., Bamberg, 1997; Ochs & Capps, 1996). For example, several authors have reported hypothetical events in stories told to and with children (e.g., Preece, 1987; Sperry & Sperry, 1996). Hypothetical talk within adult–child narrative may allow participants to play with written text or concepts, discussing what might be, given the presented circumstances, or what might have been, if the circumstances were altered – for example, if the children were called upon to make choices in their own lives similar to those confronted by biblical characters. Thus, hypothetical talk can provide a context in which children can consider the application of biblical concepts and events to their own lives, another primary socialization goal of teachers at First Baptist Church.

First Baptist Church

Hypothetical talk within Sunday School narratives involves reference to temporally sequenced, hypothetical events. In distinction to the factual or real, hypothetical speech expresses a condition that either was not met or one that is unlikely to be met (Matthew, 1997). Hypothetical talk within narratives extends the presented material by explicitly suspending the details of the text or of reality as experienced by the participants. For example, "If Jesus was walking with us today, what would he want you to do?" (Interrater reliability for identifying hypothetical talk was 100%.) That hypothetical talk was viewed as commonplace by the children at First Baptist Church is suggested by an 8-year-old girl's response to her teacher's question of how they would know that the pastor was a Christian if he were not carrying around a Bible: "He'd always be quoting scriptures and asking, 'What if, and what if, and what if.'"

As illustrated by Table 7.2, hypothetical talk occurred about as frequently as talk about personal experiences in Sunday School. Indeed, the mean percentage and SEM of narratives within Sunday School that included reference to a sequence of hypothetical events ranged up to 34% ± 7%. Table 7.2 summarizes several important characteristics of hypothetical talk within narratives in relation to personal experience talk. First, hypothetical talk, like personal experience talk, always followed and expanded the biblical text. Second, unlike talk of personal experiences, talk of hypothetical events often cast the child in a major role. In a number of instances, hypothetical event sequences were further elaborated into actual role play in which children and teachers actually "became" biblical characters, reacting and speaking in character. The following example is taken from a more extended discussion of the prophet Jeremiah and the importance of obedience to God by members of the junior class.

> SJ: If, at your age, at your age, God wanted you, Denise and Chivontee and Terranasha, to go out to downtown Salt Lake City *(girls laugh)* and tell the people that they need to live right, what would you do? *(Children struggle to respond. Teacher walks around the table and sits down directly in front of Denise.)* I'm God and I said, "Denise, *(girls laugh)* I want you to go down and, and I want you to tell Wendy and her family that they need God." How would you talk back to God? *(Children offer some responses.)* If – let's change it a few minutes – let me kinda give you an idea. You're God. And I'm sleeping at home, and God comes to me at night. . . . She's God now! *(Indicating Denise. Children laugh)* I'm asleep in bed last night, and Denise is God and she says, "Justine! Justine!" Maybe not like that. *(Children laugh.)* "I want you to go and tell Wendy and her family that they need God, right now." *(pause)* "God?" First of all I'm trying to sleep a little bit, right? Did I really hear that? *(laughter)*
> CHIVONTEE: It's a dream!
> SJ: Yeah, right! But guess what. I'm sitting up and He says it again. . . . Then what would you do? . . . Terranasha?

In the following example, Sister Justine has just scolded members of the junior class based upon a report from the previous Sunday's substitute teacher that they did not behave well. She asked the class what happens if they do not behave well in "regular school." Children report that they would get poor grades and might even fail.

> SJ: So, if you don't pay attention to your Sunday School lesson, what's gonna happen to you?
> BESS: You'll flunk it.
> SJ: But, what – what are you gonna flunk at, though?
> *(Several children answer at once.)*
> SJ: This is pretty dangerous stuff! . . . If you flunk. If you're failing in Sunday School lessons, what are you getting ready to fail at? Everybody pay attention. I want an answer to this question. There's a difference between gettin' an "F" in school, and gettin' an "F" in Jesus Christ. You get an "F" in Jesus Christ, what's gonna happen to you?
> JOSH: You're gonna go to *(pause)*.
> SJ: Where are you not goin'?

CHILDREN, IN CHORUS: Up to Heaven. *(Laughter. The class then engages in a long, very humorous role play in which they discuss and assign grades to one another on "Jesus Christ.")*

In discussing with her class the biblical text in which Jesus walks on water, Sister Justine set the following scene:

Imagine . . . if you was just lounging on the beach and all of a sudden you took your shades off, looked up, and there was somebody and they were walking on water! *(Loud laughing and hooting from the children.)* . . . You'd be afraid.

Interestingly, by the time they were in the junior class, some children began posing hypotheticals. For example, 9-year-old Javon launched the following exchange:

JAVON: What if you don't go to church and you don't believe –
SJ: Ummm. Keep talking . . .
JAVON: What if . . . you don't even go to church and you don't even know.
SJ: Ummm! Now, that's interesting. Will God touch the unsaved?

In this next example, the class had been discussing going to heaven or hell and 9-year-old LaTasha asked:

LATASHA: If, if you were good and – say you were really good.
SJ: Ahha.
LATASHA: And an angel when you were a child, but you got up and when you got grown up, you were just really mean in a gang – but then turned back over to God and then when you die – say you got shot by a gang member. . . . So where would they go then? Because their sins were there?
SJ: All you have to do is ask for forgiveness! You're saying – alright . . . this person you said went to church, came back hard-headed, then came back to church, and then got accidently killed in the line of fire of a gang member? . . . All it takes is believing . . .
LATASHA, INTERRUPTING: Yeah, but you believe yes and you believe no.
SJ: . . . You can't waiver in your faith.

Hypothetical speech also occurred in the intermediate class. A mean and SEM of $13\% \pm 3\%$ of narratives contained hypothetical talk. In the following example, Sister Ima tries to get the children to imagine an alternative world in which God does not keep his promises. The discussion began with the children describing promises that others had made to them, including Christmas presents and a trip to a basketball game.

> OK. Now, suppose those promises had been broken . . . ? You would have been heartbroken, wouldn't you? *(Children agree.)* If you got up on Christmas morning and found you didn't have all that stuff under the Christmas tree, you would've been really sick, wouldn't you . . . all those material things that you received because somebody promised you. . . . Suppose those promises had never been kept, then you would really be in a mess, right? *(Children agree.)* But not half the mess you'd be in if God had not kept his promise . . . suppose God had not promised us eternal life through his son, Jesus Christ? Would we not be in a mess?

Remarkably, even the youngest children participated in narratives referring to hypothetical events. Although extended hypothetical discussions were less typical of kindergarten and primary classes, brief hypothetical discussions did occur. Indeed, a mean and SEM of $21\% \pm 14\%$ of narratives in kindergarten classes contained some hypothetical talk. Following a discussion of Paul's letters to the Ephesians, Sister Katherine challenged her 3- to 5-year-old students:

> [If] Mommy say, "Pick up your toys," would you keep taking them out and put them on the floor? . . . If Mama say, "Make your bed!" Do you make your bed? . . . And it also says, "Parents treat your children with kindness and fairness, and raise them with Christian discipline and instruction." So, if I'm a mom, I have to be nice to you, huh? . . . If I give Matthew a cookie, I also have to give Terrance a cookie, huh? If I give PJ a cookie, do I have to give Curtis a cookie too?

Relatively few narratives within the primary class (a mean and SEM of $4\% \pm 3\%$ of narratives) contained hypothetical talk.

CONCLUSION

Consistent with scholarly work indicating that storytelling is a significant aspect of African-American culture (Gates, 1989; Hale-Benson, 1987; Hill-Lubin, 1991; Smitherman, 1977), as well as a significant context for children's socialization (e.g., Bruner, 1990; Fivush, 1993; Miller et al., 1989, 1997; Nelson, 1989), narratives were a frequent occurrence in all Sunday School classes at First Baptist Church. Although an important focus in the classes was the written biblical text or paraphrased biblical text from the Sunday School papers, these texts sometimes appeared difficult for children to understand, or not to interest them. Immediately following or during the reading of these texts, however, Sunday School teachers engaged children in emotionally vivid, lively oral narratives recounting and elaborating the central concepts of these written texts.

Although the focus of this chapter is on children's participation in storytelling with adults, it is important to note that stories were ubiquitous in a number of more adult-centered educational and worship contexts. For example, stories were told during the Sunday School teachers' meeting, adult Sunday School classes, and Sunday morning worship services. Children's Sunday School may provide a context in which children begin to actively participate in a cultural form that remains central to the construction of a belief system well into adulthood.

Narratives told within Sunday School related a variety of different types of events. A significant proportion of narratives in all classes involved oral recountings of the written text. This finding is consistent with participants' stated pedagogical goal of helping children to become familiar with the literal text, as well as with observations that literal meaning is emphasized within other African-American educational contexts (Mehan, Okamoto, Lintz & Wills, 1995), and other religious contexts (Zinsser, 1986). It is also consistent with observations of adult classes at First Baptist Church in which biblical texts frequently were recounted. When interpreting this finding, however, it is important to remember that a central spiritual goal of Sunday School was not to simply memorize the text, but to understand the relevance of those words to individuals' own, varied life circumstances.

Consistent with this goal of finding personal meaning within the biblical texts, narratives of personal experience also occurred in all classes. This finding also is consistent with Michelle Foster's (1995) characterization of effective African-American teachers as concerned with linking classroom content to students' experiences. In particular, teachers in the junior and intermediate classes told powerful, extended stories of personal experience to illustrate the lesson. Overall, however, the hourly rate of occurrence of stories involving personal experience (1.7 per hour) is somewhat lower than that reported by Sperry and Sperry (1996) (approximately 2.8 per hour), based upon their observations of young African-American children and their caregivers at home. There are a number of factors which may account for this lower rate in classrooms than in the home. First, socialization goals at home and at school may vary substantially. In Sunday School, teachers were concerned with covering particular materials and with keeping children focused on the biblical text. Children's own personal stories can be distracting to this goal. Within the junior and intermediate classes, where personal storytelling was initiated by teachers, teachers sometimes explicitly framed the purpose of the story with comments such as, "And, I just share that with you, not that you need to be worried about it, or anything like that, but that's something that happened to me that's in line with today's lesson."

In addition, teachers were concerned with protecting the privacy of families. When newcomers to the young adult Sunday School class shared too much personal information, the teacher would make gentle comments such as, "I don't want to be too nosey now . . ." This concern with privacy seems similar to Amy Shuman's (1986) discussion of the storytelling practices of adolescents in an inner-city, racially diverse junior high school. Students rigidly enforced the right to privacy, and although they sometimes revealed details of family life in offhand stories, they did not ask one another questions about such topics. Stories about families were never requested by listeners, and if they were related, rarely received a direct response.

There were, however, some contexts in which adult students were explicitly invited to share personal experience narratives in Sunday School. These contexts included discussions of conversion experiences and other mystical experiences. For example, the teacher of the young adult Sunday School class posed the question: "What was it like for you when God first spoke to you?" One woman told of a near death experience in the hospital in which her deceased father reassured her, and she slept with his hands cupped to her face. Another woman told of watching over a sick loved one when she heard the "imps of Satan" laughing and jeering at the back door. She felt her spirit rise up to protect her loved one. The next morning, he told her that he thought he was going to die in the night. A man stood at the front of the class and told of how, when he was a child and his grandmother was very ill, she recited scripture in her sleep. She recovered and lived for many more years.

Unlike narration of personal experiences, narration of hypothetical events allowed class members to elaborate biblical events and concepts and relate them to everyday life without violation of privacy or the distraction of aspects of actual personal experiences unrelated to the lesson. Furthermore, stories involving hypothetical events may be particularly compelling to children because they, rather than their teachers, typically were cast as protagonists.

Hypothetical stories also were observed in the class for young adults (age range of approximately 20 to 50). For example, in discussing conflict, the teacher, Junie, provided a hypothetical example to illustrate her point,

> Say Missy believes I said something about her, and she doesn't address it with me. She goes and talks to May . . . she keeps seeking someone to validate her. Now it gets back to me. . . . Missy won't talk to me. I can pray. I need to take some ownership for why Missy wants to believe this. I know what's on the surface is not true, but there still is a conflict between Missy and me that needs to be resolved. . . . What happens if you look in the mirror? My hair's messed, I fix it. When a Christian examines himself, he looks inside.

Data from children's Sunday School classes also suggest both developmental stability and changes in children's participation with adults in storytelling. First, the frequency of adult–child stories increased over time with children and teachers in the junior and intermediate classes telling relatively more stories than teachers and children in the kindergarten and primary classes. This increase in storytelling may be attributable to any number of factors including children's increasing competence with storytelling. Children also become increasingly competent at managing their own behavior and completing academic tasks involving reading and writing, which left greater time for other activities such as storytelling.

Second, there appears to be a developmental increase in children's participation in recounting after kindergarten. Again, there could be a variety of explanations. For example, children's increasing comprehension of and familiarity with complex Bible stories may allow their greater participation in recounting these events. Each Sunday, all classes covered the same content – for example the Genesis story – but the presentation was modified as appropriate for the age group. Thus, by the time a child reached the junior class, she may have encountered the Genesis story in Sunday School on four or five previous occasions.

Third, if one considers only personal experience events initiated by teachers (that is, nearly all personal experience sequences in the junior and intermediate classes, and almost none of the personal experience sequences in the kindergarten class), teachers' propensities to tell children about personal events also appear to increase over time. Again, there are a variety of possible explanations. For example, teachers may perceive that older children are better able to relate personal experiences to biblical texts without becoming distracted. Although the teacher of the kindergarten children did discuss narratives of personal experience as a pedagogical tool, she also pointed out that for her age group stories of personal experiences can lead to off-topic discussions as children become caught up in details of actual lived experiences unrelated to the lesson:

> They will pipe up with, "My mommy told me," you know, such and such. Usually they say what I got for Christmas, and what my birthday is, and, you know, my class is basically like that. You can't use that if I'm teaching about Noah's ark – what you got for your birthday – how is that going to help me with Noah's ark? So they want to tell me everything that Mom has done, or Camilla [baby sibling of a student] has done *(laughs)*, that's it. OK? . . . Usually it doesn't have to do with the Sunday School lessons because my kids are too young. . . . When I come to the class, I try to prepare, but how can you prepare for kids that's my age group – three and four. You know, when you walk in there and you try and say, "OK I'm going to do it this way," I can forget that, because when somebody starts to talk about what they did at a birthday party or the Galleria it kind of just gets you off track, and then how do you get everybody on track again? You go with the lesson, and then if something comes up, you say,"How can you help Mom?" Or, "How can you help your brother or sister?"

Finally, it is worth noting the apparent developmental stability in children's participation in narrative involving hypothetical events. Even children in the kindergarten class participated in relating hypothetical events. This participation may reflect both the centrality of hypothetical speech within this community, and the utility of hypothetical speech for achieving the pedagogical goals of relating biblical text to everyday life while protecting the privacy of individuals and families. Although fewer hypothetical events were related in the primary class, this may be attributed to stylistic differences across teachers rather than development. Hypothetical stories in Sunday School often had a humorous, playful element. Sister Patrice was one or two generations older than the other teachers, and she generally was more formal and less playful in her interactions with the primary-class children.

CHAPTER EIGHT

Socialization and Participation through Storytelling

In this chapter, I will focus on some social aspects of storytelling. First, I will explore the ways in which teachers and children in Sunday School participate together in storytelling. The impact of narratives on children's development depends, in part, on the ways in which children are involved in telling and listening to stories. Mehan, Lintz, Okamoto, and Willis (1995) criticized an African-American Christian academy as containing highly structured, teacher-centered classrooms in which children were not encouraged to have meaningful discussions about different perspectives. In chapter 6, adults at First Baptist Church described socialization beliefs and practices that displayed some overlap with the interpretation of Mehan et al., in that the adults viewed themselves as leading children in acquiring critical cultural knowledge. However, adults' descriptions of their beliefs and practices also differed profoundly from the interpretations of Mehan et al., in that they emphasized the importance of actively involving children in the learning process. In this chapter, I will describe the simultaneous ways in which teachers lead and children actively participate in storytelling at First Baptist Church.

Second, I will describe some socialization strategies through which teachers highlighted for children key concepts within narratives. Narratives are important to socialization, in part because stories communicate that particular events are meaningful and why (e.g., see Haden, Haine & Fivush, 1997; Labov & Waletzky, 1967; Ochs & Capps, 1996; Polanyi, 1985). Stories are told to make a point, often including the narrator's moral evaluation or critical judgments (e.g., Polanyi, 1985). When children listen and tell stories with adults, such as their Sunday School teachers, they encounter culturally significant meanings, values, and beliefs, for example, the importance of maintaining love, faith, and patience even under trying circumstances (e.g., see Nicolopoulou, 1997, for discussion of an interpretive, sociocultural perspective of narrative). In this chapter, I also will show how teachers highlight for children culturally significant meanings, values, and ideas during storytelling.

TEACHERS' AND CHILDREN'S PARTICIPATION IN NARRATIVES

In describing the ways in which teachers and children participate in storytelling, I will begin with an analysis of the initiation of stories. The ways in which individuals participate in storytelling, including who has the right to initiate stories, relates to their position within the social group (Ochs & Capps, 1996; Ochs & Taylor, 1992) and varies across cultural communities (e.g., Bruner, 1987; Michaels, 1985; Miller, Wiley, Fung & Liang, 1997). For example, in many communities, including some African-American communities (Heath, 1983; Ward, 1971), adult–child interactions are hierarchically organized, and children are not expected to interact with adults as peers, initiating interactions and participating as equals in conversation (see also Ochs & Schieffelin, 1984; Rogoff, Mistry, Goncu & Mosier, 1993). For example, Chinese caregivers initiate a relatively greater proportion of episodes of interaction with their young children than do European-American caregivers (Fung, 1994; Wang, Goldin-Meadow & Mylander, 1995), and relatively fewer caregiver–child interactions are characterized by mutuality (Miller, Fung & Mintz, 1996). In their discussions of socialization (chapter 6), adults at First Baptist Church described interactions with children that could be described as relatively hierarchically organized; that is, adults are viewed as more knowledgeable and experienced, and as having an obligation to teach children culturally important information. Thus, I expected to observe relatively more stories to be initiated by adults than by children during adult–child interactions at First Baptist Church.

Subsequent to the story's initiation, children may participate with teachers to elaborate it in any number of ways. For example, children may assume a passive or even a detached stance, contributing little to the story. On the other hand, individual children may spontaneously contribute to the ongoing story or eagerly respond to a teacher's question. In addition, children may participate as part of a class chorus during call-and-response sequences. During such sequences, the leader addresses the group, and the members respond in chorus. Call-and-response sequences have long been recognized as a central and unique part of worship within black communities (e.g., see Moss, 1988; Freedman, 1993). In addition, M. Foster (1996) has identified call-and-response sequences as part of the repertoire of some effective African-American teachers. Within a classroom context, call-and-response sequences may support the cultural values of equality and collective responsibility among children in contrast to individual competition. Given the child-sensitive stance toward socialization expressed by many teachers in chapter 6, I expected that children would be actively involved in storytelling through culturally appropriate discourse structures such as call-and-response sequences.

Teachers Initiated Narratives

The initiator of the narrative is the person who produces the first utterance of the narrative. Percentage agreement for identifying the initiator was 100%. Consistent with my expectations, teachers initiated the vast majority of narratives in all classes. (See Table 8.1.) Indeed, in the kindergarten and intermediate classes, 100% of all narratives were initiated by the teachers.

Children Actively Participated in Narratives

Active participants contribute substantive material to the narrative. For example, they describe a relevant event, make evaluative comments, provide clarifying information, or otherwise elaborate upon the topic under discussion. By this definition, merely listening, nodding, or uttering

TABLE 8.1. *The Social Conduct of Narrative Practices in Sunday School (mean percentage and SEM of narratives)*

	Katherine's Kindergarten Class (%) (3–6 years)	Patrice's Primary Class (%) (6–8 years)	Justine's Junior Class (%) (8–12 years)	Ima's Intermediate Class (%) (12–15 years)
Teacher initiated	100	80 ± 8	94 ± 8	100
No. of active child participants:				
2–3	21 ± 9	22 ± 10	34 ± 5	27 ± 5
>3	79 ± 9	40 ± 12	58 ± 7	61 ± 6
Call & response	30 ± 7	37 ± 13	30 ± 8	34 ± 8
Individual response	89 ± 5	51 ± 15	79 ± 5	85 ± 4
Spontaneous response	37 ± 16	24 ± 10	56 ± 9	27 ± 7

accompanying "uh-huhs" does not constitute active participation. Percent agreement for identifying the number of active participants was 100%.

Although teachers initiated narratives, consistent with my expectations, children did participate actively. (See Table 8.1.) For all classes (kindergarten through intermediate), the vast majority of narratives involved two or more active participants, and for most classes the majority of narratives involved more than three active participants. Children were involved in narratives in a number of ways:

Call-and-Response Sequences

Call-and-response sequences consisted of teacher-initiated questions followed by a choral response from multiple children. Percentage agreement for identifying call-and-response sequences was 100%.

Call-and-response sequences were observed in all classes, kindergarten through intermediate. (See Table 8.1.) Across all classes, a minimum mean of 30% ± 8% of narratives contained call-and-response sequences. For example, the teacher of the junior class initiated a call-and-response sequence with: "[Jesus told his disciples that] you will no longer be fishermen but you will be fishers of – ?" The class responded, in chorus "Men!!!"

Some adults at First Baptist Church appeared to use call-and-response sequences strategically. For example, in discussing unique characteristics of African-American teachers, Pastor Daniels observed:

> I think African-American teachers are, as we are in the African-American church, on a call-and-response kind of base with students. When the teacher says something, the students are expected to respond. I think other teachers, non-African-Americans, want you to hold your hand up and be recognized before you respond. And, I think it's a unique characteristic, it's a very valuable one, I think, a very good one. It helps students to speak up, almost immediately, when there's a question to be answered or a comment to be made.

When orienting a group of former junior students newly graduated to the intermediate class, Sister Ima explicitly described call-and-response sequences:

> And we do . . . call-and-response. We do a lot of incompletes. That means if I stop talking, that means you do what? *(pause)* I stop and you start.

Individual Responses

Individual responses to questions occurred after the teacher queried an individual child or an individual child volunteered to answer. Percentage agreement for identifying individual responses was 100%.

Individual responses occurred frequently in every class. (See Table 8.1.) Indeed, more than a mean of 50% of narratives in every class contained individual responses. Sometimes children actively requested to be allowed to answer. For example, a child in the junior class said eagerly, "I know how that happened! Let *me* tell you how that happened!" Sister Justine responded, "Well, tell me how that happened, then, since you know!" She also offered her enthusiastic support of the child's new knowledge, "Go girl! Go girl!! Chastity – you go girl!"

Spontaneous Contributions

Spontaneous contributions by children are not preceded by direct teacher questions or requests. They are children's unsolicited comments and elaboration. Percentage agreement for identifying spontaneous responses was 100%.

Spontaneous contributions by children occurred in all classes. (See Table 8.1.) In each class, more than a mean of 20% of all narratives contained spontaneous child contributions. In the junior class, a mean of more than half of all narratives contained such contributions. Children offered their own unsolicited interpretations and speculations, which sometimes led to rather lengthy digressions. In the following example, Sister Justine has been teaching from the New Testament (John 1:1–18), and she emphasizes that "Jesus came to help us know God."

> SJ: God must of known we were going to mess up. *(Children laugh.)* If Jesus was made in the beginning – if he was there from the beginning – He knew He would have to send Him. Isn't that amazing?
>
> 5   JAVON: You know, Justine, um –
>
> SJ: He knew we was gonna mess up. He knew Eve was gonna eat that apple *(laughs)*.
>
> JAVON: You know what – you know – if He, if He – I know He's right, but I – the thing is, why did He say whoever sins is gonna die? But
>
> 10   why do we have to die if we're-we're not – I know we're after Adam and Eve, but since their sins, why do they have to be carried on to us?
>
> SJ: OK. Now, listen to that! . . . That's a, boy, that's a good question! That is a great question! I'm gonna answer it in my intermediate

15   spirituality and religious teaching. *(Several children laugh.)* And, and
        this is strictly my opinion. We gonna have to write that question down
        and have one of the pastors answer it, but this is how I would answer
        it.

        . . .

20   *(The class embarks on an extended discussion of the knowledge of good and evil
        that came from eating from the tree of knowledge. At Sister Justine's prompting,
        children offer multiple examples of evil present today. Javon, however, is not
        satisfied and persists:)*
        SJ: Brothers and sisters are killing each other all the time.
25   JAVON: Yeah, but I'm just saying why do their sins have to pass
        onto us if we're being real Christians?
        SJ: OK. OK. There's, that's – wait a minute –
        JAVON: I know we're born after them, but –
        SJ: OK. Now listen. That's why Jesus was sent. That's what Jesus was
30   sent. We're not bearing Adam and Eve's sins anymore. . . . After
        Jesus was sent we're burying the sins – each one of us is burying our
        own sins. So when Jesus came, he gave us the chance to redeem
        ourselves from Adam and Eve. Old Testament, New Testament. Now
        all we got to do now – had he not come, we's all gonna die anyway
35   and never make it to heaven. *(Playful, high-pitched, "witch's" voice.
        Continues in serious voice.)* Had he not come – wait a minute – here,
        I've got a question for you, since you asked me that. Had he not
        come, what do you think this world would be like?
        CHILDREN: *(Several groan and exclaim, "oh, boy!" Laugh.)*
40   SJ: What do you think?
        . . .
        (Several children offer speculations. Including:)
        ROBERT: Earth would be taken over by the devil.
        SJ: If Jesus hadn't come? The earth would have been taken over by the
45   devil?
        ROBERT: Yeah.
        SJ: Umhm! Anybody else got an idea if Jesus hadn't come what would
        have happened? What do you think? If Jesus hadn't come, what do
        you think this world would be like?
50   TERRY: This world would be like Hell.
        SJ: Owwwww!!! *(Loud exclamation.)* You guys are all right. You all right!
        So, then the answer – let's get back to your [Javon's] question . . . To
        get back to your question – now – what do we get our redemption
        from? Where do we get the opportunity not to wear the sins of the
55   world, or Adam and Eve as you say? *(Children are giggling. SJ pauses,
        and then goes on in a lower voice.)* Jesus came to die for us.

. . . (The discussion continued in this vein, but Javon still was not satisfied and continued to raise questions. The discussion concluded with a story of personal experience told by Sister Justine regarding a time when her own faith wavered.)

Note that, beginning on line 4, Javon begins to question persistently, not only Sister Justine's conventional interpretations, but God ("I know He's right, but . . ."). Sister Justine not only responds to these questions with approval ("Now, listen to that! . . . That's a, boy, that's a good question!"), she energetically embarks with the children on a lengthy discussion including the Old Testament story of Adam and Eve. In the context of that discussion, Sister Justine repeatedly asks children to speculate, to extend, and to consider, "what if." For example, on line 31, she begins to pose a hypothetical question to the class, "Had he not come, what do you think this world would be like?" The children offer numerous speculations, including "Earth would be taken over by the devil" and "This world would be like Hell," to which Sister Justine responds with energetic approval. Throughout, Sister Justine recognizes diverse perspectives. For example, beginning on line 11, she responds to Javon's question, "I'm gonna answer it in my intermediate spirituality and religious teaching. And, and this is strictly my opinion." Another example begins on line 55, when Sister Justine responds to the children's speculations regarding her hypothetical questions, "Owwwww!! . . . You guys are all right. You all right!"

SOCIALIZATION STRATEGIES FOR LINKING NARRATIVE EVENTS TO EVERYDAY LIVES

The second issue addressed in this chapter concerns characteristics of narratives that may help to highlight specific events or concepts from the Bible as relevant to children's modern, everyday lives. Overall, narratives highlight the set of events recounted as meaningful. For example, the very fact that Sister Justine took time during Sunday School class to recount the crucifixion of Jesus indicates that these events are significant. Within the longer and morally complex story, however, specific actions and concepts also may be highlighted. For example, Sister Justine focused not on the role of religious leaders in Jesus' crucifixion, but on Judas's betrayal of his personal relationship with Jesus.

To highlight actions or concepts within a story, the narrator may draw upon evaluative devices from all levels of linguistic structure including

direct statements, lexical intensifiers, suspension of action, and the judgment of a third person (for examples see, Haden et al., 1997; Labov &
Waletzky, 1967; Polanyi, 1985). The specific devices employed by narrators, however, vary widely across cultural contexts and with children's
development (see Miller, Potts, Fung, Hoogstra & Mintz, 1990). They
also may vary across individual speakers within a community who prefer
particular devices from the community's larger linguistic repertoire. Sunday School teachers at First Baptist Church employed a wide range of
devices to highlight the significance of narrative events to children's
everyday lives. Some devices were common in all classes, some occurred
more frequently within particular age groups, and some seemed to be
preferred by individual teachers.

Devices Common to All Classes

There were two devices frequently used in all classes. Their frequent use
with all age levels may reflect their utility for achieving socialization
goals – in this case, communicating to children that biblical events and
concepts are significant to their own lives.

Direct Connections Regarding the Text's Relevance
One straightforward strategy for highlighting particular past events as
significant is to state directly that they are relevant. For example, Livia
Polanyi (1985) described explicit meta-comments regarding relevance
as a discourse-level evaluative device. Within European-American adult
Sunday School, a teacher routinely commented that the verses were
significant to class members' lives (Martinson, 1994). Similarly, in
European-American Christian schools, teachers used references to the
Bible as often as possible in their lessons with the explicit expectation
that students were to use the Bible as the guide for life (Peshkin, 1986).
Interrater agreement for identifying direct connections, including meta-
comments and other comments directly linking the biblical texts and
stories to children's lives, was 91%.

As shown in Table 8.2, direct connections were ubiquitous in all
classes but somewhat more typical of narratives within the kindergarten
class. A mean and SEM of approximately half of all narratives in the
primary through intermediate classes contained direct connections,
while nearly all narratives in the kindergarten class (91% ± 6%) contained such direct connections. For example, Sister Ima often intro-

TABLE 8.2. *Description of Evaluative Devices (mean percentage and SEM of narratives)*

	Katherine's Kindergarten Class (%) (3–6 years)	Patrice's Primary Class (%) (6–8 years)	Justine's Junior Class (%) (8–12 years)	Ima's Intermediate Class (%) (12–15 years)
Narratives containing				
Direct connection	91 ± 6	49 ± 13	50 ± 9	51 ± 5
Generalization	76 ± 8	45 ± 13	36 ± 5	43 ± 3
Figurative speech	0	0	51 ± 5	44 ± 5
Role-play	0	0	10 ± 4	2 ± 2
Code switching	19 ± 10	1 ± 1	40 ± 8	7 ± 1
Historical present	10 ± 6	9 ± 6	15 ± 6	30 ± 8
Music	(Singing observed in all classes.)		(Singing never observed.)	

duced a narrative with, "Remember, we read and study the Bible so we can apply it to our lives." Teachers also directly linked events in the Sunday School lesson to children's own lives through specific examples that paralleled events portrayed within the Sunday School lesson. For example, Sister Katherine commented on a story from the kindergarten children's Sunday School papers, "This little girl has a special job she has to do every day when she comes home from school. She sets the table for her mom and dad." She then challenged the children, "Can you think of something special to do at home every day to help Mom and Dad out?"

Generalizations

Another characteristic of talk within narratives that may signal to children the relevance of events to everyday situations is the generalization from one instance to the general case (Polanyi, 1985). For example, within a European-American adult Sunday School, the teacher related the lessons to members' lives by generalizing about what "we need to do," or in other words, how the lesson should affect members' subsequent experiences (Martinson, 1994).

Generalizations also were common within narratives at First Baptist Church Sunday School. These discussions were very similar to explicit connections, but rather than asserting that the text is relevant or elaborating specific examples, these discussions focused on generalizations derived from specific instances within the Sunday School texts to modern day events or conditions. For example, Sister Patrice elaborated to the primary class members:

> He [God] promised Abraham that he would make him a great nation. . . . All right now, now God made a promise to Abraham and God keeps his promise. A lot of times we don't. A lot of times we promise to do something and we don't keep our promise. But God is one person who keeps his promise.

Interrater agreement for identifying generalizations was 86%.

As indicated in Table 8.2, generalizations were ubiquitous in all classes from kindergarten through intermediate, but again were somewhat more typical of narratives in kindergarten classes. This type of talk ranged from a mean and SEM of 76% ± 8% of narratives during kindergarten lessons to a mean and SEM of 36% ± 5% of narratives in the junior classes. In the following narrative fragment, Sister Ima discusses with the intermediate class God's promise to Abraham. She then goes on to generalize:

> . . . and then we're gonna go on and do it our way, like we do so many times. We're gonna try to solve problems our way, and don't wait on God. Then we have all kinds of problems, that's why Ishmael came about. And it caused some conflicts in that household.

Devices Used Primarily with Older Children

There were a variety of devices used only in the junior and intermediate classes. Any developmental trends in teachers' use of evaluative devices may reflect their sensitivity to older children's increasing competence with, for example, abstract thinking.

Figurative Speech

The use of figurative language may help children to relate new or abstract biblical concepts to everyday life. A figure of speech is any form of expression in which the normal use of language is manipulated, stretched, or altered to extend literal meaning for rhetorical effect (Matthew, 1997). Examples include similes and metaphors. Interestingly, a number of scholars have described the use of figurative language, including metaphors, analogies, and proverbs, by effective African-American educators (Foster, 1995; Heath, 1983; Mitchell, 1986). For example, Mitchell (1986) describes the use of proverbs as a basic component of African-American religious education. Heath (1982) helped European-American teachers to enhance their effectiveness with African-American children by including in their lessons questions calling for analogic responses, such as, "What's this like?" Interrater agreement for identifying figurative speech was 77%.

By the time children reached the junior and intermediate classes, the figurative use of language within narrative was frequent. As shown in Table 8.1, figurative speech occurred in a mean and SEM of 51% ± 5% of narratives in the junior class. For example, the junior class was discussing, "What is the church?" when Sister Justine drew a person on the board and suggested that "this is the church." The children then suggested that the head of the body is God, prayer is the right hand, and so on. This metaphor was sustained and elaborated for nearly 30 minutes. For example:

> sj: Now, let me ask you something. Say this was a moving person, OK? It's functioning like it's supposed to. What would happen if I did this? *(Erases leg.)*
> JOLENE: He'd be in a wheelchair.
> . . .
> sj: So he's not working so well. . . .What happens if I take out the prayer part?
> GEOFF: "He's definitely crippled."
> *(Sister Justine continues to erase parts.)*
> sj: OK. What's missing? . . .
> GEOFF: The leg, the other arm, the head and the body.
> . . .
> sj: There's parts missing right? . . . In order for our church to work we need *(pause)*
> CHILDREN, IN CHORUS: Every part!

Figurative speech also occurred frequently in the intermediate class. A mean and SEM of 44% ± 5% of narratives contained figurative speech. In the following example, the class members are discussing how to be a Christian in difficult circumstances when Sister Ima suggests that the football players' pads and helmets are like the Christians' adherence to biblical principles. The metaphor of putting on the "whole armor of God" is then sustained throughout an extended discussion. In the following fragment, Sister Ima has begun the discussion by showing a picture of a football player.

> s1: Protection. If you leave something off, then something is gonna go wrong, right? Something is not gonna be protected. . . . Instead of [just] putting on the shoulder pads, you got to put on the helmet, too, right? You got to put both of them on. You have to put on everything that is necessary in order to be protected all the way that you will be able to stand against those things that the devil presents to you on whatever level that might be – whatever age level. If this football player has left his helmet off there's a chance he's gonna get brain damage from all that bumping that he's gonna feel. Mind you, I don't know any rules about football, but I do know that they bump a lot. *(Laughter and discussion of what happens if the football player and the Christian are not protected.)*

Figurative speech was notably absent from narratives in the kindergarten and primary classes.

Play with Roles

Another narrative device that may highlight and elaborate upon the significance of particular events is play with roles, such as when teachers enact with children a portion of a larger story. "Play with roles" is a subcategory of pretend play involving the transformation of identity, for example, players act as if they were characters in stories, or assume routine roles such as that of parent, teacher, friend, and so on. Lev Vygotsky (1978) attributed to this type of play a special significance for children's socialization into the meaning systems of their communities.

> The child imagines himself to be the mother . . . , so he must obey the rules of maternal behavior. . . . Only actions that fit these rules are acceptable to the play situation. . . . What passes unnoticed by the child in real life becomes a rule of behavior in play (Vygotsky, 1978, pp. 92–95).

In playing with particular roles, Vygotsky argued that children become more deeply rooted in a system of meanings. Recent theorists also have argued that through play with roles children also alter, comment upon, and reinterpret meaning (Vandenberg, 1986), thus contributing to cultural innovation as well as reproduction.

The extent to which adults enter into children's role play varies widely. This variation is related, in part, to variation in adults' beliefs about the role of play in development and the nature of adult–child relationships (Haight, Parke & Black, 1997). Relatively little information is available describing play with roles in African-American communities or within religious contexts. There is some evidence that fantasy talk occurs in narratives with young African-American children and their rural, working-class caregivers (Heath, 1983; Sperry & Sperry, 1996) and that role-play occurs in children's Sunday School at a European-American church (Zinsser, 1986).

Although not highly frequent in any class, role-play is another device present in the junior and intermediate classes but notably absent from the kindergarten and primary classes. For the purposes of this study, role-play is defined as the transformation, or nonliteral treatment, through talk and/or action of the here-and-now (Haight & Miller, 1993). Such transformations may include actions, objects, persons, or places. Interestingly, during an interview, Sister Justine spontaneously mentioned the practice of actually assigning class members roles, to have them "become" the biblical characters, to react and speak as the character. As she described:

> We'll do a lot of role playing, OK? "You're so-and-so, you know, and you're so-and-so, right there in the scripture. Now, your response – do you understand why your response would be this?" It's funny . . . Geoff . . . did not want to be Judas, when we were talking about Judas (*loud laughter*) . . . and he goes, "I don't want to be that dude!" So, and so, we do a lot of role-playing too. "You be that person. But, how do you think that felt? And how would you feel if that was you?"

Interrater agreement for identifying role play was 100%.

As shown in Table 8.2, a mean and SEM of 10% ± 4% of narratives in the junior class involved role-play. Sister Justine freely moved in and out of role, spontaneously assigning the children, and even the observer, to various roles. In the following example, the class is discussing Judas's betrayal of Jesus.

> sj: You guys are young babes, but this is a great story, this part. Judas is like some of your two-faced friends. Judas was a two-faced friend. You know you got two-faced friends, don't you? At school? They one

minute, they up in your face yah-yah-yah- and then the next minute
they talking about you like a dog?

CHILDREN: Ummhm.

sj: Judas did that to Jesus. He set Jesus up. If it had not been for Judas,
maybe Jesus might not have got – made it to the cross – because he
had to point him out. And guess what? He said, ah –

(Child gasps.)

sj: He – do you remember the story? . . . You guys, you guys, you guys!
This is one of the most important stories that – OK *(several children
interrupt).* We should do a little play about this. OK now look. OK if
Wendy wanted me to um – say Wendy was a police officer. No, no, no,
say Wendy – let's make it even worse. Let's make it – *(SJ has W stand
up. Baby Camilla is on her back in a backpack.)*

ARLENE: FBI!

sj: No, no. Wendy's a – a – a she's from Cuba. She's a big, she's a big
drug dealer. She's a big drug dealer. *(Children laugh loudly.)* Listen.
Listen now! Let's listen!

w: And this is my sidekick *(referring to baby Camilla).*

sj: And this is her sidekick. This is her, this is her henchperson. *(Loud
laughter from children.)* This is the person who does – this is the person
who'll wipe you out if you mess with Wendy. OK?

ARLENE: OK! *(laughing)*

sj: So, so Wendy says to me, she says to me, "You know ah – there is this
do-gooder over here in your country that ah, I got to get – we want to
assassinate him and get rid of em." And I go, "No, no! That's my main
man!" Or, "That's my main woman." Oh, oh. It's Amanda. *(Standing
near Amanda.)* We're tight. And she's cracking down, boy, she's cracking down on everything. *(Giggling from the class.)* She's saying, she's
saying, "everybody straighten up. Life is supposed to be this way, this
way, this way. I've given you the example on this, that, and the other."
But, but, she wants to be in control, see. We want to be in control now
and I'm greedy. *(Laughter from children.)* I'm just, I'm greedy. They,
they promised to pay me off. And, and, it's like, I don't care how
good . . . Amanda's talk is, it's like, "um-um, um-um, um-um [no]
I'm going with the money." So, there's this big conference and she's
[Wendy] been invited because she's a big wig and her hench woman
[Camilla] has been invited because she's a big wig. We're all at this
big ole conference *(children laughing)* and – ah – but Wendy, Wendy's
never laid eyes on this Amanda person that's causing all the trouble –
making people clean their minds up and act right. So, I say to her
like this *(whispers to W).* So we're all socializing and bla, bla, bla. Ah,
what about this thing, bla, bla, bla, bla. *(Children laughing.)* And, I'm
goin', "Hey! How are you doing, Amanda?" *(Walks over to A and hugs*

her in greeting.) Look – watch this, watch what I'm doing. "How are you doing Amanda?" *(Hugs A again.)* Now, I'm goin' back and I'm gonna socialize. I just set her up. Do you know how I set her up? Wendy's never laid eyes on her. And I didn't even say, "Amanda," I just went like, "Hey! What's up girlfriend? Nice to see you." *(Said in an exaggeratedly expressive fashion. Hugging A again. Children laughing.)* Then, I go over here, "Javon, darlin'!" *(Also exaggerated. Children laughing).* You know?

(Child says something – unintelligible. Too much laughing.)

SJ: Now she knows – she's gonna assassinate her. How do you – she's never laid eyes on her. But now she's gonna assassinate her – her henchwoman's gonna assassinate her. *(More laughter.)* Tell me, tell me how that happened. Dajon? Because you – um, you – um. *(Laughter from class.)* You – you *(Interrupted by laughing, etc.)*

JAVARIUS: You're a two-faced friend.

SJ: OK. I'm a two-faced friend. But what did I just do? OK. Judas said –

ARLENE: You, you let Wendy know who the person –

SJ: How did I let her know? "Robert! Hi! How you doing?" *(Hugs R. Exaggerated. Children laugh.)* I hugged her. I did like this, I said, "The one that I put" – I told her, "The one I'm giving the hug, that's who we're talking about."

Notice that in this example, Sister Justine explicitly related Judas's betrayal to events children may have experienced directly, such as, "Judas was a two-faced friend. You know you got two-faced friends, don't you? At school?" or modern events they have heard about, such as Cuban drug dealers. Throughout the "little play," children were highly engaged: laughing, exclaiming, jumping out of their chairs, and offering responses.

Sister Ima also used role-play, but less frequently and always as a planned activity, sometimes actually announcing at the beginning of the class that they would do a role-play around the lesson, "We're gonna have a 'little play.' A mean and SEM of 2% ± 2% of narratives involved role-play.

Device Used Primarily with Young Children

There also was a device used only with younger children in the kindergarten and primary classes. Again, any developmental trends in teachers use of particular devices may reflect teachers' sensitivity to younger children's relative immaturity.

Music

Narrators do not only rely on words to fashion an effective story, they also use paralinguistic and nonverbal means such as tone of voice, facial expression, and gesture (Miller & Moore, 1989). Another characteristic of narrative that may help to highlight particular events is the incorporation of music. Scholars of African-American culture have long noted the centrality of music to the African-American religious experience (e.g., Lincoln & Mamiya, 1990). For example, a pastor may "sing" a particularly significant, emotionally intense portion of the sermon. Interestingly, the blending of song and narrative has been reported within other non-European communities including the Xavante of Brazil and the Kaluli of Papua New Guinea (see Ochs & Capps, 1996).

Although kindergarten and primary teachers relied relatively little on hypothetical talk, personal experiences, figurative speech, or role-play to highlight events and engage children, they consistently used music. Indeed, each class period included group singing with members of both kindergarten and primary classes together. These songs told biblical stories about, for example, Noah's Ark or "Father Abraham," or reinforced basic Christian concepts, such as "Jesus loves me." As Sister Katherine noted during an interview:

> They remember [the lesson] better [when there is an accompanying song]. . . . They remember the music more than when you're sitting down telling them or reading it. Kids love music . . . that's why they can remember a song from Michael Jackson, all the words. OK? If you just do it with them they love it and can remember it and eventually it will click why you sing "King's Army" or "Noah's Ark," eventually they will know it and go – Noah, Noah, oh that's it! Eventually everything will come together.

Devices Used Primarily by Individual Teachers

There also were a number of devices that, although they were used by all teachers, were used particularly frequently by individual teachers. The use of these devices may reflect individual teachers' preferences or styles.

Code Switching

Code switching, that is, changing from standard to black English, has been described by some African-American teachers as a conscious and deliberate educational strategy (Foster, 1995). By using features of children's everyday speech, code switching may not only capture children's attention, but may encourage their identification with the characters and mark the relevance of the narrative to modern life. For example, Zuni storytellers apparently code switch from Zuni to English to mark a story's transition from past to present relevance (see Ochs & Capps, 1996). Interrater agreement for identifying code switching was 86%.

In contrast to the teachers in the primary and intermediate classes, the teachers in the kindergarten and junior class frequently enlivened their narratives through the use of code switching. The most frequent and extended use of code switching occurred in the junior classes. Indeed, a mean and SEM of 40% ± 8% of narratives contained code switching. For example, Sister Justine employed code switching when recounting the story of John the Baptist's birth.

sj: You know who [John the Baptist's] parents were?

SEVERAL CHILDREN: No.

CHASTITY: think –

sj: Think about it.

CHASTITY: – It was Elizabeth- –

sj: Ow!!!!

CHASTITY: – and Zechariah.

sj: Go girl! Go girl!! Chastity – you go girl! Now look – listen to me. Now there was something strange – there was something real weird about his parents. What was it?

CHASTITY: They were old.

sj: They was real old. *(Talking in an exaggerated, old person's voice. Children laughing.)* . . .

JAVON: I know how that happened. Let me tell you how that happened.

sj: Well, tell me how that happened then since you know! *(laughing)*

JAVON: Elizabeth was real old.

sj: Real old. Really. She was old.

JAVON: And she always for her whole life wanted to have babies so –

sj: Umhm.

JAVON: She, she – well, God made her womb back in business. *(Screams and laughter from the children.)*

sj: Go! Go! All right, go! He – do you know what else happened?

JAVON: Nope.

sj: Something happened to Zechariah didn't it. Do you remember what happened to Zechariah?

JAVON: Was he blind?

sj: No, no, no. Something did happen to him though. And it was all –

MARISSA: Oh! Oh! *(Raising hand.)*

sj: What happened? *(Several children exclaiming all together.)*

MARISSA: Um – somebody came down –

sj: It wasn't a somebody –

JAVON: I know, I know! *(Several children talking at once: "It was an angel!")*

CHASTITY: An angel came down and told Zechariah that if he wanted a baby he could have one –

sj: Ahha.

CHASTITY: But he had to wait. And, Zechariah – um – doubted him.

sj: He doubted him. Yeah. OK. And what happened to him for that?

CHASTITY: And the angel said, "You cannot talk – "

sj: " – until the baby's born." Ahhuh! Ahhuh! OK. That's just what happened. So now we know a little bit – and that was right. Because Zechariah wouldn't believe. He would say, "Ah, I don't believe you." The angel said, "Excuse me?" *(Children laugh.)* "Watch this! You won't be speaking, brother, until the baby's born!" *(laughter)* And he couldn't speak. OK? He couldn't utter nothing! He couldn't even speak at all. He would open his mouth and nothing would come out.

GEOFF: So he was like this *(noiselessly gestures as if speaking).*

sj: Ahhuh. Ahhuh. Ahhuh! *(laughter)*

sj: OK. Let's get the reading. Start with Javon.

Notice that, to the children's apparent delight, Sister Justine code switches, quoting the angel using features of black English, such as, "You won't be speaking, brother, until the baby's born!" Notice also that in this excerpt, the teacher and children appear to enjoy their interactions, and there is much laughter and many exclamations.

Historical Present

The use of the historical present is another device through which teachers may convey that past events are relevant to current lives. The historical present is the use of present-tense form with past-tense reference (Matthew, 1997). The use of the historical present is common for narrators in many speech communities. In these cases, the narrators move the story from the then-and-there to the here-and-now to indicate a continuing preoccupation with the story. The events are not contained in the past but continue to have relevance to the narrator's current life. Thus, the telling of past events is integrally linked to tellers' and listeners' concerns about their present and future lives (see Ochs & Capps, 1996). Such uses of language may function to add vividness, drama, and immediacy to biblical text. Interrater agreement for identifying historical present was 63%.

The teacher of the intermediate class did very little code switching, but she often used the historical present. A mean and SEM of 30% ± 8% of narratives within the intermediate class included use of the historical present. For example, Sister Ima began a lesson, part of a series taught from Genesis, with the question, "What's God creating today?" In another example, the children were studying from Genesis 21:1–14 when Sister Ima initiated a narrative about Isaac with the assertion, "He's gonna be born this morning." In another example, Sister Ima was preparing for a lesson from Genesis:

> SI: Now, God has created the earth. He's created all, everything . . . and the earth, the heaven, the animals that went on the earth, and then last week who came along? *(pause)* Adam and who?
> CLASS: Eve.
> SI: Eve. And they're here this morning. Can you picture them? He has created a beautiful place for them to be in . . .

The use of the historical present also occurred in other classes, although less frequently, ranging from a mean and SEM of 9% ± 6% in the primary class to 15% ± 6% in the junior class.

CONCLUSION

The account of socialization practices at First Baptist Church presented in the last two chapters differs in important ways from accounts of European-American religious contexts and other African-American educational contexts. In describing an African-American Christian academy, Mehan et al. (1995) claimed that in highly structured, teacher-centered classrooms, students are not encouraged to have meaningful discourse about different perspectives. In describing two European-American Sunday Schools, Zinsser (1986) argued that, because the Bible was taught as the word of God, children were not encouraged to think speculatively about the stories, to supply additional details out of their own imaginings, or to suggest alternative endings.

In contrast, an examination of the ways in which teachers and children told stories together at First Baptist Church reflects the growth-oriented, child-sensitive beliefs expressed by adults in chapter 6. Narratives were growth-oriented in that they clearly were *led* by teachers who posed questions and forcefully argued their positions. Teachers took very seriously their responsibility to teach information that they viewed as critical to children's lives. Children were expected to acquire this information. It would be a mistake, however, to infer either that teachers intended children to accept unquestioningly their interpretations of biblical concepts or that children were passive. Rather, narratives also were child-sensitive in that children were actively engaged. The vast majority of narratives involved two or more active child participants as well as a teacher. Children participated not only through call-and-response sequences and responses to questions posed to individuals by the teachers, but through their own spontaneous comments.

In addition, at First Baptist Church children routinely extended and related biblical concepts through their participation in hypothetical narratives. In addition, older children participated in role-play and the figurative use of language. By the time children were in the junior class (age 8), they even initiated hypothetical narratives to address real issues of concern to them. Although the Bible was taught as the word of God, church leaders also taught that God speaks through the Bible in different ways to different people, and to every individual at different times of life. Even though the pastor was widely respected, Sunday School teachers routinely admonished children and adults not to "just listen to what the pastor has to say," but to go home and meditate on the Bible for themselves. Thus, a wide variety of responses were acceptable, and expected, to routine questions regarding the application of Bible verses to life.

Furthermore, children's active engagment with learning was valued by some adults. For example, when describing her 8- to 12-year-old students, Sister Justine noted with obvious pride:

> I can't believe how inquisitive they are! They're extremely inquisitive, and I let them ask their questions, and sometimes they ask really precarious questions, and so I'll run up and get Reverend (Daniels). . . . They get down in, they're debating. Extremely debated. . . . It's like, let's get into the lesson. . . . Let's pick this apart, analyze it, and apply it. And I think that's making them grow. I think they're doing a lot of growing.

Sunday School teachers used a number of socialization devices within stories to link biblical concepts and texts to children's everyday lives. The prevalence of these devices suggests their utility for meeting teachers' socialization goals; in this case, helping children to understand that biblical concepts are relevant to their own lives. Frequent in all classes from kindergarten through intermediate were: (1) "direct connections" linking past events to the child's experiences, either through meta-comments or parallel examples, and (2) "generalizations" derived from specific instances within the Sunday School texts and then generalized to modern-day events or conditions. Interestingly, narratives in the kinder-garten classes contained a particularly high percentage of direct connec-tions and generalization, perhaps reflecting teachers' perceived greater need for explicit instruction with young children. The centrality of direct connections and generalizations to instruction, however, was apparent in all classes. Indeed, direct connections and generalizations even were observed in adult Sunday School classes. For example, when members of the young adult Sunday School class discussed "dealing with difference," the teacher asked,

> How does the way that Paul deals with conflict apply to our lives today? The setting for this lesson is First Baptist Church. How many of you don't see eye to eye with somebody in the church? – I'm not dipping into business now – What emotions are associated with conflict? . . . People want to be right. . . . We want to be right. We don't want to take ownership for conflict. We can't resolve conflict by exalting ourselves and humbling others.

Certain evaluative devices, however, appeared to be more common in the junior and intermediate classes. These devices may reflect teachers' sensitivity to children's emerging competence with, for example, abstract reasoning. In particular, figurative speech frequently accompanied narra-tives told to and with children in the junior and intermediate classes, but not in the kindergarten and primary classes. It is possible that younger children have difficulty relating the relevance of the Sunday School text to their lives through figurative speech. Indeed, the extensive use of complex metaphor and other figures of speech appeared to be quite challenging to the younger children in the junior class. For example, there are a number of examples in the transcribed texts of Sunday School classes in which young 8-year-olds appeared to misinterpret metaphors as literal.

Complex figures of speech and extended analogies were very frequent in classes for adults. For example, during a discussion of "Micah: Prophet of Righteousness" in the Sunday School teachers' class, Pastor Daniels made a distinction between covering up versus repenting of sins: "We painted over a room with a lighter color. At first it looked great, but then the darker color began to show through and we had to paint over it again." This metaphor was developed and elaborated throughout the class as members responded to the lesson.

Play with roles also occurred in the Sunday School classes of the older children, but was noticeably absent in the kindergarten and primary classes. Observations of kindergarten and primary children in other contexts – for example, at picnics and other informal social gatherings – suggested that these young children clearly were capable of, and many shared a love of, social pretend play with roles. Furthermore, as discussed below, adults did engage in role-play with older children. There are two other factors that may explain the absence of adult–child play with roles in Sunday School classes for young children. First, as discussed above, teachers of the younger children were concerned with keeping them focused on the lesson. Role-play, because it is so highly engaging to young children, may have been too distracting. Second, like teachers of young children in public schools and elsewhere, kindergarten and primary teachers were concerned with encouraging what they considered to be proper classroom conduct. One of the teachers even explained to a group of kindergarteners who had asked to play that, in school, there are other ways to have fun. To have fun in school, children must take direction from their teacher and participate in structured activities in an orderly manner.

Role-play also was observed in adult Sunday School classes, suggesting that children in junior and intermediate classes were participating in a cultural form that retains its relevance into adulthood. For example, the topic of pride came up in the adult Sunday School class. To the amusement of the class, the teacher, Sister Junie, and several students spontaneously engaged in a humorous role-play:

> SJ: Why can't Addie act right?" *(Said with exaggerated, teasing intonation while smiling.)*
> ADDIE: I wish I knew! *(Said with exaggerated despair.)*
> SJ: *Why* can't Addie act right?
> ADDIE: Lord, help me!"
> *(Another student comments that the teacher has on a new sweater.)*
> . . .
> SARAH: Your sweater's better than anybody else's in here!
> SJ: It's brand new! It's beautiful . . . *(strutting around the room, pretend bragging).*

A socialization device also was present in the kindergarten and primary classes, but not in the classes for older children, perhaps reflecting teachers' sensitivity to the unique support needed by young children for learning. More specifically, although music was a regular part of Sunday School classes for the younger (kindergarten and primary) children, it was noticeably absent from classes for older (junior and intermediate) children. Within the larger church, music was an integral part of worship services. As in other African-American churches, sermons were "sung," as were the prayers of the pastor and deacons; spirituals were spontaneously sung by the church mothers at appropriate moments during the service, congregational singing was frequent, and the excellent choirs (including a children's choir) were major attractions. Furthermore, group singing was a regular component of the opening and closing of Sunday School for all age groups. Music within the kindergarten and primary classes, however, may have served a different function than music in other contexts at First Baptist Church. The songs sung during kindergarten and primary classes typically were not selected from *The New National Baptist Hymnal,* or from the broader repertoire of spiritual or gospel music, which emphasizes themes distinctive to African-American religious music, such as liberation. Songs sung during Sunday School were chosen from a repertoire of children's religious music and seemed to function to reinforce children's acquisition of biblical narratives (e.g., "Noah's Ark") and Christian concepts (e.g., "Jesus loves me"). They may be similar to those sung within European-American Sunday Schools (e.g., see Zinsser, 1986). This interpretation is consistent with Sister Katherine's comments during an interview that children remember new concepts better when they are presented in song.

Certain socialization devices were used more frequently by individual teachers, which may reflect stylistic differences. Some code switching and use of the historical present was observed in all classes. Code switching, however, was noticeably more frequent in Sister Justine's narratives to the junior class. Sister Justine's high rate of code switching seems consistent with her colorful, playful teaching style, which also included the most frequent use of figurative speech, role-play, and hypothetical speech. That code switching may be a feature of teacher style rather than a developmental aspect of narratives is suggested by the relatively frequent use of code switching by the teachers of the kindergarten and junior children, and by the relatively infrequent use of code switching by the teachers of the primary and intermediate children. Code switching also was observed in other church contexts, including Sunday School classes for young adults and Sunday School teachers, and during worship services.

Frequent use of the historical present also may be stylistic. The teacher of the intermediate class made use of the historical present noticeably more often than the other teachers. The frequent use of the historical present seemed to fit with Sister Ima's quiet but intense discussions of her Christian faith. Other adults also used the historical present in other church contexts.

In conclusion, a distinguishing features of African-American theology is the intertwining of the pragmatic and the sacred. Life in the contemporary black church is "earth-oriented though heaven-bound" (Lincoln & Mamiya, 1990, p. 374). Nowhere is this characteristic more apparent than in children's Sunday School where basic religious beliefs are presented, elaborated, and applied to everyday situations in a compelling, growth-oriented and child-sensitive manner. Through narratives told to and with children, children from the ages of 3 to 15 years are helped to "bring the gospel to bear on human lives."

CHAPTER NINE

Adult–Child Verbal Conflicts

In the following excerpt, 13-year-old Mamie challenges Sister Ima regarding her interpretation of the Adam and Eve story:

> MAMIE: Eve should of just picked up a stick and whooped that snake and we would still be in that garden.
> SI: Maybe God wanted us to know that we could have redemption.
> MAMIE: Slap him [snake] up against one of them trees! Stomp on his neck! *(While enacting.)*
> SI: God intended us not to be – God made other provisions for us.
> MAMIE: Hey, but I didn't do nothing!
> *(They continue to debate the meaning of the Adam and Eve story and the concept of sin.)*

Throughout this book, I've elaborated upon adults' growth-oriented, child-sensitive stance toward socialization and children's active participation in church. As Mamie's challenge to Sister Ima's traditional interpretation of original sin suggests, adult–child conflict is an excellent context in which to observe children's active participation in Sunday School. Children, as well as adults, had viewpoints on the particular beliefs and practices they encountered during Sunday School, and sometimes these viewpoints differed from those of their teachers. Adult–child verbal conflicts provide a unique glimpse into the rich diversity of children's perspectives. Verbal conflicts also provide a window into child-sensitive aspects of socialization practices. As we will see in this chapter, some children explicitly disagreed with teachers and elaborated their opposing views. The extent to which children were free to disagree with adults may reflect their status as active interpreters of biblical texts. In this chapter, I will describe verbal conflicts between children and teachers in Sunday School. As described in chapter 7, these analyses are based on approximately 3 hours of kindergarten lessons, 4½ hours of primary lessons, 9 hours of junior lessons, and 9 hours of intermediate lessons.

Learning to argue appropriately within Sunday School, or any other context, involves the acquisition of cultural norms much like learning to tell a story. Within British and European-American communities, these norms include a preference for agreement (Levinson, 1983). In contrast, within some African-American contexts, oppositional speech is positively valued (e.g., Corsaro, 1996; Goodwin, 1990) and related to the development of friendships (Corsaro, 1996). For example, William Corsaro (1996) presented a longitudinal case study of Zena, a young African-American child. Within her predominantly black Head Start classroom, Zena had positive relationships with her peers and teachers. In this context, children engaged in frequent oppositional talk, which was positively valued as part of the verbal enrichment of everyday play routines. Children seldom responded negatively to oppositional talk, but rather responded in kind – often accompanied by appreciative laughter and comments.

Cultural discontinuities in interactive and communicative styles, including norms for oppositional talk, have led to relationship difficulties between teachers and children of European-American descent and African-American children (see Mehan et al., 1996). For example, within the context of her predominantly white first-grade class, Zena had difficulty interacting with other children and with the teacher who perceived her as tough and mean. Cultural discontinuities in norms for conflict talk may contribute to children's feelings of failure and eventual disengagement from learning, and to adults' feelings of frustration, failure, and eventual disengagement from certain children. Fortunately for Zena, her communication and relationship difficulties abated the next year when she returned to a predominantly black second-grade classroom (Corsaro, 1996). To the extent that educators and social service providers can anticipate and understand possible discontinuities in norms for conflict talk, interpersonal difficulties such as those encountered by Zena, her classmates, and teachers may be minimized.

THE FREQUENCY OF ADULT–CHILD VERBAL CONFLICT

Background

The extent to which children are allowed or encouraged to disagree actively with adults may vary across social and cultural communities, and may reflect their social status. Home observations revealed that young, middle-class, European-American children frequently participated in verbal conflict with their mothers and that mothers generally expressed an interest in supporting children's self-expression of viewpoints divergent from their own (Haight, Garvey & Masiello, 1995). Middle-class, African-American parents and their pre- and young adolescents also reported frequent everyday conflicts of mild intensity (Smetana & Gaines, 1999). Relatively little research, however, has examined children's verbal conflicts with adults outside of the home.

First Baptist Church

For the purposes of this study, conflict talk is defined as overt and mutual verbal opposition; that is, "A" opposes "B," and "B" opposes "A" in return (Haight et al., 1995; Shantz, 1987; Vuchinich, 1987). Oppositional moves include verbal denials, refusals, objections, disagreements, conflicting claims of intentions, and contradictions in response to the partner's utterance (Eisenberg, 1992). Occasionally, oppositional moves also include provocative claims (e.g., "I'm not a Christian") or insults (e.g., "Stupid"). A conflict began with the first oppositional move and continued as long as the chain of disagreement continued. The conflict ended when both partners had ceased opposing for a minimum of one turn.

To identify the occurrence of verbal conflict in the transcribed texts, two coders independently coded all conflicts in eight randomly selected classes: two classes each from the kindergarten, primary, junior, and intermediate classes. Interrater agreement for identifying the occurrence of conflict talk was 95%. Disagreements were resolved through discussion. For all other analyses reported in this chapter, two coders independently coded 20% each of all identified conflicts randomly selected from the kindergarten, primary, junior, and intermediate classes. (Percentage agreement for these reliability checks will be reported in the text.)

As shown in Table 9.1, teacher–child conflict talk was a routine part of all Sunday School classes, but clearly did not dominate verbal interactions. The rate of teacher–child verbal conflicts ranged from 0.7 per hour in the intermediate class to 2.9 per hour in the junior class.

CONFLICT INITIATORS

Background

Within a middle-class, European-American community, children freely initiated verbal conflicts with their mothers (Haight et al., 1995). Rela-

TABLE 9.1. *The Frequency and Initiation of Teacher–Child Conflict Talk in Each Class*

	Katherine's Kindergarten Class (3–6 years)	Patrice's Primary Class (6–8 years)	Justine's Junior Class (8–12 years)	Ima's Intermediate Class (12–15 years)
Hourly rate	1.7	1.1	2.9	0.7
Child-initiated conflicts (%)	80	80	39	50

tively little research, however, has examined the initiation of adult–child conflict talk in other communities. We know that children in other communities engage in conflict with adults, but we know very little about the characteristics of such exchanges, including the extent to which children are free to initiate these disputes.

First Baptist Church

For the purposes of this study, the initiator of the conflict is the person who produces the first oppositional move. Percentage agreement for identifying the initiator of the conflict after the conflict was 100%.

As shown in Table 9.1, children made the first oppositional move in a significant percentage of teacher–child verbal conflicts. Children's active initiations of verbal conflicts ranged from 39% in the junior class to 80% in the kindergarten and primary classes.

TOPIC OF CONFLICT

Background

Several authors have described the topics of conflicts between children and adults in European-American (e.g., Eisenberg, 1992; Haight et al., 1995) and British (e.g., Dunn & Munn, 1987) families. In these groups and contexts, adult–child conflicts included disputes over verifiable facts, child conduct, and fairness. Middle-class, African-American parents and their pre- and young adolescents reported frequent arguing about everyday details of family life such as the child's choice of activities, doing chores, and the child's room (Smetana & Gaines, 1999). What adults and children argue about, however, may vary across contexts and communities.

First Baptist Church

For the purposes of this analysis, the "topic" of the conflict refers to the topic in dispute at the initiation of the conflict. Note, however, that conflicts may revolve around multiple topics and may change over the course of the dispute. Interrater agreement for identifying the topic of the conflict at initiation was 90%.

As indicated in Table 9.2, children and teachers disputed a range of topics. The most frequently initiated conflict topic for both younger (kindergarten and primary) and older (junior and intermediate) children was "facts." These disputes centered on verifiable facts, such as a child's birth date, the proper spelling of a word, or a sequence of events within a Bible story. The second most frequently initiated conflict topic for both younger and older children was "application." These disputes centered on interpretations of the application of biblical lessons and passages to the children's own lives. In the following example, a 4–year-old boy disputes Sister Katherine's interpretation of the implications for his life of a Sunday School lesson on prayer:

> SK: You should always say your prayers at night.
> JUSTIN: I didn't say my prayers at night *(loudly)*.
> SK: No. We should always say our prayers at night.
> JUSTIN: I'm not scared.
> SK: No, you're not scared. But, you're showing that you love God. Do you love God?
> JUSTIN: Yes!
> SK: All right! Are you thankful for everything God does? *(Child nods.)* Then you should say your prayers at night, and say thank you. How about that? Can we remember that?
> JUSTIN: Yes.

In the next example, a series of two verbal conflicts, a 13-year-old boy disputes Sister Ima's interpretation of a lesson's implications for his arguments with his younger sister.

> SI: See. Now, that's something [arguing with sister] you can work on based on the lesson that we studied today.
> DARIEN: I always blame it on my sister.

TABLE 9.2. *The Percentage of Child and Teacher Conflict Initiations in Each Content Category in Classes for Younger and Older Children*

	Kindergarten and Primary		Junior and Intermediate	
	Child (%)	Teacher (%)	Child (%)	Teacher (%)
Facts	50	100	54	24
Conduct	0	0	0	43
Application	38	0	31	5
Other interpretation	0	0	8	14
Other	13	0	8	14

SI: When things come up, now, are you gonna continue to blame them on your sister? . . . Think about that, Darien, really.

DARIEN: But, she keeps blaming it on me.

SI: Well, then maybe you can enlighten her that she's responsible for her actions –

DARIEN: But she always –

SI: If you will stop blaming, she will stop blaming, then that will help both of you, right?

DARIEN: Wrong!

SI: Since you're older, now that you know better, you can apply this lesson. You're gonna tell her the same thing, right?

DARIEN: Yeah.

SI: "I'm gonna stop blaming you for everything."

DARIEN: Yeah. If she starts, I'm starting.

SI: Well, OK, now. That's why we study. Are you gonna work with this? Are you gonna try?

DARIEN: I'm gonna try. I'm gonna try! *(earnestly)*

SI: You're responsible and held accountable for your own actions. OK?

DARIEN: Yeah. If she starts in, then I have to start in again. Then, we go back and forth.

SI: But see! OK, now you just said, "If she starts it, then I'll have to start it again." "If *she (with emphasis)* starts it. I have – "

DARIEN: If I start it, then she'll start it again. I'm not gonna try to start it. If she starts it, I start it. If she starts –

SI: But, you're giving somebody else the responsibility for your actions.

DARIEN: I'm giving her a chance, here –

SI: You said, "If she does, then I."

DARIEN: I will.
SI: That's still giving somebody else your responsibility.
DARIEN: OK.
(The discussion continues.)

Athough not as frequently, older children also initiated conflicts surrounding interpretive issues other than "application," for example, possible reasons for a teacher's behavior, and why a family moved from the area.

Similar to the children, teachers initiated a significant proportion of conflicts about verifiable facts. "Verifiable facts" was the largest topic category for teachers of the younger children, and the second largest category for teachers of the older children. The largest percentage of conflict initiations for teachers of the older children centered around the children's conduct, for example, polite behavior and classroom routines. Teachers initiated relatively few conflicts focusing on children's interpretations of biblical concepts.

PLAYFUL CONFLICTS

Background

From a sociolinguistic perspective, conflict is a product of participants' interactive, interpretive work. The dimensions of the talk itself allow the participants to negotiate "what it is we are doing," and also provide a window for interpretive research (Garvey & Shantz, 1992). Focusing on the interactive processes through which actual conflicts emerge and develop, Garvey and Shantz (1992) extracted common dimensions that organize the diversity of conflict talk, including a serious or nonserious orientation (Garvey & Shantz, 1992). During serious oppositions, participants represent themselves as speaking truthfully and literally. They are not playful or joking or being "silly." Furthermore, they refer to the real world, not an imaginary one, and their speech is organized on the basis of conversational principles of coherence, sequencing, and turn construction. The nonserious dimension involves oppositional speech produced as playful, joking, kidding, or teasing. Specific signals may include: (1) paralinguistic, prosodic, or nonverbal cues, such as laughter; (2) semantic, propositional, or pragmatic cues, such as distortion of veridical reference in outlandish claims and insults known to be untrue; (3) explicit comments, such as "I'm just teasing"; (4) interactional or discoursal cues, including flagrant abrogation of procedural preferences such as providing justification for one's opposition, downplaying a disagreement, or providing a partial agreement before disagreeing (Garvey & Shantz, 1992; Haight et al., 1995).

Nonserious options are important for at least two reasons. First, they can serve as a stimulating and colorful form of verbal play as, for example, in the exchanges of Zena and her classmates. Second, they provide flexibility for disagreeing, which can change the tenor of an interaction from hostile to playful (Haight et al., 1995; Holden & West, 1989; Katz, Kramer & Gottman, 1992; Maynard, 1985), thus avoiding escalation and the coercive cycles of the clinical samples described by Gerald Patterson (1982). For example, European-American mothers drew upon nonserious options to reframe increasingly negative, serious conflict as mutual play and cooperation (Haight et al., 1995).

The use of the nonserious option in adult–child conflict has been observed in a number of cultural communities. S. Boggs (1978) described a "contradicting routine" initiated by both young Hawaiian children and their parents. This routine was formed of sequences made up of a playful insult or teasing assertion followed by a loud and emphatic denial, usually in the form of "Not!" Judy Dunn (1988) provided examples of British toddlers smiling and laughing during confrontations with their mothers. Within a working-class, European-American community, Peggy Miller and Linda Sperry (1987) observed mothers spontaneously initiating playful teasing with their 2-year-old daughters. Although playful teasing has been reported between peers (e.g., Corsaro, 1996), to my knowledge, systematic research has not described the use of the nonserious option in the conflict of African-American adults and children.

First Baptist Church

Interrater agreement for identifying conflicts containing nonserious options was 95%. As shown in Table 9.3, with the exception of children in the junior class, all conflicts initiated by children were serious. In the following example of a serious opposition, Javon disputes Sister Justine's request for children's addresses and telephone numbers:

> sj: OK. I want everybody – before the class is over I'm gonna pass this around [note pad]. Let me borrow a pen real quick. This is what I want on it. I want your name, your address, OK? And your phone number.

TABLE 9.3. *The Percentage of Child- and Teacher-Initiated Verbal Conflicts That Are Nonserious in Each Class*

	Katherine's Kindergarten Class (%) (3–6 years)	Patrice's Primary Class (%) (6–8 years)	Justine's Junior Class (%) (8–12 years)	Ima's Intermediate Class (%) (12–15 years)
Child	0	0	56	0
Teacher	100	100	39	67

JAVON: You got one of them church things that they give out every year –

SJ: I don't know – there's different people in here. This is for my class. There are different people that aren't in that register. I'm not in that register.

. . .

JAVON: Yeah you are.

SJ: No I'm not.

JAVON: Yeah you are. I got that. That's how I – that's how I found out where you live.

SJ: Am I? The last one I wasn't in.

JAVON: It's a big – it's a big thing. Well, maybe you don't have it cause just the officers might have it.

SJ: Yes.

Notice that in opposing Sister Justine, Javon provides support for her opposition, ". . . that's how I found out where you live," which Sister Justine accepts. Then, Javon politely suggests a possible explanation for Sister Justine's error.

In contrast to the children, all teachers initiated conflicts with nonserious oppositions ranging from 39% to 100% of the teacher's total initiated conflicts. In the following nonserious conflict, Sister Justine threatens to assign the children a difficult writing assignment:

SJ: OK. Here's the third question. Let me make this one real hard. *(Said in a funny, "witch" voice.)*

CHILDREN: No! *(In chorus.)*

SJ: Yes! Let's see –

DENISE: Make it in between.

TEACHER: OK. The title of our lesson is, "Jesus came to help us know God," right?

Notice that Sister Justine marks her playful threat, prosodically, by speaking in an exaggerated, "witch's" voice. The children immediately oppose her in chorus, and they agree that the question will be neither too hard nor too easy.

Most typically, "nonserious conflicts" involved a mixture of serious and nonserious oppositions. In the following example, Sister Justine criticizes Javon's use of "rude words" with a classmate:

> SJ: There's key words. Matter-of-fact, I think I'll make me a, a rude word list. . . . Some of the words – there's different ways you can say it – *(Several children are interrupting.)* Listen! There's different ways you can say what you're trying to say and not be so rude about it. "Shut up" is real rude.
>
> JAVON: No it's not, it's just like –
>
> SJ: *(Interrupting)* Yes it is, Javon. . . . "Be quiet, please." "Excuse me please, but that's annoying." That's not – "Shut up" isn't communicating.
>
> JAVON: Yeah it is.
>
> SJ: No it is not. *(Several children are giggling and interrupting.)* No it isn't. Don't you hate it when somebody screams at the top of their lungs and tells you to "Shut up"?
>
> . . .
>
> JAVON: I tell 'em to shut up back.
>
> SJ: No, no, no. If it's an adult, don't that bug you?
>
> JAVON: No. I tell 'em to "shut up" back.
>
> SJ: Oh, well, you need your little butt whipped. *(Sister J. and children laugh loudly.)* That's what you need! *(More laughter.)* That's what you need.
>
> JAVON: Except for my grandparents and my mom.
>
> SJ: Well. Well, I mean, in general, adults. Don't that bug you when somebody screams at you –
>
> JAVON: No.
>
> SJ: – and tells you to shut up? *(Lots of children join Javon in denying.)* You lying. *(Children laughing.)* I have to tell you to be quiet and you tell me – scream back at me – cause you and me is going around! *(Lots of children talking and laughing.)*
>
> . . .
>
> JAVON: Unless they elderly people.
>
> SJ: You and that word, "elderly." Why don't you just say – she called me elderly today! *(Loud laughter.)* I don't see it. "You elderly women go first." I was like, "Excuse me!" *(Lots of laughter.)* "When did I get all

included in this?" *(More loud laughter.)* "After you. The elderly women go first," and Reverend Young was sitting there looking at me. I say, "Thanks, Javon." *(Fake annoyed voice. More laughter.)* "I guess I'm old *(shaky, old voice)* now. Gee whiz." I am getting older, though. Letta turned fifteen, yesterday. I can't believe that.

TERRANASHA: Who turned fifteen?

SJ: My daughter. She'll be driving next year. Oh LORD!

Notice that the conflict begins with a serious opposition to the use of "rude words." Javon then challenges Sister Justine. When Javon refuses to concede, Sister Justine reframes the disagreement as playful, "Well, you need your little butt whipped." After much loud laughter, Javon concedes that she would not talk back to her grandparents or mother. She continues, however, to oppose the general point that rudeness is unpleasant. Sister Justine again reframes the argument as playful, "You lying!" Javon then concedes that she would not talk back to "elderly" people. Sister Justine then teases Javon about her use of the word "elderly" and launches into a story involving herself and Javon. Finally, she makes references to her teenage daughter, conceding that she may indeed be getting old. Notice that Sister Justine remains in charge throughout the challenge from Javon, apparently enjoying a stimulating interaction, and that she continues to treat Javon with affection.

In the following example, Sister Justine uses the nonserious option when fielding a challenge from Adrian, who is reluctant to complete his written assignment.

SJ: "One of the valuable Christian skills is having support in our lives to help us cope. Fill in the names of your support, above. Who supports you in your Christian life?" *(Reading from the Sunday School book.)*

ADRIAN: I'm not a Christian.

5   SJ: Yes you are.

. . .

ADRIAN: I'm not a Christian. *(Pause, no response.)* I'm a Mormon.

GEOFF: I'm Methodist.

SJ: We're gonna have to – that's gonna be a whole different lesson.

10   Methodists are Christians too.

ADRIAN: Well I'm a – I'm a Mormon.

SJ: They're Christian too.

EDNA: My sister was a Mormon!

(Children talking at the same time.)

15 SJ: You don't get this! See, he – he almost missed the whole purpose of
       this lesson! He's missed the whole purpose of this lesson! What are
       the Catholics – *(child interrupts)* – wait a minute, listen! What are the
       Catholics, the Baptists, Methodists, Lutherans – what have we all got
       in common?

20 BESS: We're all –
    EDNA: *(Interrupting)* We all go to church.
    BESS: We all go to the same church like-kinda.
    SJ: OK. What are you trying to say? You're close.
    BESS: We have the same God.

25 SJ: There you go! There you go! We're all what? A part of what does
       the verse say: "One in body and one in spirit."
    ADRIAN: I don't go to church.
    SJ: There's people that don't go to church that are still part of this
       body.

30 ADRIAN: I'm not a part –
    SJ: We're all believers.
    ADRIAN: Well I – I believe in ah –
    SJ: Adrian! Will you stop being goofy and just do what I asked you to
       do? Everybody silent and work on your worksheet.

35 . . .
    BESS: I do not know what to put in here.
    SJ: Who supports you?
    BESS: My mom.
    SJ: Put "Mom" on number one.

40 BESS: All right!
    ADRIAN: Are you sure?
    SJ: Yeah, I know your Mom.
    ADRIAN: What's her name?
    SJ: Boy, I know your Mom, . . . You know I know your mother, stop

45   being goofy! Gee whiz.
    ADRIAN: You don't know her.
    SJ: Yes I do. Adrian, I've known your grandma longer than you've
       known your grandma. I'm older than you. That's got to be true. And
       your cousin is my niece. So how in the heck do I not know you?

50 ADRIAN: What cousin.
    SJ: Katrina.
    ADRIAN: Oh!
    SJ: – is my brother's – is my deceased brother's child. Give me a break.
    ADRIAN: Oh, that egg head? That egg head? *(laughing)*

55 SJ: You look just like her. . . . Where is she, by the way? *(More talking
       about time, etc.)*

sj: Come on. I want this . . . worksheet finished. I want this . . . worksheet finished. *(Talking above children. Children continue talking and
working.)*

Notice that in line 4, Adrian makes the claim, outrageous in this context,
that he is not a Christian. Sister Justine responds minimally with a denial
of Adrian's claim. Adrian, however, persists, adding the apparently more
outrageous claim that he is Mormon. Sister Justine responds, beginning
in line 15 and again in line 26, by emphasizing a main point from the
lesson. Adrian, however, persists in his opposition, including the patently
false claim in line 26 that he does not go to church. By line 31, Sister
Justine responds by reframing Adrian's challenge as playful, "Will you
stop being goofy?" By line 42, Sister Justine asserts her kinship relationship to Adrian. Despite his obvious attempts to provoke her, and her
continued opposition to his outrageous assertions, Sister Justine continues to treat Adrian with affection throughout. Eventually, he does
complete the worksheet.

CONCLUSION

In summary, teacher–child verbal conflicts provide a glimpse into adults'
growth-oriented, child-sensitive stance toward socialization and children's unique perspectives as active participants. Within Sunday School,
adult–child conflicts were a routine and acceptable form of social interaction. Even the youngest children initiated verbal conflicts with their
teachers, and teachers did not correct children for engaging in topic-
relevant verbal opposition. Teachers did, however, retain their status as
more knowledgeable adult class leaders during class conflicts. In addition, when conflicts were playful, they typically were initiated by teachers,
not children. Indeed, with the exception of three students in the junior
class, children did not initiate nonserious conflicts with their teachers.
Teachers seemed to use playful teasing to reframe potentially negative
exchanges, to enliven the classes, and to engage children in mutually
enjoyable, affectively positive social exchanges.

Interestingly, humorous teasing also was used by adults in the "young
adult" Sunday School class, possibly to enliven social exchanges or to
defuse tension. For example, the young adults were discussing conflict
resolution when a newly married man provided an example of a conflict
with his wife in which he portrayed himself as the head of the family. This

brief narrative was followed by much laughter and good-natured teasing by several women in the class who challenged his apparent assumption that he knew more than his wife.

The relatively high level of conflict in the junior class, including the relatively frequent challenges of three children and their initiation of nonserious conflicts, may be related to Sister Justine's status as a relatively new junior class teacher. In other words, these children may have been testing Sister Justine's resolve to engage in serious work. In addition, Sister Justine's general playfulness and sense of humor also may have encouraged some children to engage in somewhat higher levels of conflict and teasing than they did with other teachers.

Children and teachers argued about a variety of topics. These topics provide a glimpse into children's perceptions of the socialization messages and practices of Sunday School, as well as teachers' concerns. Teachers and children both initiated conflicts over verifiable facts. These findings are consistent with teachers' concerns with relaying information about the Bible to children. They also are consistent with descriptions of the topics of parent–child conflicts in European-American and British families (e.g., Dunn & Munn, 1987; Eisenberg, 1992; Haight et al., 1995).

Teachers of the older children also frequently initiated conflict over children's conduct. These findings seem consistent with the teachers' goal of encouraging exemplary behavior by their students. They also are consistent with Judith Smetana and Cheryl Gaines' (1999) description of middle-class, African-American parents' and their pre- and young adolescents' reports of frequent arguing about everyday details of family life, such as the child's choice of activities, doing chores, and the child's room (Smetana & Gaines, 1999). The relatively lower percentages of teacher-initiated conflicts over conduct with younger children does not mean that teachers did not address issues of conduct with younger children. Younger children, however, may have been less likely to oppose their teachers on these issues.

Interestingly, children initiated conflicts not only about verifiable facts, but also about teachers' interpretations of the implications of biblical concepts and stories for children's own lives. In particular, children sometimes challenged teachers over the appropriateness and utility in their families and schools of central Christian tenets, such as "turning the other cheek," or other nonaggressive responses to verbal and physical confrontation. The fact that children initiated these conflicts, and that teachers treated them with seriousness, suggests that children were not viewed as passive recipients of teachers' knowledge, but as active interpreters of biblical text and concepts.

In conclusion, further study of adult–child conflict can teach us much more about adult–child relationships and children's unique perspectives and reactions to routine socialization messages. Such knowledge, while important in its own right, also has the potential to reduce confusion and misunderstandings when adults and children from different cultural communities interact in educational, social service, and other contexts.

CHAPTER TEN

Other Contexts for Socialization and Participation

As discussed in chapter 1, in addition to Sunday School, children participated with adults in a wide variety of emotionally compelling weekly,
monthly, and yearly events at First Baptist Church. Similar to Sunday
School, in these contexts, the importance of applying biblical concepts to
modern life was highlighted through story, song, and prayer. As discussed
in chapter 3, these multiple contexts of observation allow for a more
complete account of adults' socialization practices and children's participation. These observations contextualized Sunday School within the
larger community and suggest the unique, as well as the redundant,
socialization functions of Sunday School. They also provided critical
checks on interpretations of practices observed in Sunday School and
beliefs articulated during interviews.

KEY WEEKLY EVENTS: THE CHILDREN'S STORY

During one Sunday School lesson, Sister Justine asked the children in the
junior class why they attended church. Amanda stated that she comes to
church because her grandfather, who was an associate reverend, sometimes told children's stories. The others quickly agreed that children's
stories were an important reason to attend church.

Children's stories, also referred to as "Children's Sermons," occurred
midway through the Sunday morning worship service. Pastor Daniels, or
the associate reverend, invited children aged 10 and under to come
down to the front and center of the sanctuary. As the congregation sang
"Jesus Loves Me," the children gathered in a circle around the teller.
During the children's stories, the teller drew a parallel between African
or African-American culture and history, and biblical concepts.

Although the stories were addressed to the children, the adults also were involved. They sang "Jesus loves me" as the children filed to and from the center of the sanctuary, they applauded and laughed at clever responses, and they voiced their agreement with the storyteller through enthusiastic "Amen!"

Animal Tales

The most frequent and perhaps favored stories were tales in which human characteristics were attributed to animals. These stories illustrated the safety of adhering to, and the dangers of straying from, Christian principles of behavior. For example, Pastor Daniels elaborated a traditional African folk tale of a spider and antelope to emphasize the protective features of helping others. In summary, a spider asked an antelope for help during a brush fire. The antelope allowed the spider to jump into his ear and whisked him away to the edge of the forest. At the edge of the forest stood a hunter. The antelope then asked the little spider for help. The spider asked to be let down from the antelope's ear, and he quickly wove a web in the antelope's tracks. When the hunters came to the tracks, they decided that the tracks were old and called off the hunt. Following a scripture reading, the children were admonished to "do unto others as you would have others do unto you."

In this next example, told right after Christmas time, Pastor Daniels elaborated upon the dangers of being greedy. Notice that the telling involved singing as well as speaking, and a good deal of laughing and responsiveness from the adults.

> PASTOR D: A friend of mine went hunting. One day he couldn't find anything to kill. What do you think he should do?
> JUSTIN: Go home! *(Laughing from the congregation.)*
> PASTOR D: He looked up in a tree and saw caterpillars. How many of you have been hungry? *(Several children raise their hands.)* Well, this man's family was hungry. He thought, "At least I can take home some caterpillars for my bird." Then, a little bird in a tree sang, "Share what you have, or lose what you have." *(Pastor Daniels actually sings this warning.)* But, the man paid no attention. The next day he came back, and it was the same: "Share what you have, or lose what you have" *(sung)*. All of a sudden, a limb on the tree jumped up and bit the man on the arm!! And my friend started home because he knew he had been bitten by a snake. He was greedy. He didn't leave any caterpillars for the little bird. And his bow arm was paralyzed, so he couldn't pull the hunting bow anymore. "Share what you have, or

lose what you have" *(sung)*. This story reminds me of Christmas because lots of us get lots of things at Christmas, but we don't share. Being greedy doesn't work in the long run. *(Pastor Daniels asks who wants to sing a solo. Many children raise their hands, and he invites 2-year-old Olivia to sit on his lap and sing, "Yes, Jesus Loves Me" into the microphone while the other children return to their seats.)*

Occasionally, the children's story was told by an associate reverend. In the following excerpt, Reverend Charles uses the characteristics of animals to illustrate the importance of following Jesus' good example. He begins by asking children to differentiate good examples from bad. He holds up a picture of a little boy pretending to be a doctor, and the children describe it.

REV. C: What do we know about doctors?

CHILDREN, IN CHORUS: They help.

REV. C: They help. They are good, doctors. Well, just like we've got . . . people, people that act like good ones. We've also got some bad ones. You know, out in the woods there's a, there's a, an old snake that crawls around on the ground and he spreads his head out and acts – imitates like he's gonna attack somebody, but he's really not gonna hurt anybody. He just acts – swells all up, blows all up. They call him a blow snake because he just blows all out and he acts awful fierce. And then there's a little animal called an opossum. Do you children know what an opossum is? *(Murmurs from the adults, "Oh, yeah!")* Ever seem a picture of an opossum? Looks like a little raccoon – a rat – something like that. *(Loud laughing from the adults.)* Anyway, anyway an opossum. What does he do? Do you know anything about him? What does he do? What does he do? He plays what? He plays dead. Whenever he's attacked or gonna be attacked he rolls over and acts like he's dead. Whenever something – maybe a badger or something is gonna attack him – another big animal that's badder than he is – he just rolls over and plays dead. He just gives up. You know. And then there's an old monkey. A monkey he acts – he just cuts the fool and acts the fool. And he *(loud laughter from adults)* – he really acts – acts like he's somebody sometimes. All . . . those are bad examples. But you know Jesus Christ wants us to be good examples.

ADULTS: Yes!

REV. C: What kind of example does he want us to be?

ADULTS: Good examples.

REV. C: There's a few words in the Bible, in first Peter. And it talks about being an example, being good, being imitating – acting like somebody. I'm gonna ask Reverend Gates if he'll read that passage of scripture. Listen to what Reverend Gates is gonna read.

REV. GATES: "For to this you are called because Christ also struggled for us, leaving us an example that we can follow to the death."

REV. C: So what can we do? Follow what?

CHILDREN (*in chorus*): The example.

REV. C: Follow the example of who?

CHILDREN, IN CHORUS: Of Jesus.

REV. C: Give me one example of how you can follow the example – how you can act like Jesus. Tell me one thing you can do. Who'd like to tell me one example, of what they can do to act like Jesus. . . . What are things that people do, and someone would look at you and say, "You, know, that's like Christ Jesus." (*The children give several examples including helping other people, being good, being nice, and doing what your parents say. Examples are accompanied by "Amen" from the adults.*) Jesus wants us to act like someone that's good. Be like him – he's acting like a doctor [boy in picture].

. . .

(*Rev. Charles leads the congregation in prayer to be and to follow good examples.*) God bless you. Be good examples this week. God bless you. (*Children return to their seats as the congregation sings "Jesus Loves Me."*)

These two examples of children's sermons led by Pastor Daniels and Reverend Charles share a variety of features with stories told in Sunday School. First, they illustrate biblical concepts in an engaging manner (in this case through the use of animals). Then, they go on to draw parallels and to ask children to draw parallels to their own lives, such as when Reverend Charles said, "Give me one example of how you can follow the example – how you can act like Jesus." Next, the story is presented and led by an adult, but the children are actively involved. They participate as part of a class chorus during call-and-response sequences, and as individuals. Notice that adults also respond actively to the story. This genuine engagement may communicate to children the importance of the presented material. Finally, the inherent value of the children is communicated in multiple ways: they are "blessed," they are the center of attention, and the congregation sings "Jesus Loves Me" to them.

Famous African-Americans

Also popular were stories featuring famous African-Americans. These stories were used to illustrate how adherence to biblical principles can enhance success.

PASTOR D: Good morning to all of you. Good morning to all of you!

CHILDREN, IN CHORUS: Good morning!

PASTOR D: I appreciate your coming down and talking with me for a few minutes. I want to ask you if you know who this person is that I'm gonna talk to you about, and then I'm gonna ask you how much you really know about – anybody ever see this person before? *(A child asks if the picture is of Pastor Daniels.)* Anybody know – is that me? *(Laughter from the adults.)* You know, I'm glad you asked that question because it looks almost identical to the way my father looked when my father died, but that's not me, no. Anybody know who this is? Any of you know who this is? *(Several children say, "No.")* How about any of you adults who can see this. Anybody know who this is? Who'd like to tell us who this is.

ADULT: Dr. George Washington Carver.

PASTOR D *(to children)*: Did you hear anybody say anything?

CHILDREN, IN CHORUS: Yes.

PASTOR D: What'd they say?

CHILDREN, IN CHORUS: Dr. George Washington Carver!

PASTOR D: Dr. George Washington Carver. Now, anybody know anything about him, now that you know his name, you know anything about that person? *(Several children say, "No.")* Ever heard anything about him? He was a great scientist. You like to eat?

(Several children call out, "I do!" Adults laugh.)

PASTOR D: Now, who said they like to eat?

CHILDREN, IN CHORUS: Me! *(More laughter from the adults.)*

PASTOR D: Now listen, I'm gonna ask you a question. Have you ever eaten potato bread? You haven't eaten potato bread? How many of you have eaten potato bread?

(Several children say, "me.")

PASTOR D: How many of you eat peanut butter? *(Lots of children raise hands, adults laugh.)* I knew we'd hit one sooner or later. George Washington Carver is the person who first taught the world to make sweet potato bread and peanut butter. And what he did was, Dr. George Washington Carver was hired at Tuskeegee, and the farmers were all planting cotton, right? But, the boll weevil came. How many of you have seen a boll weevil? You haven't seen a boll weevil? How many of you have seen a boll weevil? But the boll weevil came and Dr. Carver said, "You need to change the crops that you grow, and you need to change them because you're not gonna make much money planting cotton because the boll weevil is gonna do so much harm." And he said to the farmer, "Plant sweet potatoes and plant peanuts. Plant sweet potatoes and peanuts." Anybody have any idea why Dr.

Carver recommended those two things? Matthew? Why those two things? Why sweet potatoes, or why peanuts? Chris?

CHRIS: Maybe because they would grow.

PASTOR D: *(Nods)* Because these were things that he believed a market could be created for. And, by the way, he got, he got these notions from the Bible, and Reverend Young's gonna read a passage of scripture, this is one of Dr. Carver's favorite passages of scripture that helped him to share with the farmers what they ought to do. Well, he told them that if they would plant peanuts, and they would plant sweet potatoes, that in a year's time he would create the market to make sure they could sell what they grew. And so at the end of a time he had invented some three-hundred different products that come from peanuts, including peanut butter and peanut oil. And there's a hair product that people use on their hair, and there's lots of other things. And then he also created a market for sweet potatoes. He made one-hundred different products that farmers – that could be made out of sweet potato. And Dr. Carver did all of this, and he always wore, wherever he went, he always had something live attached to the lapel of his coat: a piece of cedar, a leaf of the tree – *(Small child crying, "No!")* Yes, he did. *(Adults laugh.)* He always had something live attached because Dr. Carver believed that whatever you did in life ought to be about life, ought to be about living. *(Adults, "Amen.")* And there's a passage in Psalms twenty-three, that all of you probably know, it was one of Dr. Carver's favorite passages of scripture. Reverend Young's gonna read it to you.

REV. YOUNG: Psalms twenty-three and two. "He maketh me to lie down in green pastures, he leadeth me beside the still waters."

PASTOR D: One of Dr. Carver's favorite passages was, "He maketh me to lie down in green pastures, he leadeth me beside the still waters." And he believed that life had to do with green things and with having plenty of water. Now, I want to suggest to you, that if you're trying to have a good time in life, learn to appreciate the things that are right around you, the green things, the water, things that we take for granted, because in a few years, if we're not careful, we may not have any decent water to drink. *(Adults, "That's right.")* And if we don't have any decent water to drink then we also won't have anything that will be green.

This is Dr. George Washington Carver. Now, remember him, and the next time you do a book report, maybe you can do a book report on Dr. Carver. All right. Thank you. We're gonna stand, and we're gonna have a word of prayer. . . . OK, let's hold our hands together. Let's pray. Dear God, our father, we thank you for these young people, for these children, we thank you for their eagerness to learn. And we pray that you'll help us to learn from those who are our previous examples. Allow you, your word, and then your will in our lives. Bless us now. And help us to learn and appreciate who we are. In Jesus' name, Amen. Thank you for coming, you may be seated. *(Piano playing "Jesus Loves Me" as children sit down.)*

In stories like this one featuring famous African-Americans, biblical concepts such as an appreciation for living things were related to children's black heritage. One important function of such stories may be to provide children with black role models they otherwise might not encounter in their public schools. In this example, Dr. George Washington Carver's lasting contributions were described, as well as more personal characteristics with which children might identify, for example, that he wore a piece of something living on his lapel and that Psalms 23 was his favorite Bible verse. The relevance of Dr. Carter's direct contributions to the children also was conveyed through a discussion of common products invented by Dr. Carter and through the pastor's encouragement that they write about Dr. Carver for their school book reports. As with other children's stories, this discussion communicated the inherent value of the children in multiple ways. First, they are African-American like the famous American described. Also, in this example, Pastor Daniels explicitly thanked the children for their attention, and he thanked God for them in his closing prayer.

Church Etiquette and Christian Behavior

Occasionally, the teller would deliberately teach some aspect of church etiquette or Christian behavior via a clever demonstration or verbal game. In the following example, Pastor Daniels teaches about tithing:

> PASTOR D: Come on. If you're ten years old or younger come on down. And if you want to be ten, you can come down too. *(Pastor D. and the congregation singing "Jesus Loves Me" as children move forward.)* Tell you what, I've got a little gift for everybody *(dimes)*, and I'll give it to these young people *(several children)*, and they're gonna give it to everybody. They're gonna give everybody one. You keep one, and give everybody else one. *(Pause, children passing out dimes.)* Come on you all, speed up, act like you're in a hurry! *(Loud laughter from adults.)* Has everybody got one? Who didn't get one? You all got some left? There's lots of folks back there that don't have one. Those of you

whose got the gifts, stand up and go back there and give those one.
You don't have one? You got one? Take these *(to child)* and make sure
everybody's got one. Stand up and do it. Hurry, hurry, hurry. *(Pastor
D. begins singing "Jesus Loves Me." The piano and congregation join in as
children continue passing out dimes.)* Don't give it to those adults, now,
they got plenty of those. *(Laughter, continues singing).* Thank you. I
appreciate my helpers. They gave everybody a gift. Who did not get a
gift? Great, everybody's got one. Now, if you'll just hold it in your
hand. Oh, thanks, there's some left over. Great! Great! This'll go
back in my pocket, now. Great. *(Laughter from adults.)*

Now, everybody's got a gift. I want to ask you a couple of questions.
You guys up to answering a question for me? How many of you have
ever been robbed? *(A number of children raise their hands. Adults laugh.)*
How many of you have ever been robbed? One, two, three, four, five
of you have. Tell me about when you were robbed?

JUSTIN: My cousin, Lawrence, took some money of mine. *(Loud laughter from the congregation.)*

PASTOR D: I guess maybe we better leave that alone. *(More loud laughter.)* We gonna get some – all kinds of family stories here. *(More
laughter.)* You get robbed?

JAVARIUS: My brother took my money from me.

PASTOR D: Your brother took your money from you? Oh. All right,
brother, where are you? *(Calling out, teasing. Lots of laughter from
adults.)* Well, anyway. I wanted to ask you that question because – how
many of you say you've been robbed? Hold your hands up again.
Great. Put your hands down. Now, how many of you have ever robbed
anybody? *(More laughter from adults.)* Just four of you? *(More laughter
from adults.)* Anybody got any idea what ought to happen if you get
robbed? If – if somebody else rob you? What ought to happen to the
person that robs you? Anybody know? What do you think ought to
happen?

JUSTIN: They get put in jail.

PASTOR D: They get put in jail. You would like your brother put in jail?
(More laughter from adults. Child nods.) Well, I guess I better leave that
alone. The reason I ask you the question is because there's an interesting story in the Bible, in the book of Malachi. Malachi. M-a-l-a-c-h-i.
In the third chapter, verse eight, nine, and ten, and those verses say
that, they ask the question, "Will a man rob God?" And then they say,
"All of those people who have robbed God have been cursed." And
then the third verse says, instead of robbing God, from now on, what
you ought to do is give God one-tenth of whatever it is that you have.
Now, who can tell me, of the gift I gave you this morning, how much
of that ought you give to God? If you're gonna give one-tenth of what

I gave to you this morning, how much of that would you give to God?
Yes, sir. How much?

MATTHEW: Twenty cents.

PASTOR D: That would be great, that would be great, huh?

MARRISA: A penny.

PASTOR D: One penny. You give God one penny. I gave each of you a
dime, right? And one-tenth of a dime would be one cent. And so of
every dime that you get, you ought to give one cent of that to God.
OK? How many of you are willing to do that? *(A few children raise their
hands.)* OK. What about the rest of you. *(Adults laugh.)* Now, if you
don't give God that one cent that is in that dime, then you're robbing God. So, let's don't be robbers, all right? Is that fair? Great.
Thank you. I appreciate you listening to me, and you can have the
gift. And if anybody didn't get one, you tell them to come see me. I
think I got ten more left. *(Begins singing, "Jesus Loves Me," and the piano
and congregation join in.)* Thank you, you may go to your seats. *(The
singing continues as the children return to their seats.)*

In the following excerpt, Pastor Daniels plays a clever word game to
emphasize the importance of looking outward toward others in love:

PASTOR D: How many of you have ever seen a one-eyed man? *(Draws a
picture on chalkboard of head with one eye, nose, mouth, eyes, hair.)* I can tell
you what makes a one-eyed man. *(Writes "EVIL" on the board.)* But, do
you know how you can change a one-eyed man into a two-eyed man?
(Pause.) What does that word *(evil)* spell backwards? L-i-v-e. *(Writes on
other side of board.)* It means, "live," doesn't it? And so you take that
word, "live" *(writes, "love" below)*, how bout that? What does that spell?

CHILDREN: Love.

PASTOR D: That spells love. So you take – you take "evil" and turn it
around so that it's not backwards, so that it spells *(pause)* l-i-v-e, right?
And then you change the "i" to an "o."

Now, here's the real problem with the one-eyed man. He's always
looking at himself. *(Adults laugh)* That's the real problem – the reason we can't see the other eye is it's always looking inside, looking at
himself. And so if you change the "i" to an "o" and that means
"others." *(Writes on the board, below, "love.")* So instead of looking at
oneself, he can look at others, right? Right? OK. So, we're gonna get
rid of all the one-eyed people that exist and make sure that they do
what?

CHILDREN: Love!

PASTOR D: That they love. Great! Great! And I just want to say to all of
you boys and girls that it's a good idea to practice loving one another,

and even if you don't particularly agree with somebody else, it's a good idea to love them. And if they don't look like you, and if they not smart like you, or if they don't live the way you live, it's still a good idea to love everybody. OK? *("Amens" from the adults.)* And there's a little verse in the scriptures that talks about that, and that verse in the scriptures, and Sister Williams is gonna read it, because what it does is it changes us from to evil to live, and then from live to love, and love is always centered on others. Sister Williams.

SISTER W: "Beloved. If God so loved us, we ought also to love one another."

(Lots of affirmations from the adults.)

PASTOR D: Beloved. Or, another way of saying beloved is, "Little children, if God so loved us, then we ought to love *(pause, and the adults say, "others")* – others." We ought to love one another. And so I – I like to look at one-eyed people. But I also want to change all the one-eyed people that I see, so that they have two eyes. Let me see if I can draw one with two eyes. *(Lots of laughter as Pastor Daniels draws a smiling stick figure with two eyes.)* Hey, listen, I'm going to art school. *(Loud laughter.)* I'm gonna start selling my art work. *(More loud laughter from adults and comments.)* And so the real person is one like this, who has two eyes and a nose and a mouth, has arms and legs and all kinds of things and that's because that person cares, not just about themselves, but about others. And I want to really recommend to you that you learn how to care about other people. And how do you do that? How do you show that you care about other people? Can somebody tell one way that you can show you care about somebody else?

MARRISA: Because you love them.

PASTOR D: Because you love them. And how do you show them that you love them? How can you show them that you love them? Yes?

MATTHEW: By helping them out.

PASTOR D: By helping them out. So, learn to help others out. And, how can you show your friends that you love them, those who you play with?

JAVARIUS: By being nice.

PASTOR D: By being nice. And how about your toys? Can you show that you love them with your toys? *(pause)*

MARRISA: Share your toys.

PASTOR D: Share your toys. And what do you do in terms of your parents to show them that you love them?

DENISE: Do chores for them.

PASTOR D: Do chores for them. Boy, where are my kids? Did they hear that? *(Loud laughter from adults.)* Do chores for them. So, all I really wanted to say to you today, is it's a good idea not to be evil, how many

of you want to be evil? Good, I'm glad to see that none of you want to
be evil. So just turn evil around and you have live, and then if you
change that "i" to "o," representing others, then you have love.

PASTOR D: *(Begins singing "Jesus Loves Me," and the piano and congregation join in.)* Thank you boys and girls, I appreciate you coming and
sharing. . . .

In these two examples, lessons were infused with engaging verbal play,
teasing, laughter, and respect for the children. In the second example,
children were "beloved" and, in addition, generated examples of how
they could show their love to others.

KEY MONTHLY EVENTS: YOUTH EMPHASIS DAY

The third Sunday of every month was "Youth Emphasis Day" at First
Baptist Church. Activities during Youth Emphasis Day communicated in
many ways the inherent worth of children. For example, the children
ushered, carried out the devotions, read reports on African-American
history, and sang. For many children, the opportunity to perform legitimate service to the community was a source of pride and self-esteem.

In addition, children were celebrated and honored during Youth Emphasis Day. For example, Pastor Daniels might invite all the "young people" to come down and sit in the front pews, or he might recognize an
individual child for good behavior or achievement in school. Throughout the service, Pastor Daniels made comments such as, "We are celebrat-
ing our youth because without them you and I would be just passing on."

Further, the sermon on Youth Emphasis Days addressed young people. For example, on one Youth Emphasis Day, Pastor Daniels began by
telling a funny story about how he was going to show his son (a high
school track star) how to run. Unfortunately, he pulled a muscle just a few
steps after starting. He then noted that someday "your speed and
strength will be like my pulled muscle," but you can still be in the race
because the race doesn't always go to the fastest. "The race sometimes is
given not to the swift or strong, but to the connected." Pastor Daniels
then told another funny story of a classmate of his from high school who,
on the surface, appeared to be a "boy from nowhere going nowhere."
But, he was connected to other people. And now that boy is mayor of a
town in Georgia where his parents, years before, were not even allowed to
vote. This theme of developing connections to others was used to lead
into a sermon on Moses' leadership of the Israelites.

KEY YEARLY EVENTS: CHRISTMAS AND EASTER PROGRAMS, VACATION BIBLE SCHOOL

There were several yearly events at First Baptist Church that revolved around children and may have further reinforced a belief in the dignity and worth of each individual, and the application of biblical text to everyday life: the Christmas program, the Easter program, and Vacation Bible School. Adults participated in all three of these programs, but the focus was definitely on the children. For example, during a Christmas program in which adults as well as children participated, the mistress of ceremonies began by reading from Mark 10:13–14, "Suffer the little children to come unto me." She then invited the congregation to celebrate the children on that day.

The Christmas Program

The Christmas program was a much anticipated and widely enjoyed event. Children began preparation for the Christmas program in Sunday School the Sunday following Thanksgiving when they received copies of their individual "speeches" to memorize and began planning group skits, songs, or presentations. In addition, practices were held on the three Saturdays preceding the program. The actual Christmas programs were held in the sanctuary during Sunday School hours the Sunday before Christmas. The church would be filled with church members, their relatives, and friends. Additional chairs would be set up in the aisles to accommodate the eager audience.

During 1993, the Christmas program began with a "Good morning" from the Sunday School superintendent, Brother Brown, and a reminder that the gathering was to "celebrate Jesus' birthday." One of the adult classes then led the devotions. The class for older women led the congregation in singing "Go Tell It on the Mountain," read from the gospel of Luke about Jesus' birth, and led a group prayer to Jesus to "keep your arms wrapped tightly around us as you were held in the manger."

Children from the kindergarten and primary classes presented their individual, memorized speeches. Each child walked to the front of the church and spoke into the microphone. For example, 6-year-old Matthew's speech was:

> Christmas means many things to people everywhere. Some think of only presents and the gifts that they may share. But when I think of

Christmas, I think of God above and how he sent us Jesus with his everlasting love.

Every child was applauded loudly before and after his/her speech, regardless of the quality of the performance. A few of the youngest children had their mothers come up with them, and one cried. Overall, however, children appeared proud and happy to contribute. After the last child spoke, the entire class was again applauded. Then the kindergarten and primary class sang a song, "Hosanna," together, while performing the words in American Sign Language. Next, the primary class presented their individual speeches. Again, each child was applauded both before and after his/her speech, and the entire class was applauded after the final speech.

Children in the junior and intermediate classes put on skits. For example, the junior class contributed a modern-day rendition of the Christmas story, complete with home boys (the three wise men), a very hip angel ("Hey, dudes! Don't sweat it"), a rap, and a homeless Mary who gave birth underneath the freeway overpass. Unlike the younger children, children in the intermediate class incorporated actual biblical scripture into their skit. Their play, "The most precious gift," also was a modern-day rendition of the Christmas story. The adult classes also made presentations including skits, songs, and biblical readings.

Intermixed throughout these presentations was congregational singing of traditional hymns, such as "Silent Night," and other musical activities; for example, the mistress of ceremonies taught a call-and-response song to the congregation. The program ended with song, "We Wish You a Blessed Christmas" and "Happy Birthday to Jesus," and words from the pastor. Pastor Daniels thanked everyone for participating in the program. He told a funny story of a young preacher, dependent on his notes, who was at a complete loss when the lights went out. He then encouraged the children to memorize as much as they could of God's word "because no one can take away from you what's in your head."

Easter Program

The Easter program was one of the biggest celebrations of the year. Preparations would begin weeks in advance in the Sunday School classes and on the three Saturdays preceding the program. The actual program would be held in the sanctuary during the 1½-hour period of Sunday School before Easter morning services. The messages of the pastor reinforced much of what the children were learning in Sunday School. For example, when opening an Easter program, Pastor Daniels spoke of the need to understand the resurrection so that "we can apply the lessons to our own lives." Many children participated in Easter programs with more than 60 delivering speeches on any given Easter Sunday. For example, 6 ½-year-old Matthew recited "The Reason":

> The birds outside are happy, and I am happy too. There surely is a reason, I'll tell it now to you. Christ lives! He lives forever. He rose on Easter Day. That's the reason I am happy, and what I'd like to say, Happy Easter.

Once again, children received ample applause. Children who had difficulty during previous programs would receive particularly enthusiastic cheers. For example, after crying during her Christmas speech, 3-year-old Olivia delivered a very loud, enthusiastic Easter speech followed by actual cheering from the congregation. Her parents praised her, and she beamed as she returned to sit on her older brother's lap. Children in the junior and intermediate classes and adults also made presentations, including skits, songs, and biblical readings.

Vacation Bible School

The Vacation Bible School occurred on five weeknights in August from 6–9 P.M. Each year, the school focused on a particular theme, such as "Let's go with Jesus." Written lessons, crafts projects, games, and songs were coordinated around this theme. For example, children's written lessons were taken from the "Loyal Travellers Workbook" and included topics such as "Praying under Pressure." The new song children learned was, "Let's Go with Jesus," which focused on following Jesus "anywhere He leads me." Vacation Bible School also included some major social events. For example, on Friday, all children aged 9 and over participated in a sleepover at the church followed by a church picnic in the park the next day.

The organization of Vacation Bible School was very similar to that of Sunday School. It began with an opening song and prayer led by the teachers. Then, the participants divided into classes by age: kindergarten (3–5 years), primary (6–8 years), junior (9–11 years), teens (12–18 years), and adults. Vacation Bible School typically involved between 50 and 60 students. Classes were taught by members of the church, including regular Sunday School teachers. The adult class was taught by the pastor. Within these groups, approximately one hour was devoted each day to Bible study. The children also did arts and crafts projects and played games. Then the entire group reassembled to watch a video, listen to presentations, and participate in closing services. Videos included presentations on African-American children at school, self-esteem, and Bible stories. The actors on the videos were African-American. For example, one video featured a group of African-American children acting out Bible stories with their teacher, "Griot." Presentations included the "rules of conduct" for church, taught by the pastor's adolescent son. He presented one rule per night, written on a big card: "Be on time," "Listen when the preacher or teacher is talking," "Walk don't run in the church building," "Be polite in God's house," "Get a drink and use the restroom before services." Closing services included a prayer, a salute to the Christian flag, a salute to the Bible, and, finally, a salute to the American flag.

Vacation Bible School culminated on Sunday with an evening program. Each class performed before the assembly. All of the children were given certificates of participation, "Let's go with Jesus" t-shirts, and a gift. The kindergarten class sang "Jesus Loves the Little Children," and the primary class presented memorized speeches. For example, 7-year-old Matthew's speech was:

> Jesus wants us to excel and be the best that we can be just like Mae Jamison, who became the first female, African-American astronaut.

The junior class showed some of their crafts, and the teens performed a skit. Their teacher articulated the goal of the class as showing how the lessons applied to everyday life and engaging in some "down-to-earth" discussions. The adults discussed "ordinary people doing extraordinary things" through God. They described for the assembly the biblical characters they had studied. Four women presented on the strengths of Debra, emphasizing that women are not "second-class citizens" in God's eyes. Following the presentations there was an invitation to join the church, accompanied by the song "I Have Decided to Follow Jesus." Pastor Daniels then introduced a visiting pastor who said a few words. He emphasized that "Vacation Bible School and Sunday School are very important. . . . If we don't teach the children, who will?" At the close, children attending Vacation Bible School for the first time were given live birds or fish.

SPECIAL EVENTS: BAPTISMS AND BLESSINGS

Children also participated actively in special events such as baptisms and blessings. By the age of 8 or 9, some children chose to be baptized. At First Baptist Church, children were not automatically baptized at a certain age, and individuals participated in the church community for years without being baptized (although baptism is a prerequisite to formal church membership). Baptism was viewed as a highly personal choice, determined by an individual's relationship to God. To pressure another to be baptized would be to take away from that person an opportunity to choose actively to be "born again."

The decision to be baptized began with an acceptance of the invitation to join the church. This invitation was issued at the closing of Sunday School and during regular Sunday morning church services. The pastor would declare that the "doors of the church are open," and the congregation would sing the spiritual, "Pass Me Not Oh Gentle Savior": "Pass me not Oh gentle Savior. Hear my humble cry. While on others Thou art calling, do not pass me by." At that time, anyone desiring to join the church would come forward and be received by the pastor who would ask him/her several questions regarding faith. Then, the church officers would make arrangements for baptism, usually held within a month's period.

Within the Baptist church, the total immersion baptism symbolizes the death by drowning of the old, sinful soul, with the subsequent laying on of hands symbolizing the entrance of the new spirit into the world (Sobel, 1998). The actual ceremony at First Baptist Church in the sanctuary took place during Sunday morning worship services. Elevated behind the pulpit was a large tub suitable for holding a fully submerged adult, as well as the pastor and two adult attendants. Ordinarily this tub was shielded from view by red velvet curtains. On the day of the baptism, these curtains were drawn aside. The person to be baptized, dressed in white, was led into the water and baptized while the congregation sang in quiet, low voices the beautiful spiritual, "Wade in the Water." With the refrain of "Wade in the water. Wade in the water, children, wade in the water. God's a-going to trouble the water," the song also includes a series of verses in a call-and-response format; for example:

LEADER: O, see that host all dressed in white,
RESPONSE: God's a-going to trouble the water.

LEADER: The leader looks like the Israelite.
RESPONSE: God's a-going to trouble the water.

Although baptism is an active choice made by the individual, the "blessing" is a ritual that formally drew the infant and his or her family into the community. Like baptism, the blessing occurred during regular Sunday morning worship services. The infant was asked to "bring" his or her family and friends to the front of the sanctuary. Pastor Daniels talked to the parents about the joys and responsibilities of parenthood. Then, the godparents and other friends and family, as well as the entire congregation, were asked to pledge their support of the parents and child. Finally, the child was "introduced" (held up for all to see by Pastor Daniels), and the congregation sang "Jesus Loves Me."

OTHER WAYS OF RECOGNIZING CHILDREN

There were a number of other ways in which children were actively recognized during regular Sunday morning worship services. Approximately twice a month, a child presented "a little bit of black history." For example, 11-year-old Christopher read his school report on Rosa Parks. He discussed her exposure as a child to the Ku Klux Klan, her work as a field hand, her ability and efforts as a student, her activism for voting rights, and, of course, the bus boycott. Christopher concluded that Rosa Parks "moved blacks from the back of the bus to the front of America's consciousness." Pastor Daniels went on to "pay tribute" to Christopher for the great job he does at home and at school.

Children also were recognized routinely during church services for school achievement and for good behavior. For example, a 10-year-old boy was recognized for receiving three awards in school. He was asked to stand up, and the awards were announced to an approving congregation amid much nodding, commenting, and clapping. The awards were listed in the following order: (1) Being on time every day for the entire term, (2) Outstanding citizenship, (3) Honor roll. During another Sunday morning worship service, Pastor Daniels "paid tribute" to 9-year-old LaTasha in recognition of her outstanding work and behavior at school. She wrote for the school paper and had "tremendous" behavior. Pastor Daniels concluded with: "Congratulations, and keep up the good work. . . . LaTasha is just one example of the young people in our church that we are all proud to know."

CONCLUSION

In conclusion, other contexts in which children actively participated at First Baptist Church highlighted and reinforced the socialization messages they heard during Sunday School – particularly the relevance of biblical concepts to everyday life and the value and promise of each individual child. In contrast to Sunday School, where the relationship between the child and the biblical concepts typically was made at a personal level, certain other contexts tended to link children to biblical concepts at a cultural/historical level, for example, the inclusion of African folk tales and stories of famous African-Americans in the children's sermons.

PART THREE

RELATIONSHIPS OF RESEARCH AND PRACTICE

CHAPTER ELEVEN

The Computer Club

Implications of Research for Practice

Collaborations between researchers and practitioners promise significant mutual gains. First, social service practice and education provide a perspective to stimulate critical thinking about human development research and theory. As researchers strive to articulate the complex interplay between human development and context, practice provides critical exemplars of the ways in which individuals, families, and communities function within diverse contexts. In foregrounding the daily struggles of real families dealing with issues such as unmet educational or mental health needs, substance abuse, poverty, child abuse and neglect, and the culture of social service agencies, practice pushes for more complex, inclusive, and adequate theoretical models of human development.

On the other hand, research also has the potential to support more effective practice. First, research can expand the knowledge base from which practitioners draw in addressing issues encountered by children and families (e.g., Reid, 1995; Sigel, 1998; Thornton & Garrett, 1995). Research also provides a perspective and method that can stimulate critical thinking about everyday problems. For example, the scientific method can provide a means to assess interventions and to consider systematically alternative explanations for particular patterns of outcomes (e.g., Reid, 1995). The ethnographic method can provide a set of tools for developing knowledge about a specific community, thus providing a bridge to multicultural practice (Thornton & Garrett, 1995).

Despite the potential for significant mutual gains, collaborations between researchers and practitioners can be problematic. Tensions can result from individuals' differences in experience and communication styles. In addition, Irving Sigel (1998) describes the relationships of some researchers and practitioners as involving "mutual disrespect." Many researchers and practitioners have been educated in institutions – for example, some research universities – where applied research and practice are devalued. As a result, researchers may assume an elitist stance in relation to practitioners, and practitioners may feel defensive, devalued, and unheard. This dynamic may be particularly problematic in contexts where researchers are European-American and practitioners are of color. For example, Lisa Delpit (1988) quotes an African-American public school teacher frustrated both with her European-American colleagues and with European-American researchers:

> It becomes futile because they think they know everything about every-body. What you have to say about your life, your children, doesn't mean anything. They don't really want to hear what you have to say. They wear blinders and earplugs. They only want to go on research they've read that other White people have written. (p. 281)

In this chapter, I will describe the Computer Club as an example of a collaboration between practitioners and researchers. This collaboration was not without its flaws, but two primary characteristics facilitated its success. First, we (Pastor Daniels, other community members, and I) identified our common values and goals, including supporting the educational achievement of African-American children, before embarking on the collaboration. This goal remained at the forefront even during some initial difficulties, including my failure to deal effectively with certain equipment problems or to keep noise from the children down to a reasonable level. Second, we developed mutual respect. The respect that I had gained for Pastor Daniels and community members through my ethnographic research worked against any tendencies of mine toward elitism. Pastor Daniels's primary commitment was to practice, but he also was respectful of education and scholarship.

RESEARCHERS AND PRACTITIONERS IN COLLABORATION

The Computer Club, an educational intervention focused on children's computer literacy, was informed by knowledge gained from the ethnographic data described in this book. These data were interpreted and applied in collaboration with the pastor, other adult informants, and children.

The Goals of the Intervention

The primary objective was to provide educational opportunities for children who did not have ready access to computers. Consistent with the strong value African-American communities historically have placed on academic achievement and educational attainment (e.g., Billingsley, 1992; Comer, 1988; Wilson, Cooke, & Arlington, 1997), adult informants stressed the importance of increasing the educational opportunities of African-American children (see chapter 6), a goal that I shared. In particular, adults were concerned that many children at First Baptist Church did not have ready access to computers at home or at school and hence were at a distinct educational disadvantage.

A secondary objective (to be discussed in chapter 12) was to provide an educational context for European-American college students of child development, many of whom would soon begin professional training in social work, counseling, education, or health care. Adults in charge of Sunday School (see chapter 6) and I believed that European-American students entering the helping professions of education, health care, and social service were not being adequately prepared to effectively serve the increasingly multicultural community of Salt Lake City.

Most broadly stated, our goals were to strengthen community–school and community–university linkages. From an ecological perspective, we were concerned that the links between the African-American community at First Baptist Church, and the public schools and university were very weak; for example, many African-American adults expressed distrust of the public schools, and local African-American students rarely elected to attend the local university. We reasoned that positive experiences with university faculty and students would support community members' consideration of the local university as an educational resource. Likewise, we intended that the supervised participation of European-American college students within the African-American community would support their understanding, empathy, and openness to others from diverse cultural communities, which ultimately would be reflected in their professional practice.

The Physical Context and Logistics

Pastor Daniels arranged to have a small basement office at First Baptist Church rewired to accommodate computers, and he provided tables and chairs. Another church member donated an IBM PC and printer. Additional donations of computers and a variety of software programs came primarily from faculty at the University of Utah who were upgrading their equipment. We received approximately three times the number of computers and printers as we could physically fit in the office occupied by the Computer Club. The extra computers were stacked in my office at the university to be "cannibalized" for parts, or rotated into the Computer Club as needed. At any given time, there were approximately nine MacIntosh computers, two IBMs, and three printers in use at the Computer Club. The computers and printers sat on tables lining three walls in the office. Children sat at the tables, one to three per computer.

To facilitate children's attendance, Computer Club hours and activities were regularly announced by Pastor Daniels. For example, during Sunday church services, Pastor Daniels would encourage children to sign up for the Computer Club with an assistant reverend after church services. This request also appeared in written form in the church bulletin. In addition, the Computer Club was coordinated to overlap with other activities at the church in the hope that this would enhance children's abilities to find transportation with adults attending those activities. Regular Computer Club hours were Thursday evenings and Saturday mornings.

The Social Context

During the final three years of my fieldwork, the Computer Club was used on a regular basis by approximately 50 children ranging in age from 3 to 18. Children's attendance varied from 2 or 3 children on some quiet Thursday evenings, to more than 20 on some very busy Saturday mornings, with an average of approximately 12 children. Many of these children attended First Baptist Church. Other children lived around the church, or were friends and relatives of church members.

There always were a variety of adult helpers available to assist children during Computer Club hours. We generally were able to maintain a ratio of one adult for every two or three children. Thus, each child received individual attention and instruction during each Computer Club session, and also worked together with two or three friends. Adult church members always were on hand to help resolve disputes, provide snacks, phone parents, or engage young children bored with the computers. Adult church members with computer skills also assisted children and helped keep the machines up and running. The bulk of the educational assistance, however, was provided by undergraduate students from the University of Utah. Over a 3-year period, approximately 200 different European-American undergraduate students assisted at the Computer Club. The majority of these students had been raised within and practiced the Mormon religion. At the time of their participation they were enrolled in an upper division (junior and senior) course for psychology majors,

Introduction to Child Development. These students received extensive preparation and supervision which will be described in chapter 11.

Undergraduate students and children were supervised by at least two professionals or graduate students from the University of Utah. I regularly supervised children and students. In addition, a physician completing his residency in Psychiatry at the University of Utah, and three graduate students from the University of Utah, two with specific interests in multicultural education, regularly volunteered to help children.

The Content of the Intervention

The content of the intervention was mutually determined by child interests, adult objectives, and available software. Consistent with their focus on spirituality, church members donated software with biblical themes, such as a Bible trivia game. Consistent with their focus on supporting education, other church members donated educational games (such as "Oregon Trail," a history and problem-solving game for school-aged children) and literacy games (such as "Reader Rabbit" or "Playroom" for preschool-aged children). Other donated software reflected the interests of the children in graphics (used to construct greeting cards, banners, etc.), music, and arcade games.

Once every several months, there were special events associated with the Computer Club. For example, children worked for several weeks using the graphics programs to generate artwork for a Computer Club art show displayed in the church. At another time, children enjoyed earning Computer Club membership cards for demonstrating competence with basic computer skills (e.g., booting up disks and using software) and knowledge of the club rules (e.g., no food or drinks at the computer tables).

Conducting the Intervention

My observations of adult–child interactions in Sunday School and other church contexts, as well as adults' beliefs, were considered when planning how to present the computer literacy materials. First, we obtained materials on which several children could work together, cooperatively. For example, one game required that several pioneers work together to solve problems as they travelled the Oregon Trail. Second, student volunteers were encouraged to drop what some perceived to be a "professional," i.e., emotionally distant and task focused, stance toward the children for a less formal relationship that included, for example, the sharing of stories about school experiences.

CONCLUSION

I view service as an integral component of ethnographic research. Service provides the ethnographer both with a role inside of the community and with a means to contribute. There are, however, many challenges to integrating research and practice. It would be inaccurate to leave the impression that the Computer Club operated completely smoothly. There were misunderstandings and miscommunications. On occasion, the noise from the Computer Club disturbed adult study groups in adjacent rooms. Sometimes there were too many children to accommodate, and some went away disappointed. In general, the room was too small, and adult volunteers complained of headaches from the noise and press of too many bodies in such a small space. Given the respect and trust between researchers and practitioners, however, none of these problems grew larger than our mutual commitment to the children. A key to a successful collaboration between research and practice may be a genuine partnership in which all participants play a critical role in reaching a mutually defined goal.

At the time of this writing, the computer club was in its eighth year. It has become integrated into both the church and university communities as a thriving collaboration. The Lowell Bennion Public Service Center at the University of Utah provided training and guidance to an advanced, undergraduate student "project director," who oversaw a team of university student volunteers who staffed the club on Thursday evenings and Saturdays. In addition, the Computer Club was integrated into the larger church community through a newly developed "Saturday School." The Saturday School was organized by church members who provided tutoring and ongoing classes in self-esteem and African-American dance and music for children. The Computer Club, however, remained a favorite activity of children, many of whom became sophisticated computer users who helped to train the new college student volunteers. In addition, the Computer Club remained very popular with college student volunteers, many of whom reported that the privilege of participating at First Baptist Church was a transforming experience.

In conclusion, the Computer Club is one example of how knowledge and perspective gained from ethnographic research informed the development of an educational intervention for children. It is important to stress, however, that just as research can contribute to practice, so practice can contribute to research. As scholars take seriously a contextual model of human development in which the individual and the context are mutually defining, and in which the various pathways to development are a central point of interest, then the real-life issues dealt with by social workers, educators, and health care professionals become pivotal to the development of research questions. Attending to the wisdom of those who are "on the front lines" can expand the horizons of researchers, allowing us to see dimensions and domains of experience that are currently neglected or omitted from study entirely (Miller, 1999). In chapter 12, I will describe how experiences solving practical problems that arose within the Computer Club contributed to research on the development of multiculturalism.

CHAPTER TWELVE

Enhancing University Students' Understanding and Appreciation of Cultural Diversity

Implications of Practice for Research

One of the reasons for organizing the Computer Club was to provide European-American university students intending to enter the helping professions with meaningful participation within the local African-American community. When asked to explain the low achievement of many African-American children in Salt Lake City's public schools, adult informants discussed a lack of interest in African-American children by local educators and an inadequate coverage of African-American history and culture in the curriculum (see chapter 6). In addition, we shared the concern that the understanding and empathy of many European-American helping professionals toward African-American children needed enhancement. These concerns also were echoed by recent interviews with experienced black teachers (Delpit, 1988; Foster, 1994), who generally viewed their white colleagues as both unsuccessful with the overwhelming majority of black students and unresponsive, "They're [white colleagues] so headstrong, they think they know what's best for everybody, for everybody's children. They won't listen" (Delpit, 1988, p. 282).

As the population of the United States continues to diversify, an understanding of cultural diversity is increasingly necessary for all helping professionals. Professionals in Salt Lake City are no exception. Population statistics indicate that more and more people from diverse cultural communities are arriving in Salt Lake City, many fleeing the violence and weakening economy of the West coast (Mathews & Wright, 1994). Yet many middle-class, European-American students have relatively little

Material from this chapter was originally published in Haight, W., Rhodes, J. & Nicholson, M., "Cross-race mentoring: Perspectives of mentors over time and strategies for support," *The Mentor: Journal of Mentoring and Field Experiences* (in press). Reprinted by permission.

knowledge and experience with issues such as racism. For example, Salt Lake City, like other large, American cities, is racially segregated with all but approximately 3% of the people of color residing on the West side. Thus, the majority of European-American students entering the helping professions have little or no informal, day-to-day contact with people of color. Coleman (1981) suggests that such limited exposure places European-American Utahns at particularly high risk for stereotyping people of color.

CROSS-RACE HELPING RELATIONSHIPS

Helping relationships in which a European-American adult professional or volunteer and a young person of color are matched are increasingly common across the United States. Despite its challenges and possible limitations, in certain contexts cross-race matching serves important functions. For example, in many successful mentoring programs, youth requesting services far outnumber available adult volunteers. As a result, vulnerable youth, who presumably could benefit from the immediate attention of a caring adult, may experience extended waiting periods. For example, youth applying to Big Brothers/Big Sisters wait an average of 18 months before they are assigned a mentor (Freedman, M., 1993). In part to minimize waiting periods, many programs pair youth with mentors of different races rather than wait until same race mentors become available. The most typical cross-race match involves an African-American youth and a European-American mentor. Indeed, over three quarters (76%) of the youth of color in a nationally representative Big Brothers/Big Sisters sample were mentored by European-Americans (Tierney, Grossman & Resch, 1995).

The challenges of cross-race helping relationships are suggested by recent discussions within the field of social work. Although the Council on Social Work Education has mandated that undergraduate and master's level education programs include content on racial diversity (see Carrillo, Holzhalb & Thyer, 1993; Thornton & Garrett,1995; Van Soest, 1995), the success of such programs in preparing students for practice in an increasingly pluralistic society appears mixed. For example, critics argue that particular social work interventions are not culturally appropriate (Thornton & Garrett, 1995); that certain practices within the social welfare and child welfare systems are racist (see Van Soest, 1995); that the practice literature addressing people of color generally is naive and superficial (McMahon & Allen-Meares, 1992); and that many

European-American, middle-class social workers display little understanding of the implications of cultural sensitivity for practice (see Van Soest, 1995) or willingness to challenge seriously their own biases (McMahon & Allen-Meares, 1992).

Empirical research describing the experiences of European-Americans also points to the challenges of cross-race helping relationships. In a study of 43 students working toward a master's degree in social work and taking a course on diversity and oppression, many students reported intensely negative, self-critical emotions reflecting the pain involved in acknowledging and processing one's own attitudes about oppression (Garcia & Van Soest, 1997). A large-scale study of 108 predominantly European-American university students participating in community service projects mainly within African-American communities (Neururer & Rhoads, 1998) indicated that many students struggled with their own discomfort, for example, in receiving hospitality and generosity from those they envisioned serving. Rarely did a European-American student comment that he or she enjoyed or benefited from experiencing the world from an African-American's perspective, and students had difficulty grasping such concepts as mutuality, diversity as an ideal, and dialogical encounters with others as a means of bridging communities.

The challenges of cross-race helping relationships also are reflected in empirical research describing outcomes of professional helping relationships. Studies of psychotherapy suggest that same-race client–therapist matches typically are more sustained than cross-race matches (Sue, Fujino, Hu, Takeuchi & Zane, 1991; Yeh, Eastman & Cheung, 1994). In the context of higher education, African-American students paired with African-American faculty generally have more positive attitudes about their environment, research, and academic careers than do African-American students paired with European-American faculty (Frierson, Hargrove & Lewis, 1994; Kalbfleisch & Davies, 1991). Discrepancies between communication patterns of teachers and children can impede education (Mehan et al., 1995).

On the other hand, when teachers and social service providers are educated regarding cultural variations in patterns of interaction and communication and adjust their practices accordingly, their effectiveness can be enhanced. For example, Heath's (1983) classic ethnography conducted in the Piedmont Carolinas included a detailed description of normative patterns of communication between adults and young children within African-American and European-American communities, and between teachers and students at school. Within European-American, middle-class families, adults posed to young children many "known information" questions. For example, they asked children to label objects and identify features of things. Within an African-American, rural community, adults frequently used statements and imperatives when addressing young children. When adults did ask questions, the questions called for nonspecific comparisons or analogies as answers. Within the classroom, teachers asked questions similar to those common within the middle-class European-American families. In contrast to the young African-American children, European-American children participated actively in class discussions led by their teachers. However, when teachers were taught to modify the types of questions they initially asked of children to include those common within the African-American community, these children's participation increased.

A FRAMEWORK FOR FACILITATING UNIVERSITY STUDENTS' UNDERSTANDING AND APPRECIATION OF DIVERSITY

Facilitating university students' understanding, empathy, and openness to others from diverse cultural communities requires attending to students' complex cultural beliefs. Cultural beliefs are taken-for-granted ideas about the nature of reality (Harkness & Super, 1996) shared by members of particular communities. Beliefs provide a frame of reference within which individuals interpret experience, assess problems, and formulate goals and strategies for living.

A closer look at belief systems and their development suggests four factors important to supporting students' emerging understanding of the relations of culture and behavior. First, beliefs include cognitive components. As members of particular communities, students are presented with "social representations," "cultural models" (Goodnow, 1988), or "folk psychologies" (Bruner, 1990) of human behavior and development. This exposure occurs through multiple sources, including the media and face-to-face interactions (for example, with "experts," such as grandparents, pastors, and social workers). The cultural models presented to European-American students, particularly regarding people of color, may contain omissions and inaccuracies. Thus, the frame of reference within which they interpret their cross-race experiences, assess problems, and formulate goals and strategies may be inadequate, as well as discrepant with that of their clients. More subtly, anthropologists have long recognized the importance of multicultural information in illuminating the cultural bases of human behavior. Exposure to culturally diverse practices helps to lay bare the assumptions about human behavior and development underlying the taken-for-granted practices within one's own community and reflected in professional practice.

While cognitive content is a necessary condition of effective multicultural education, it is not sufficient. There simply are too many cultures about which to provide meaningful content (see Thornton & Garrett, 1995). In addition, by focusing on specific content, students may develop stereotyped views (Gould, 1995) that will not serve them well in dealing with individual clients. Finally, when focusing on cognitive content, mainstream students may fail to appreciate the role of racism in their own lives (King, 1991; Ladson-Billings, 1995).

Effective multicultural education also requires attention to affective components of belief systems – feelings and values related to various social practices, which can interact with cognitive components. For example, European-American, middle-class individuals may experience powerful negative emotions such as guilt and defensiveness in relation to issues of oppression (e.g., Garcia and Van Soest, 1997). Such emotions can interfere with learning (e.g., King, 1991; Tatum, 1992) through distortion of the "facts" and dampen motivation for continued multicultural learning. For example, European-American teachers criticized African-American master teachers as inappropriately strict and rigid with children, despite evidence of the effectiveness of their methods and the quality of their relationships, including with African-American children experiencing difficulties with European-American educators (M. Foster, 1994). However, the role of emotion in the development of cultural beliefs typically has not been explicitly addressed in discussions of multicultural education in social work or related fields.

Third, the development of beliefs is an active process that continues into adulthood. As Cynthia Lightfoot and Jaan Valsiner (1992) explain, "Belief systems that exist within a collective culture do not have an effect in the sense of being copied directly (or appropriated) by individuals. Instead, they constitute resources from which active persons construct their own (personal) belief structures" (p. 395). The ways in which students actively interpret new multicultural materials relate to their own unique life experiences – including past and ongoing interactions with members of particular groups – and to their individual interests and strengths. Issues of adult development, particularly of changes over time in students' active interpretations of multicultural materials, have not figured prominently in discussions of multicultural education in social work or related fields.

Fourth, beliefs emerge in a variety of contexts. In particular, cross-cultural learning experiences are integral to developing a multicultural world view (Gould, 1995; Thornton & Garrett, 1995). Fortuitously, face-to-face interactions with members of culturally diverse communities are increasingly characteristic of field placements in social work, education, and clinical psychology. The challenge is to use such experiences, systematically, to enhance students' understanding, particularly of emotionally difficult interactions. Simply immersing students in cross-cultural field placements can result in the further entrenchment of preexisting prejudices. Indeed, the current "wisdom of practice" within multicultural teacher-education suggests that the most effective cross-cultural field experiences include planned debriefings and guided reflections (King, 1991; Ladson-Billings, 1995). Despite the potential significance of the meanings students construct during face-to-face encounters with culturally diverse clients, however, multicultural education in social work and related fields remains focused upon students' understanding of academic materials in classroom discussions.

In this chapter, I will describe the multicultural experiences of European-American university students, advanced undergraduates, the majority of whom planned to enter the helping professions of social work, education, psychology, or medicine. I use students' experiences in a "service learning" course to consider the issues that may challenge other European-American, middle-class students entering into the helping professions. In particular, I describe students' own reported responses to the course, and then suggest strategies for most effectively facilitating students' experience both within and outside of the classroom.

SERVICE-LEARNING AT THE UNIVERSITY OF UTAH

Service-Learning

Service-learning is an educational philosophy based on the integration of academic coursework and community service. Typically, service-learning involves student participation in community service with additional learning objectives associated with the student's program of study; for example, a social work student enrolled in a class on child welfare might mentor a foster child. Service-learning also includes specific experiences designed to help students process their experiences, for example, small group discussions and journal writing (e.g., Myers-Lipton, 1996; Rhoads, 1998).

Service and service-learning programs have a long tradition in the United States but have received increased attention in the past decade. For example, in 1990, the National and Community Service Act allocated $275 million for mostly service-learning programs at the K–12 and higher education levels. In the past 5 years, more than 600 articles have been published in professional social work, education, and psychology journals on service-learning. Some outcome research suggests that participation in service-learning enhances university students' academic development (e.g., Astin & Sax, 1998) and sense of civic responsibility (e.g., Astin & Sax, 1998; Myers-Lipton, 1996), and decreases their racism (Astin & Sax, 1998).

Overview of the Course

"Introduction to child development" was an upper-division (junior and senior), elective university course. Each quarter, several sections of the course were available from different instructors with diverse perspectives on child development. The course catalogue indicated that community service was a requirement of the section of the course from which students were recruited. More specifically, it was described in students' registration materials as a "service-learning" course. The service component of the course was participation in the Computer Club, which students described in journals (discussed in the following section).

The course met twice a week for approximately 70 minutes during a 10-week quarter. During the quarter in which the data were collected, as well as the preceding quarter, the section I developed was taught by an advanced graduate student in developmental psychology. He was advised by me, and assisted by an upper-division, undergraduate teaching assistant. The teaching assistant was trained and sponsored by the Lowell Bennion Community Service Center at the University of Utah. This arrangement served several important functions. First, during the preceding quarter, the graduate student benefited from a "run through" of the course, thoroughly familiarizing himself with the materials and visiting the Computer Club. Second, I was able to seek students' voluntary participation in the research project and to assure them that their decisions to participate in the research project or not would not affect their grades.

Indeed, their instructor would not participate in the Computer Club during the quarter of data collection and would not see their journal entries. The teaching assistant would respond to students' ungraded journals at midterm and the end of the course, and would assist me in the supervision of students at the Computer Club.

The course was developed and taught four times over a 2-year period prior to data collection. Course readings and lecture-discussions presented students with an interpretist framework in which human development and the sociocultural context are viewed as inseparable (see Gaskins, Miller & Corsaro, 1992). In short, humans actively co-construct with others meaning from available social, physical, and intellectual resources. Thus, understanding development requires examination of the sociocultural context in which the individual develops, for example, the social resources available and the roles toward which the child is socialized. Furthermore, understanding culture as a dynamic system of shared ideas and practices requires examination of the processes through which meanings are created and recreated. To facilitate students' understanding of development in sociocultural contexts, several texts were used. The main course text was *The Development of Children* (Cole & Cole, 1992), which integrates cross-cultural research with discussions of language, cognitive, social, and physical development. Students also read Heath's *Ways with Words* (1983), an ethnographic study of language socialization within African-American and European-American communities in the Piedmont region of the Carolinas. Also assigned was Spencer, Brookins, and Allen's (1985) edited collection of works describing the social and affective development of black children, as well as a variety of other articles. Crucial to setting the stage for open discussions of students' own cross-community experiences were Beverly Tatum's (1992, 1994) descriptions of college students' racial identity development. Tatum's framework places intense feelings, such as anger, shame, sadness, and guilt, within the scope of normal developmental processes.

A central feature of the course was the opportunity it provided students for face-to-face interactions with individuals from diverse cultural communities. Students were required to engage in a minimum of 8 hours of community service. Typically, this service took the form of four 2-hour sessions at the Computer Club. During this time, the Computer Club was used on a regular basis by approximately 50 children (46% were girls), ranging in age from 3 to 16 years (mean age = 9.1 years), on Thursday evenings and Saturdays. As described in chapter 11, children's attendance varied from two or three children on some Thursday evenings to more than 20 on some busy Saturday mornings, with an average of approximately 12 children per session. Children learned to use a variety of educational software programs, and they participated in a variety of special projects. Typically, children were supported by four university students at each session. University students facilitated children's acquisition of basic computer literacy skills and their positive learning experiences, but, more importantly, they developed relationships in which perspectives and experiences were shared. In addition to playing educational computer games, students and children produced a computer-generated art show, went on a picnic, had a party, and played outdoor games. A graduate student and myself were present at each session to provide supervision to the university students.

Informal observations of, and sometimes even participation in, church activities scheduled concurrently with the Computer Club also became important aspects of many university students' experiences. When the Computer Club became too crowded, or the students simply needed a break from many excited, active children, they observed or participated in choir rehearsals for adults and for children, African dance rehearsal for children and adolescents, or prayer time; or they simply interacted, informally, with a variety of community members. For example, one student remarked, in reference to the adult choir, "It was amazing to me because I had never before seen such enthusiasm in a church choir." University students also were affected simply by the physical decor:

> I walked around and looked at some of the pictures hanging on the walls. There was a massive display of African-Americans who have made a difference in society or who were examples of excellence and integrity. It was like taking a mini-course in Black History.

In addition to participating in the Computer Club, university students listened to, and many interacted with, two members of First Baptist Church – the pastor and a senior deaconess – during in-class presentations at the university. During the second week of the course, Pastor Daniels presented his oral history and discussed African-American history and culture. In his oral history, Pastor Daniels described his childhood and young adulthood during segregation including attending all-black schools in Georgia, eating in all-black restaurants, riding in designated seats on buses, and using separate bathrooms and drinking fountains. He focused on his involvement as a young college student at

Tuskegee in the civil rights movement, including working with Dr. Martin Luther King, Jr. He also described his personal experiences with racism in Salt Lake City, for example, difficulties finding a landlord to rent to his family. Pastor Daniels also gave a brief history of the African-American experience from slavery to the present, again focusing on the civil rights movement. Next, he discussed the history and characteristics of the African-American community in Utah and of First Baptist Church. Finally, an important part of Pastor Daniels's visit was the opportunity he provided for students to ask him questions and engage with him in discussion.

During the sixth week of the course, Mrs. Hudley, a 72-year-old church deaconess, presented her oral history focusing on her childhood (see Hudley, Haight & Miller, in press). The sixth of eight children, Mrs. Hudley grew up on a rural Texas farm. As a child she engaged in manual labor, including picking cotton. By the time she was 12, Mrs. Hudley could pick 100 pounds of cotton per day for $1.00. Beginning at the age of 7, Mrs. Hudley attended segregated school. Although the supplies were inadequate, indeed the school building itself was burned down repeatedly, she was an excellent student. When Mrs. Hudley was 10 years old, her mother died and she assumed much responsibility for helping her father and for raising her younger brothers. As a young adult, Mrs. Hudley moved to Oakland, California, where she continued to work at a variety of jobs and to raise two sons. Approximately 5 years before her participation in the service-learning course, Mrs. Hudley had moved to Salt Lake City with her third husband. Given Mrs. Hudley's challenging life, her optimistic and hopeful comments were powerful: "All that you do, do with your might. Things done by half are never done right."

Faith was the major theme of Mrs. Hudley's oral history. She stated that "without faith I wouldn't be here." This faith was nurtured through family prayer and parental guidance, and strengthened by several events that she characterized as "miracles." Also, after her mother's death, Mrs. Hudley recalled seeing the spirit of her mother on three occasions. On the third occasion, she saw her sitting next to her brother's bed with her hand on his face. Her father said that this was a warning that something would happen to her brother. The next day, her brother became ill with appendicitis. No surgeons were available. In his pain, her brother also saw their mother. To this day, Mrs. Hudley's mother is credited with the child's miraculous recovery. Interestingly, no student challenged Mrs. Hudley's miracles or visions; rather, they generally responded with acceptance and respect. One student commented,

> I used to smirk when people would talk about "miracle healings" and
> things such as this. For some strange reason, I believed Mrs. Hudley.
> Whether the bleeding really stopped with the keys, I don't know. But
> she believes it, and she remembers it, and she has faith in it. This allows
> me to believe it and have faith in it, too.

Another student commented that, "Her faith was so strong, not to believe
[the miracles] seemed a sacrilege."

Another major theme in Mrs. Hudley's oral history was love. Mrs.
Hudley's stories revealed that she has been the object of others' hate and
overt discrimination. For example, as a young woman she hoped to attend night school and, eventually, to become a nurse. These plans, however, were derailed by her employers who, upon learning of her activities,
demanded that she work for them in the evening. They believed, cor-
rectly, that if she were to become educated, then she would leave her
position as their maid. Given this context, Mrs. Hudley's discussion of
hate was powerful: "Never hate because hate will destroy you. . . . Build
hope, trust, love, charity, and forgiveness and you will be successful."

As with Pastor Daniels's presentation, an important component of
Mrs. Hudley's visit was the opportunity she provided for students to talk
with her and to ask her questions. Indeed, she invited students to interact
with her, responding with interest to all questions and comments.

Following their experiences at the Computer Club and visits from
Pastor Daniels and Mrs. Hudley, students participated in planned
debriefings and guided classroom discussions in which they were actively
encouraged to reflect upon their experiences. For example, immediately
subsequent to their participation in the Computer Club, usually just
before they left the church, we attempted to reflect informally with students upon their experiences. Individual students were asked how they
felt the session went, and if they had any concerns. In addition, class time
was set aside approximately once every 2 weeks for guided discussions.
During these discussions, led by the teaching assistant, students
described their experiences, including their emotional reactions, and
attempted to integrate them with the academic materials.

University Students' Responses to Service-Learning

All 26 upper-division university students enrolled in the human development course agreed to keep ungraded, anonymous journals describing
their experiences in and reactions to the Computer Club, as well as to
classroom presentations/discussions by Pastor Daniels and Mrs. Hudley.

Students ranged in age from 19 to 43 years (mean = 26), and 14 (49%) were women. With the exception of two Asian foreign exchange students (whose responses are not included here), all of the students were European-American. There were no African-American students.

Each student contributed five to six separate journal entries (typically, four 2-hour sessions at the Computer Club and the two classroom presentations) spread out over the 10-week quarter. Their instructions were to describe the activity in which they were involved, its relation to the course readings and classroom discussions, and their own reactions. Given the apparent emotional obstacles to European-American students' understanding and appreciation of cultural diversity (e.g., Garcia & Van Soest, 1997; King, 1991; Tatum, 1992), this chapter focuses on students' reported emotional reactions to the Computer Club and to the class presentations/discussions by Pastor Daniels and Mrs. Hudley.

Students' reported emotions were described based upon their use of several linguistic devices: (1) *Emotion labels* are explicit verbal labels of emotion, for example, "I was really nervous" and "I felt so sad." (2) *Emotion displays* explicitly portray actions indicative of emotion, for example, "I was crying" and "My hands were shaking." (3) *Evaluations* are descriptions in which emotion is implicit, such as name calling, "He was such a jerk," and critical comments, "They were so rude."

Each journal entry was first coded as neutral, negative, positive, or mixed (both positive and negative) in emotional valence. (Note that this coding refers to experience and does not imply judgment of the emotion as good or bad.) Then, those specific negative emotions reported by three or more students were coded. (Definitions and examples of codes are provided below.) Students sometimes expressed a variety of specific negative emotions in a single journal entry, and all were coded.

Following training using actual journal entries, intercoder reliabilities were obtained for all emotion codes using 20% of journal entries randomly chosen from each student, excluding those entries used during training. One of the two independent coders was unaware of the research questions. Disagreements were resolved through discussion. Kappas ranged from .97 to 1.0.

Emotional Valence

The emotional valence and complexity expressed in students' journal entries were consistent with Tatum's (1992, 1994) reports of undergraduate university students' responses to a course on racism. As shown in Table 12.1, across contexts, only 7% percent of the total journal entries were "neutral" or completely "negative" in tone. Neutral entries described no particular emotion. Negative entries included several specific emotions, described in the following subsection, including anger and fear. Approximately one-third of entries were positive in tone. Positive entries described feelings of inspiration, admiration, respect, self-efficacy, love, and joy. For example, one student wrote in relation to Mrs. Hudley's oral history,

> It was so inspiring to hear her speak that she actually brought tears to my eyes. . . .When she was talking . . . I got goose bumps.

The majority of journal entries (approximately 59%), however, contained complex mixed reports of both highly positive and highly negative emotions. For example, the student might express loving feelings toward a child, but anger at the child's adult caregiver.

Table 12.1 also shows some variation in the emotional valence reported by students in response to different classroom presenters. The majority of journal entries reporting on Mrs. Hudley's presentation were positive, while the majority of journal entries reporting on Pastor Daniels's presentation were mixed. Although Mrs. Hudley conveyed personal experiences and beliefs unfamiliar to students, including racially motivated hate crimes and a belief in miracle cures, students appeared to identify easily with her values. Indeed, 68% of the students spontaneously quoted her admonition, "All that you do, do with your might. Things done by half are never done right." An equal number (68%) of the students quoted her caution against hatred, "Don't hate because hate will destroy you. Build hope, trust, love, charity, and forgiveness and you will be successful. Hate will only hold you down." In addition, students typically responded to Mrs. Hudley's focus on love and faith with warmth and admiration. For example, one student wrote, simply,

> It was really weird, but immediately I felt this great love for her. . . .

Another student wrote,

> I was very taken with [Mrs. Hudley], she is a very wise and loving woman. . . . Toward the end of her talk, my eyes started to water, and my heart filled because I could feel the love from her so strongly. . . . . Sometimes people are able to get strength from those hard times and become more loving and caring people. I believe that [Mrs. Hudley is]

TABLE 12.1. *Emotions Reported by Students in Each Context and across Contexts*

			Contexts				Total across Contexts
	Mrs. Hudley	Pastor D.	CC1	CC2	CC3	CC4	
	(N = 22)	(N = 25)	(N = 26)	(N = 26)	(N = 25)	(N = 22)	(N = 146)
Emotional Valence (percentage of journal entries)							
Neutral	5	0	0	4	4	0	2
Negative	0	4	8	4	8	5	5
Positive	68	20	19	35	36	32	33
Mixed	27	76	73	58	52	64	59
Specific Negative Emotions (percentage of total negative emotions)							
	(N = 8)	(N = 31)	(N = 27)	(N = 27)	(N = 21)	(N = 23)	(N = 64)
Angry/critical of African-Americans	25	13	19	19	29	39	48
Nervous/fearful	0	3	59	26	10	22	45
Sad/sorry	25	16	4	15	10	30	34
Angry at racists	13	26	0	0	5	0	16
Embarrassed/ashamed	25	10	7	4	0	0	13

Note: In the column heads, CC1 = first visit to the Computer Club, CC2 = second visit, CC3 = third visit, and CC4 = fourth visit.

one of those people, and I am very glad I took this course, otherwise I never would have had the pleasure of her presence and her wisdom.

According to one student:

Today's class was the most memorable period this quarter for me. . . . I'm amazed that a person who has walked the road she has walked can stand up and express such a powerful faith in her God and in herself. . . . She came from such a destitute and humble background . . . I have tremendous respect for her. I think she is a powerful example of someone who loves life in spite of the challenges it has handed her.

The identification these European-American, middle-class university students felt toward Mrs. Hudley, including their positive feelings of love and inspiration, seemed to help them to "hear" her perspective on difficult issues involving oppression. For example, Susan's journal included an early entry questioning the existence of racism. After Mrs. Hudley's presentation she wrote:

She [Mrs. Hudley] spoke of her work as a maid and her employer's obstruction of her going to school to become a nurse. . . . Racism kept her from bettering herself and achieving a higher education. It makes me so angry! People are such pigs. . . . The fact that her employers purposely kept her from achieving a higher education makes me steam! I would like to slap those people silly.

It is also important to note that while this report focuses on group trends, there was substantial individual variation in students' reported responses to the very same materials. For example, Frank "heard" Mrs. Hudley tell a very different story from Susan:

She [Mrs. Hudley] gave a story about how the "whites" kept her from finishing school. . . . I could not believe that . . . [Mrs. Hudley] was blaming the whites [for not] getting an education. I understand that employers have goals in mind when hiring employees. Employees must also keep their own lives under control.

Students generally responded to Pastor Daniels's presentation with admiration, mixed with mild distress, perhaps because he explicitly addressed institutionalized racism. In reference to Pastor Daniels's description of segregation, one student commented:

It's really difficult to believe or understand why such behavior existed in this country just a short time ago. That description sounds like a completely different America compared to what I'm experiencing today.

Another student wrote:

My personal reaction to the lecture was one of extreme surprise. He brought up many points and subtly made many others of which I had little to no previous knowledge. One question I remember starkly was his question about the Emancipation Proclamation. He asked if anyone knew how many slaves it set free. I did not know and, as I looked around the room of college students, I realized no one else knew any more than me. . . . One of the most important documents in American History and no one knew a thing about it. . . . The things I learned [from Pastor Daniels's presentation], I am sure, will stick with me for a long time.

One student summed up his experience:

I don't know how one's life could be the same after listening to Pastor [Daniels]. He sure broadened my perspective and made me more aware of African-American History through his personal experiences.

Specific Negative Emotions and the Role of Context

Table 12.1 also suggests that the specific negative emotions reported by students varied across contexts. In contrast to the anger at racists and shame described by Tatum in classroom contexts (1992, 1994), a relatively high proportion of negative emotions described in relation to the Computer Club were fear and nervousness, and anger toward individual African-Americans. For example:

Since today was my first visit to the church, I was very nervous. In fact, I was so apprehensive about this situation that I put it off for quite a while. I think the reason that I was so scared was that this was a totally unfamiliar experience for me . . . I have never been around African-American people before.

Another student observed a man spank a toddler for touching a computer:

I felt . . . angry at J. for hitting her, she was so small and I didn't feel J. had to do what he did. Because she was just curious about the computers and what was going on.

Students also expressed sadness and pity in this context, as well as during the classroom presentations. For example, one student wrote in relation to a musically talented teenager whose single mother could not afford piano lessons for him, "I felt sorry for this guy. . . . It makes me so sad."

As would be expected from previous studies (Tatum, 1992, 1994), the classroom presentations by Mrs. Hudley and Pastor Daniels evoked some feelings of anger at racists, as well as embarrassment or shame.

The Role of Development

As suggested by Table 12.1, students were engaged in a developmental process over their four visits to the Computer Club. Overall, they did not become more positive, negative, neutral, or mixed in their responses to the Computer Club, but their reports of specific negative emotions did change. Students' expressions of nervousness and fear, while they did not dissipate entirely, did decrease over time – from more than half of all mixed or negative entries for the first session at the Computer Club to less than one-quarter of all negative or mixed entries for the final Computer Club visit. Interestingly, students' expression of sadness and pity also increased over time, from less than 5% to nearly one-third, perhaps reflecting an increased empathy toward the individuals whom they came to know. Other emotions, such as anger at individual African-Americans, anger at racists, and shame did not change over time.

It is also important to note that some students reflected upon changes in emotional response even within a particular session. For example:

I was nervous and I think it was because of my perceptions of my purpose there. What am I going there for anyway? . . . We are supposed to interact and observe. "Okay, so I'm going to this African-American Baptist church to interact and observe. I'm here folks, please do something 'African-American' so I can observe, and let's interact while we're at it." I guess I was just a little self-conscious about exactly what I would do there. These feelings of nervousness and uneasiness about my role that night quickly disappeared. As I began playing games and talking with T. and the other children there, I became very comfortable and the time really flew. As I look back now, I really wonder why I had these feelings I just described. I can't wait to go back.

CONCLUSION

In this chapter I have described European-American students' reflections upon their own reactions to a supportive, educational intervention designed to enhance their insights into African-American culture in Salt Lake City and racism. Their responses have several implications for how multicultural education may be enhanced for European-American students entering into the helping professions. First, students' responses underscore the importance of attending to *affective* as well as cognitive components of students' developing beliefs. Students expressed complex and intense emotions, including anger at African-American clients. If not explicitly addressed, such negative feelings may lead to an entrenchment of preexisting, racist beliefs. For example, Robert apparently reverted to preexisting stereotyped (or, overtly racist) thinking during a problematic personal encounter at the Computer Club:

> They [older boys] both were trying to act tough with me, so I wrestled with them for fun but not enough to scare or hurt them. Suddenly one of them took a shot at my groin. I luckily dodged it and ended up with a big bruise on my thigh. . . . I did not feel comfortable with the two boys' aggression that night. My personal reaction . . . is that the African-American culture cannot be as aggressive and tough. If these boys' parents and culture are teaching them to always be tougher than someone else then there is no way they can learn to cooperate within their community or in the United States. . . . These kids have to stop their tough image because in this world it pays to be intelligent and not tough. . . . No wonder there are so many African-Americans and Hispanics in gangs. I think toughness and machismo might be part of their culture.

Robert's response underscores the importance of processing with students their reactions to cross-cultural interactions. The challenge is to help students to use uncomfortable feelings such as fear and uncertainty to motivate learning and greater self-awareness. In this study, students were encouraged during guided classroom discussions and individual supervision to reflect upon their own reactions. For example, following a small group discussion, Terry reflected upon her initial reactions to children's choir rehearsal, an activity that was scheduled at the same time as the Computer Club:

> The adult women struck me as unnecessarily harsh, critical and direct. . . . When the women leading the singing were so abrupt with

the children, it surprised me. One of my closest friends is an African-American man. I had mistakenly assumed that because I know him well, I also understand his culture. This is not true. I realized that he is dealing with me in my cultural context. He is playing our friendship by my rules. It really unsettled me that the First Baptist women did not act like the women I remembered from my Sunday School. . . . It would be easy to mistake different cultural behavior norms for different basic human values. . . . [Are] African-Americans moms . . . just as likely to judge my mothering as fake or sugary sweet, as I am to judge them as too harsh and critical?

The contrast between Terry's and Robert's responses suggests that students enter into cross-cultural experiences with very different beliefs, and it underscores the importance of tailoring the preparation and guidance of students to their own *development*. Students underwent a developmental process reflected in changes in their emotional responses over time. For example, initially, the vast majority of students reported anxiety, discomfort, and even fear when participating at the Computer Club. Educators can anticipate and normalize such responses for students, for example, by simply stating that, initially, most students feel anxious, but become much more comfortable, usually after their first visit.

Students' responses also underscore the importance of tailoring the preparation and guidance of students to the *context* in which the educational experience occurs. Students found particular multicultural contexts challenging in different ways. In particular, the high level of angry and critical responses toward African-Americans during face-to-face interactions at the Computer Club suggests that European-American, middle-class students may require considerable preparation and guidance in assuming the stance of *learners* in preparation for assuming the stance of "helper." Such preparation may include formal discussions of emotion in fieldwork (e.g., see Denzin & Lincoln, 1994), as well as the informal sharing of the problematic, personal experiences of European-American, middle-class educators.

Finally, student responses suggest the importance of educating students on strategies for social change. As Tatum (1992) observed, heightening "students' awareness of racism without also developing an awareness of the possibility of change is a prescription for despair." In this study, students reported increased feelings of sadness and pity as they developed relationships with clients and as their understanding of how oppression affects individual lives deepened. Several students described their own motivation for continued learning and involvement as strengthened through their active participation in an effective intervention program and through their involvement with African-American church leaders and antiracist white faculty supervisors who served as important role models of cross-racial collaborations.

Clearly, this chapter also leaves unaddressed many important issues. In particular, future research should consider the emotional responses of the child recipients of "service." Clearly, many children, particularly older boys, had complex and conflicted feelings. The failure to attend to these feelings may result in further entrenchment of racist attitudes, no less for the children than for the college students. How, for example, did the boys understand Robert's attempts to roughhouse with them? Another university student wrote:

> I talked to the young man that attempted to knee Robert in the groin. I patted him on the shoulder as I walked by him and he said something like, "You guys are all mean." I stopped and asked him what he meant and he proceeded to tell me how Robert had tried to choke him . . . and so he had kneed him in the balls. I was interested to see the difference in their perspectives on what had happened and that their conclusions were allot [*sic*] the same. Both seemed to generalize that what happened was attributable to entire races of people.

In conclusion, multicultural education can deeply challenge many students' beliefs about race and racism in the United States. By better understanding these challenges, professionals can more effectively educate and support students entering into the helping professions, thereby enhancing the goal of facilitating the development of children.

PART FOUR

CONCLUSION

CHAPTER THIRTEEN

Some Final Points

> Our hopes are centered on the little child. Is it possible that that little
> babe in the manger could be the Messiah? Today I want to say . . . be
> careful how we treat the little children. You don't know what's possi-
> ble for that baby. That baby, that little child may be the next
> leader. . . . "Suffer the little children to come unto me and forbid
> them not . . ." Without the little child we will never see God. . . . The
> kingdom of God is for the childlike. . . . We all need to learn to be
> childlike.
>
> Pastor Daniels

In this excerpt from his 1992 Christmas sermon, Pastor Daniels used the
child as a symbol of hope both for change in this world and for spiritual
salvation. At First Baptist Church, children are treasured as the hope for
the future and for the central role they play in the present as models of
love and trust. In Sunday School and other church contexts, children are
nurtured as future leaders. To be given such respect in the community
can contribute powerfully to children's resilience, particularly their sense
of self-worth and efficacy. Children also are given a place as legitimate
community members whose current contributions are meaningful. To be
given opportunities for genuine, legitimate participation can result in
the development of many competencies, as well as opportunities to form
meaningful relationships with caring adults.

BELIEF SYSTEMS CAN BE PROTECTIVE FACTORS

The African-American church has a long history of providing support to
individuals and families. A large body of literature has documented and
described the importance of concrete aid offered by churches to individuals and families in need, as well as to communities. In this book, I have

considered another level of protection provided by the black church: the cultural belief systems developed over hundreds of years in relation to the unique and changing circumstances associated with being African-American.

A hallmark of the belief systems elaborated with children at First Baptist Church is the inherent worth of each individual. This worth exists independently of material success and social status. In the words of a popular hymn, each individual is a "Child of the King" with unique, God-given gifts. As such, each child is entitled to love and respect and, with opportunity and effort, will go far. As elaborated within the stories told in Sunday School, Vacation Bible School, and other church contexts, however, the journey will be difficult. Just as many were blind to Jesus – a powerful, personal role-model for many African-American children – many will not see the black child's inner resources and strengths. Just as the Egyptians enslaved and oppressed Moses' people, some will attempt to oppress the black child. The stories told with children, however, also stress that with faith, effort, and community, they too, like the ancient Hebrews, eventually can prevail. The challenge is to remain a loving and moral person throughout the journey, and to maintain a deep optimism in the ultimate rewards of a successful journey.

Another hallmark of the belief systems elaborated with children at First Baptist Church is the utility of spiritual beliefs in everyday life. Religious beliefs – such as the inherent worth of each individual and the value of freedom, justice, and forgiveness – are spiritual and pragmatic lifelines. It is critical that children be familiar with them so that they may reach for them in times of need. Familiarity with religious teachings, however, is not adequate. Children – even very young children – must understand how these concepts may be used in their everyday lives. In the words of Sister Ima, children must know how to "put on the armor of God." This protection can be carried inside of each child to the neighborhood, to school, to work, to the mall, and so on. Through stories involving personal experiences and hypothetical events, Sunday School teachers and other adults strived to help children apply protection effective for meeting the difficulties in their individual, everyday lives.

A third hallmark of the belief systems elaborated with children at First Baptist Church is the centrality of community. Children are valued members of a cultural community stretching back in time and including members of the church highly esteemed for their wisdom and spirituality. Each child can participate in meaningful ways beside these esteemed community members, for example, by ushering worship services, leading devotions, singing in the choir, or providing service to families in need. Children also learn about the challenges and accomplishments of community members from earlier times, for example, through children's stories told during regular Sunday morning worship service and through the study of black history during Vacation Bible School. These individuals, who share a heritage with the children of First Baptist Church, have faced great challenges and prevailed.

Clearly, there are many pathways for future research concerned with cultural belief systems as protective factors. For example, future research could explore the extent to which practical helping, community support, and acceptance/affirmation are emphasized in other religious communities, and the culturally specific ways in which these and other beliefs are applied to children's religious socialization. The hallmarks of the belief system elaborated at First Baptist Church to meet the particular needs of this African-American community also may serve as protective factors across other religious groups.[1] Although the application of these beliefs is unique in that it protects from racism and draws on particular oral narrative practices, the basic beliefs themselves may not be unique. For example, many successful churches wed theology with real world practical applications and foster a strong sense of community. Furthermore, the belief in the "inherent dignity and worth of each individual" also is a central tenet of the Unitarian Universalist faith, selected precisely because of its broad appeal (Johnson, personal communication, 2001). Thus, in considering what is special about First Baptist Church, something more general about the social functions of churches also may be reflected. In other words, the universal is discovered in the particular.

Future research also could explore the extent to which practical helping, community support, and acceptance/affirmation are apparent in nonchurch contexts, and the culturally specific ways in which these and other beliefs are applied to the socialization of African-American and other children. In addition to churches and other religiously affiliated institutions, African-Americans have formed a variety of other kinds of supportive communities. Carol Stacks (1996) described mutual help in rural, southern communities to which African-Americans have returned bringing with them the skills they learned while living in northern, urban areas. Gregory Dimitriadis (1999) described an urban community center as a protective context in which African-American children and youth drew upon relationships with adults and peers, as well as resources from

---

[1] I am indebted to Carl Johnson for this point.

popular culture, to develop their self-identities and to resist racism. Shirley Brice Heath (1995) described a number of nontraditional and ethnically mixed contexts in which children and youth are supported, for example, in a "Teen Feed" program that provided a free evening meal and a context in which street children could form supportive relationships with other youth and with caring adults.

RELIGIOUS SOCIALIZATION AND PARTICIPATION ARE CHILD-SENSITIVE AND GROWTH-ORIENTED

My primary goal has been to describe how religious belief systems were actually elaborated with children growing up in Salt Lake City through routine adult–child interaction in Sunday School and other church contexts. Overall, the picture of socialization and participation at First Baptist Church that has emerged contrasts sharply with portrayals of African-American teachers as intellectually understimulating, interpersonally harsh, and ineffective (see Foster, 1995, for discussion). It also contrasts sharply with portrayals of religious instruction as emphasizing literal meaning at the expense of children's active questioning and speculating (Zinsser, 1986).

At First Baptist Church, adults' socialization practices and children's participation are both child-sensitive and growth-oriented. Adult–child interaction in Sunday School, Vacation Bible School, and other church contexts described in chapter 10 is growth-oriented in that it typically is adult-led, emphasizes mature conduct, and does prioritize knowledge of biblical text. Adults retain their status as leaders, setting and enforcing high standards both for children's learning and for their conduct. These values and practices are comprehensible when viewed within a social and historical context in which the opportunities of African-American children in the wider society have been limited, second chances for African-American children exhibiting immature academic or social behavior remain scarce, and religious beliefs have provided critical lifelines. For example, numerous adults at First Baptist Church commented on the very real dangers that befall young African-American males who misbehave in public. Given the realities of the sociocultural context, for adults to fail to set and enforce high standards of learning and conduct, or to fail to pass along religious lifelines, would be reprehensible.

At the same time, however, socialization beliefs and practices are child-sensitive. They focus on each child's inherent worth, value children's unique perspectives, consider children's emotional needs and relative

immaturity, and prioritize positive adult–child relationships as a prerequisite to effective socialization. For example, when asked to describe the
characteristics of a "good teacher," adults at First Baptist Church did not
list intellectual attributes or accomplishments. A "good teacher" loves
and listens to children. Adults in a variety of church contexts also engage
children's active participation through a number of culturally specific
communication practices such as call-and-response sequences, assertive
questioning, and verbal conflict; and they draw upon a rich tradition of
metaphor and story to enrich and relate biblical concepts to the joys and
challenges of children's everyday lives.

While the beliefs and practices of all Sunday School teachers at First
Baptist Church could be broadly characterized as child-sensitive and
growth-oriented, individual teachers also were distinct. All teachers held
a lasting love, respect, and concern for the children and a deep commitment to living the values inherent in biblical texts. All of the teachers had
as central goals to help children to understand and then to apply biblical
texts to their own everyday lives. The ways in which such child-sensitive,
growth-oriented characteristics were expressed through teachers' approaches to developing relationships and teaching children, however,
were diverse. Sister Justine and Sister Katherine were playful and informal in their approach to the children: they teased and joked, engaged in
code-switching, and Sister Justine even led children in spontaneous role-
play. Sister Patrice and Sister Ima were more reserved and structured in
their approach to relationship building and teaching. They too, however,
told engaging stories and through various devices – such as the use of the
historical present – brought the biblical text to life. In developing strong,
loving relationships with children, Sister Patrice emphasized careful listening, and Sister Ima focused on mutual respect, practical helping, and
counsel about succeeding academically and socially in junior high.

Again, there clearly are many possible pathways for continued inquiry.
For example, future research could examine the extent to which child-
sensitive, growth-oriented socialization beliefs and practices are apparent
in other cultural communities. Some of the socialization beliefs and
practices reported by adults at First Baptist Church seem culturally
distinct – such as the concern with racism – but others seem to overlap
with beliefs and practices reported in other cultural contexts. In
Catherine Lewis's (1995) ethnographic study of Japanese teachers' beliefs and socialization, she found that many of their beliefs converged
with dominant American beliefs about early childhood education. The
centrality of knowing and listening to one's students, affirming children,

and supporting their participation may be basic to good educational and socialization practices across cultural contexts.

Further research also could examine within-community variation in child-sensitive, growth-oriented socialization beliefs. Within-community variation may occur across individuals, as discussed with respect to the different styles exhibited by Sunday School teachers at First Baptist Church. Within-community variation also may occur across contexts. For example, university students working at the Computer Club occasionally described what they perceived to be harsh treatment of a child by an adult. These observations suggest that there may be contexts in which adults behave in a relatively more "growth-oriented" and a less "child-sensitive" manner, such as in public spaces as opposed to at home or at Sunday School. These observations also caution against looking at adult–child interaction too globally and suggest the importance of directing attention toward specific contexts and practices within cultural communities.

CHILDREN'S PARTICIPATION AT FIRST BAPTIST CHURCH IS STABLE AND CHANGING

In this book, I also have begun to explore stable and changing patterns of children's participation at First Baptist Church. The apparent stability of children's participation across classes may reflect the centrality of specific communicative practices within this community. It also may reflect the utility of particular practices for meeting teachers' basic socialization goals, such as helping children to relate biblical concepts to their everyday lives and to be actively involved in the lessons. For example, even children in the kindergarten class participated in narratives with their teachers, including narratives involving hypothetical events. Also, children in all classes participated in narratives through call-and-response sequences, through spontaneous responses, and through verbal conflict with their teachers. Children's changing patterns of participation may reflect their developing competencies, as well as teachers' sensitivity to those changes. For example, children increasingly participated in storytelling with teachers, especially in the recounting of biblical stories. Teachers of older children initiated more personal experience stories and used more figurative speech.

Future research into children's participation might investigate more directly the belief systems children are developing through their participation in narrative, verbal conflict, and other practices at First Baptist

Church, including the various stances taken by individual children toward these beliefs. Future research also could focus on identifying consequences of children's religious socialization and participation for other aspects of their development and functioning. For example, longitudinal research could examine the relations among children's perceptions of key religious beliefs, their participation in religious practices, and their social and academic functioning at school.

RESEARCH AND PRACTICE ARE INTIMATELY RELATED

Another purpose of this book has been to consider the relationships between research and practice. Chapters 11 and 12 illustrate how ethnographic data and perspectives informed the development of specific, supportive interventions for children at First Baptist Church. The perspectives developed here, however, also may be relevant to the development of culturally sensitive interventions in other contexts – not in the sense that they prescribe particular interventions, but because they enlarge our repertoire of educational and therapeutic approaches. For example, adults at First Baptist Church were concerned with helping children to understand and apply biblical concepts to their everyday lives. Helping children to understand, retain, and then apply new concepts is basic to any successful educational or therapeutic intervention across cultural communities. Teachers and therapists strive not only to help children to understand new concepts from basic arithmetic to cognitive restructuring, but to retain and generalize this knowledge to other contexts. The teachers at First Baptist Church provide a model of how new ideas can be made meaningful to children and how children can be encouraged to apply this new knowledge to everyday situations. Teachers provided numerous examples of creative strategies for engaging children's humor and interest, as well as encouraging cooperation and mature conduct. Certain of these strategies – for example, the collaborative telling of hypothetical stories – may be effective in a variety of educational and therapeutic contexts with individual children from a range of cultural communities.

In addition, this book underscores the centrality of true collaboration with community leaders to effective interventions. Programs that draw upon the natural resources of a community may be more likely to offer sustained and meaningful support to children and families than are those grafted on from the outside. In this case, the Computer Club built upon community members' preexisting concerns about and commitment to children's education, and the physical and social resources within a trusted institution, First Baptist Church. It is these community resources that have sustained and developed the Computer Club over the years following my study.

Finally, the perspectives developed within this book reinforce the importance of understanding the operation of context-specific risk and protective factors before attempting to develop and implement interventions for children and their families. For example, African-American children in Salt Lake City, like children in other African-American communities, encountered racism at school and in their neighborhoods and larger communities. In Salt Lake City, racism was shaped, in part, by culturally specific beliefs embedded within the dominant Mormon community – for example, that blacks have the "mark of Cain." Clearly, educational and therapeutic interventions must be prepared to address context-specific risk (and protective) factors.

It also is critical to reemphasize that just as research can inform practice, so practice can inform research. For example, my experience with the Computer Club led to empirical research on the limitations of multicultural education in the university classroom. Although practitioners increasingly have incorporated knowledge from research into practice – as seen in modern trends in social work toward "empirically-based practice" – researchers generally have been slower to embrace "practice-wisdom" in developing their research agendas. However, as scholars increasingly recognize the importance of a contextual model of human development in which the individual and the context are mutually defining, and in which various pathways to development are a central point of interest, then the real-life issues addressed by social workers, educators, and health care professionals become pivotal to the development of research and theory. Attending to practice wisdom can expand the horizons of researchers, allowing us to see dimensions and domains of experience that are currently neglected, or omitted from study entirely.

"RESILIENCY" HAS LIMITATIONS

In conclusion, this book has focused on socialization beliefs and practices that may support the development of children's resilience. In thus prioritizing the development of children's psychological resilience, it also is very important to emphasize the social and cultural contexts of these resources. Given sufficient stress from external factors, any child's inner resources will be taxed. "Resilient" does not mean "invulnerable." Further, even the most "resilient" individuals may experience a deep and lasting sadness in relation to the hardships they've experienced. The lessons that psychologically resilient children and adults have to teach us regarding healthy strategies for coping with life's challenges are significant, but our intervention efforts simultaneously must include the reduction of preventable social and cultural risk factors, such as poverty, racism, and inadequate educational opportunities.

References

Allen-Meares, P., Washington, R., & Welsh, B. (1996). *Social Work Services in Schools* (2nd ed.). Boston: Allyn and Bacon.

Angelou, M. (1969). *I Know Why the Caged Bird Sings.* New York: Random House.

Arnold, M. S. (1995). Exploding the myths: African American families "at promise." In B. B. Swadener & S. Lubeck (Eds.), *Children and Families "at Promise": Deconstructing the Discourse of Risk.* Albany: State University of New York Press.

Astin, A., & Sax, L. (1998). How undergraduates are affected by service participation. *Journal of College Student Development, 39,* 251–263.

Baker-Fletcher, G. K. (Ed.) (1998). *Black Religion after the Million Man March: Voices of the Future.* New York: Orbis Books.

Bamberg, M. (1997). A constructivist approach to narrative development. In M. Bamberg (Ed.), *Narrative Development: Six Approaches.* Hillsdale, NJ: Lawrence Erlbaum Associates.

Banks, J. A. (1993). Multicultural education: Historical development, dimensions, and practice. In L. Darling (Ed.), *Review of Research in Education.* Washington, D. C.: AERA.

Banks, J. A., & Banks, C. M. (1995). *Handbook of Research on Multicultural Education.* New York: Macmillan.

Becker, H. (1996). The epistemology of qualitative research. In. R. Jessor, A. Colby, & R. Shweder (Eds.), *Ethnography and Human Development: Context and Meaning in Social Inquiry.* Chicago: University of Chicago Press.

Becker, W. H. (1997). The black church: Manhood and mission. In T. Fulop & A. Raboteau (Eds.), *African American Religion: Interpretive Essays in History and Culture.* New York: Routledge.

Bernstine, C. A. (1989). *How to Develop a Department of Christian Education: A Congregational-Enablement Model.* Tennessee: Sunday School Publishing Board.

Billingsley, A. (1992). *Climbing Jacob's Ladder: The Enduring Legacy of African-American Families.* New York: Simon & A. Schuster.

Boggs, S. T. (1978). The development of verbal disputing in part-Hawaiian children. *Language in Society, 7,* 325–344.

Boykin, W. (1994). Harvesting talent and culture: African-American children and educational reform. In R. Rossi (Ed.), *Schools and Students at Risk: Context and Framework for Positive Change.* New York: Teachers College Press.

Briggs, J. L. (1992). Mazes of meaning: How a child and a culture create each other. In W. A. Corsaro & P. J. Miller (Eds.), *Interpretative Approaches to Childhood Socialization*. San Francisco: Jossey-Bass.

Britt, G. C. (1995, April). Children's coping with everyday stressful situations: The role played by religion. Paper presented at the biennial meeting of the Society for Research in Child Development, Indianapolis, IN.

Bronfenbrenner, U. (1979). *The Ecology of Human Development*. Cambridge, MA: Harvard University Press.

Brown, D. R., & Gary, L. E. (1991). Religious socialization and educational attainment among African Americans: An empirical assessment. *Journal of Negro Education, 60(3)*, 411–426.

Bruner, J. (1986). *Actual Minds, Possible Worlds*. Cambridge, MA: Harvard University Press.

Bruner, J. (1987). Life as narrative. *Social Research, 54*, 11–32.

Bruner, J. (1990). *Acts of Meaning*. Cambridge, MA: Harvard University Press.

Bullis, R. K. (1996). *Spirituality in Social Work Practice*. Washington, D.C.: Taylor & Francis.

Canda, E. R., & Furman, L. D. (1999). *Spiritual Diversity in Social Work Practice: The Heart of Helping*. New York: Free Press.

Carrillo, D., Holzhalb, C., & Thyer, B. (1993). Assessing social work students' attitudes related to cultural diversity: A review of selected measures. *Journal of Social Work Education, 29*, 263–268.

Chow, R. (1994). Beyond parental control and authoritarian parenting style: Understanding Chinese parenting through the cultural notion of training. *Child Development, 65*, 1111–1119.

Church Historical Committee. (1976). Calvary Missionary Baptist Church. Unpublished manuscript.

Clark, C. D. (1995). *Flights of Fancy, Leaps of Faith: Children's Myths in Contemporary America*. Chicago: University of Chicago Press.

Clayton, L. (1988). The impact of parental views of the nature of humankind upon child-rearing attitudes. In D. Thomas (Ed.), *The Religion and Family Connection: Social Science Perspectives*. Provo, UT: Brigham Young University.

Cole, M., & Cole, S. (1992). *The Development of Children* (2nd ed.). New York: W. H. Freeman.

Coleman, R. (1981). Blacks in Utah history: An unknown legacy. In H. Z. Papanikolas (Ed.), *The Peoples of Utah*. Salt Lake City: Utah State Historical Society.

Coles, R. (1990). *The Spiritual Life of Children*. Boston: Houghton Mifflin.

Coles, R. (1995). The profile of spirituality of at-risk youth. In R. Coles, D. Elkind, L. Monroe, C. Shelton, & B. Soaries (Eds.), *The Ongoing Journey: Awakening Spiritual Life in At-Risk Youth*. Boys Town, NE: Boys Town Press.

Comer, J. (1988). *Maggie's American Dream: The Life and Times of a Black Family*. New York: Plume.

Corsaro, W. A. (1985). *Friendship and Peer Culture in the Early Years*. Norwood, NJ: Ablex Publishers.

Corsaro, W. (1996). Transitions in early childhood: The promise of comparative, longitudinal ethnography. In R. Jessor, A. Colby, & R. Shweder (Eds.), *Ethnogra-*

phy and Human Development: Context and Meaning in Social Inquiry. Chicago: University of Chicago Press.

Corsaro, W., & Miller, P. (1992). Editors' notes. In W. Corsaro & P. Miller (Eds.), *Interpretive Approaches to Children's Socialization. New Directions in Child Development, 58,* San Francisco: Jossey-Bass.

Cowger, C. (1992). Assessment of client strengths. In D. Saleebey (Ed.), *The Strengths Perspective in Social Work Practice: Power to the People.* White Plains, NY: Longman.

Cowger, C. (1994). Assessing client strengths: Clinical assessment for client empowerment. *Social Work, 39,* 262–268.

Daly, A., Jennings, J., Beckett, J., & Leashore, B. (1995). Effective coping strategies of African Americans. *Social Work, 40,* 240–248.

Davis, F. (1997). *Light in the Midst of Zion: A History of Black Baptists in Utah, 1892–1996.* Salt Lake City, UT: University Publishing.

Delpit, L. D. (1988). The silenced dialogue: Power and pedagogy in educating other people's children. *Harvard Educational Review, 58,* 280–298.

Denzin, N., & Lincoln, Y. (Eds.) (1994). *Handbook of Qualitative Research.* London: Sage Publications.

Dimitriadis, G. (1999). *Popular Culture and the Boundaries of Pedagogy: Constructing Selves and Social Relationship at a Local Community Center.* Unpublished dissertation, University of Illinois at Urbana-Champaign.

Du Bois, W. E. B. (1961). *The Souls of Black Folk.* New York: Fawcett Publications.

Dunn, J. (1988). *The Beginnings of Social Understanding.* Cambridge, MA.: Harvard University Press.

Dunn, J., & Munn, P. (1987). Development of justification in disputes with mothers and siblings. *Developmental Psychology, 791– 798.*

Eisenberg, A. R. (1985). Learning to describe past experiences in conversation. *Discourse Processes, 8,* 177–204.

Eisenberg, A. (1992). Conflicts between mothers and their young children. *Merrill-Palmer Quarterly, 38,* 21–43.

Ellison, C. (1993). Religious involvement and self-perception among black Americans. *Social Forces, 71,* 1027–1055.

Ellison, C. (1997). Contemporary African American religion: What have we learned from NSBA? *African American Research Perspectives, 3,* 30–39.

Engel, S. (1995). *The Stories Children Tell: Making Sense of the Narratives of Childhood.* New York: W. H. Freeman.

Ewalt, P., Freeman, E., Kirk, S., & Poole, D. (1996). Introduction. In P. Ewalt, E. Freeman, S. Kirk, & D. Poole (Eds.), *Multicultural Issues in Social Work.* Washington, D. C.: National Association of Social Workers Press.

Fisher, C. B., Jackson, J. F., & Villarruel F. A. (1998). The study of African American and Latin American youth. In I. Sigel & K. Renninger (Eds.), *Handbook of Child Psychology* (5th ed., vol. 4). New York: John Wiley.

Fitts, L. (1985). *A History of Black Baptists.* Nashville, TN: Broadman Press.

Fivush, R. (1991). The social construction of personal narratives. *Merrill-Palmer Quarterly, 37,* 59–81.

Fivush, R. (1993). Emotional content of parent–child conversations about the past. In C. A. Nelson (Ed.), *Memory and Affect in Development: Minnesota Symposia on Child Psychology*. Hillsdale, NJ: Erlbaum, Broadman Press

Foote, J. (1886). A brand plucked from the fire: An autobiographical sketch. In H. Gates, Jr. (Ed)., *Spiritual Narratives*. (1988). New York: Oxford University Press.

Foster, M. (1989). "It's cookin' now": A performance analysis of the speech events of a black teacher in an urban community college. *Language and Society, 18,* 1–29.

Foster, M. (1994). The role of community and culture in school reform efforts: Examining the views of African-American teachers. *Educational Foundations, Spring,* 5–26.

Foster, M. (1996). African American teachers and culturally relevant pedagogy. In J. Banks & C. Banks (Eds.), *Handbook of Research on Multicultural Education*. New York: Macmillan.

Foster, S. (1994, December 10). Dance class: A cultural communion. *The Salt Lake Tribune.*

Fowler, J. W. (1981). *Stages of Faith: The Psychology of Human Development and the Quest for Meaning*. New York: Harper Collins.

Franklin, J. H. (1969). *From Slavery to Freedom: A History of American Negros* (3rd ed.). New York: Vintage Books.

Fraser, M. W. (Ed.) (1997). *Risk and Resilience in Childhood: An Ecological Perspective*. Washington, D.C.: NASW Press.

Frazier, E. F. (1964). *The Negro Church in America*. New York: Schocken Books.

Freedman, M. (1993). *The Kindness of Strangers: Adult Mentors, Urban Youth, and the New Voluntarism*. San Francisco: Jossey-Bass.

Freedman, S. (1993). *Upon This Rock: The Miracles of a Black Church*. New York: Harper Perennial.

Frierson, H. T., Hargrove, B. K., & Lewis, N. R. (1994). Black summer research students' perceptions related to research mentors' race and gender. *Journal of College Student Development, 35,* 475–480.

Fulop, T. E., & and Raboteau, A. J. (Eds.) (1997). *African American Religion: Interpretive Essays in History and Culture*. New York: Routledge.

Fung, H. H. (1994). *The Socialization of Shame in Young Chinese Children*. Unpublished doctoral dissertation, University of Chicago.

Garcia, B., & Van Soest, D. (1997). Changing perceptions of diversity and oppression: MSW students discuss the effects of a required course. *Journal of Social Work Education, 33,* 119–130.

Garland, D. R. (1995). Church social work. *Encyclopedia of Social Work*. Washington, D. C.: National Association of Social Workers Press.

Garmezy, N. (1985). Stress-resistant children: The search for protective factors. In J. E. Stevenson (Ed.), *Recent research in developmental psychopathology. Journal of Child Psychology and Psychiatry Book*. (Supplement No. 4, 213–233).

Garmezy, N., & Rutter, M. (1983, 1988). *Stress, Coping, and Development in Children*. New York: McGraw-Hill.

Garvey, C., & Shantz, C. (1992). Conflict talk: Approaches to adversative discourse. In C. U. Shantz & W. W. Hartup (Eds.), *Conflict in Child and Adolescent Development,* (pp. 91–121). New York: Cambridge University Press.

Gaskins, S., Miller, P., & Corsaro, W. (1992). Theoretical and methodological perspectives in the interpretive study of children. In W. Corsaro & P. Miller (Eds.), *Interpretive Approaches to Children's Socialization: New Directions for Child Development.* San Francisco: Jossey-Bass.

Gates, H. L. (1989). Introduction. In L. Goss and M. E. Barnes (Eds.), *Talk That Talk: An Anthology of African-American Storytelling.* New York: Simon and Schuster.

Geertz, C. (1973). *The Interpretation of Cultures.* New York: Basic Books.

Göncü, A. (Ed.), (1999). *Children's Engagement in the World: Sociocultural Perspectives.* Cambridge: Cambridge University Press.

Goodnow, J. J. (1988). Parents' ideas, actions, and feelings: Models and method from developmental and social psychology. *Child Development, 59,* 286–320.

Goodnow, J. J. (1990). The socialization of cognition: What's involved? In J. W. Stigler, R. A. Shweder, & G. Herdt (Eds.), *Cultural Psychology Essays on Comparative Human Development.* New York: Cambridge University Press.

Goodnow, J. J., & Collins, W. A. (1990). *Development According to Parents: The Nature, Sources, and Consequences of Parents' Ideas.* Hillsdale, NJ: Lawrence Erlbaum Associates.

Goodwin, M. (1990). *He-said-she-said: Talk as Social Organization among Black Children.* Bloomington: Indiana University Press.

Gould, K. (1995). The misconstruing of multiculturalism: Stanford debate and social work. *Social Work, 40,* 198–205.

Greenfield, P. (1994). Independence and interdependence as developmental scripts: Implication for theory, research, and practice. In P. Greenfield & R. Cocking (eds.) *Cross-cultural Roots of Minority Child Development.* Hillsdale, NJ: Lawrence Earlbaum Associates.

Haden, C., Haine, R., & Fivush, R. (1997). Developing narrative structure in parent–child reminiscing across the preschool years. *Developmental Psychology, 33,* 295–307.

Haight, W. (1998) "Gathering the spirit" at First Baptist Church: Spirituality as a protective factor in the lives of African American Children. *Social Work, 43,* 213–221.

Haight, W., Garvey, C., & Masiello, T. (1995). Playing with conflict: A longitudinal study of varieties of spontaneous verbal conflict during mother–child interaction at home. *Social Development, 4,* 92–107.

Haight, W., & Miller, P. J. (1993). *Pretending at Home: Early Development in a Sociocultural Context.* Albany: State University of New York Press.

Haight, W., Parke, R., & Black, J. (1997). Mothers' and fathers' beliefs about and spontaneous participation in their toddlers pretend play. *Merrill-Palmer Quarterly, 42,* 271–290.

Haight, W., Wang, X., Fung, H., Williams, K., & Mintz, J. (1999). Universal, developmental, and variable aspects of young children's play: A cross-cultural comparison of pretending at home. *Child Development, 70,* 1477–1488.

Hale-Benson, J. (1987). The transmission of faith to young black children. Paper presented at the Conference on Faith Development in Early Childhood, Henderson, North Carolina.

Harding, S. (1992). After the neutrality ideal: Science, politics, and "strong objectivity." *Social Research, 59,* 567–587.

Harkness, S., & Super, C. (1996). Introduction. In S. Harkness & C. Super (Eds.), *Parents' Cultural Belief Systems: Their Origins, Expressions, and Consequences*. New York: Guilford.

Heath, S. B. (1983). *Ways with Words: Language, Life, and Work in Communities and Classrooms*. New York: Cambridge University Press.

Heath, S. B. (1995). Ethnography in communities: Learning the everyday life of America's subordinated youth. In J. A. Banks & C. M Banks (Eds.), *Handbook of Research on Multicultural Education*. New York: Macmillan.

Heath, S. B. (1996). Ruling places: Adaptation in development in inner-city youth. In R. Jessor, A. Colby, & R. Shweder (Eds.), *Ethnography and Human Development: Context and Meaning in Social Inquiry*. Chicago: University of Chicago Press.

Hellendoorn, J., van der Kooij, R., & Sutton-Smith, B. (Eds.) (1994). *Play and Intervention*. Albany: State University of New York Press.

Hermans, J. M. (1997). Self-Narrative in the Life Course: A Contextual Approach. In M. Bamberg (Ed.), *Narrative Development: Six Approaches*. Hillsdale, NJ: Lawrence Erlbaum Associates.

Hill-Harris, M. (1998). *Religious Socialization and Educational Attainment among African Americans*. Unpublished master's thesis, California State University: Hayward.

Hill-Lubin, M. A. (1991). The African-American grandmother in autobiographical works by Frederick Douglass, Langston Hughes, and Maya Angelou. *International Journal of Aging and Human Development, 11*, 173–185.

Holden, G. W., & West, M. J. (1989). Proximate regulation by mothers: A demonstration of how differing styles affect young children's behavior. *Child Development, 60*, 64–69.

Hudley, E., Haight, W., & Miller, P. J. (in press). *His Eye Is on the Sparrow: The Life and Childrearing Wisdom of Edith V. P. Hudley*. Chicago: Lyceum Press.

Hurd, E. P., Moore, C., & Rogers, R. (1995). Quiet success: Parenting strengths among African Americans. *Families in Society, 76*, 434–443.

Hymes, D. H. (1982). *Ethnolinguistic study of classroom discourse: Final report to the National Institute of Education*. University of Pennsylvania, Graduate School of Education.

Jessor, R., Colby, A., & Shweder, R. A. (Eds.) (1996). *Ethnography and Human Development: Context and Meaning in Social Inquiry*. Chicago: University of Chicago Press.

Johnson, J. W. (1955). *God's Trombones: Seven Negro Sermons in Verse*. New York: Penguin Books.

Jones, J. H. (1993). *Bad Blood: The Tuskegee Syphilis Experiment*. New York: The Free Press.

Kalbfleisch, P. J., & Davies, A. B. (1991). Minorities and mentoring: Managing the multicultural institution. *Communication Education, 40*, 266–271.

Katz, L., Kramer, L., & Gottman, J. (1992). Conflict and emotions in marital, sibling, and peer relationships. In C. Shantz and W. Hartup (Eds.), *Conflict in Child and Adolescent Development*. New York: Cambridge University Press.

King, J. (1991). Dysconscious racism: Ideology, identity, and the miseducation of teachers. *Journal of Negro Education, 60*, 133–146.

Labov, W., & Waletzky, J. (1967). Narrative analysis: Oral versions of personal experience. In J. Helm (Ed.), *Essays in the Verbal and Visual Arts*, (pp. 12–44). Seattle: University of Washington Press, American Ethnological Society.

Ladson-Billings, G. (1990). Culturally relevant teaching: Effective instruction for black students. *The College Board Review, 155*, 20–25.

Ladson-Billings, G. (1995). Multicultural teacher education: Research, practice, and policy. In J. Banks & C. Banks (Eds.), *Handbook of Research on Multicultural Education*. New York: Simon & Schuster.

Lave, J., & Wenger, E. (1991). *Situated Learning: Legitimate Peripheral Participation*. New York: Cambridge University Press.

Leashore, B. R. (1995). African Americans overview. *Encyclopedia of Social Work*. Washington, D. C.: National Association of Social Workers Press.

Lee, C., & Slaughter-DeFoe, D. (1995). Historical and sociocultural influences on African American education. In J. Banks & C. Banks (Eds.), *Handbook of Research on Multicultural Education*. New York: Macmillan.

Lerner, G. (Ed.) (1972). *Black Woman in White America: A Documentary History*. New York: Vintage Books.

Levine, L. W. (1997). Slave songs and slave consciousness: An exploration in neglected sources. In T. E. Fulop & A. J. Raboteau (Eds.), *African-American Religion: Interpretive Essays in History and Culture*. New York: Routledge.

Levinson, S. (1983). *Pragmatics*. New York: Cambridge University Press.

Lightfoot, C., & Valsiner, J. (1992). Parental belief systems under the influence: Social guidance of the construction of personal cultures. In I. E. Sigel, A. V. McGillicuddy-DeLisi, & J. J. Goodnow (Eds.), *Parental Belief Systems: The Psychological Consequences for Children*. Hillsdale, NJ: Lawrence Erlbaum Associates.

Lincoln, C. E. (1974). *The Black Experience in Religion*. Garden City, NY: Doubleday.

Lincoln, C. E. (1999). *Race, Religion, and the Continuing American Dilemma*. New York: Hill and Wang.

Lincoln, C. E., & Mamiya, L. H. (1990). *The Black Church in the African-American Experience*. Durham, NC: Duke University Press.

Lomotey, K. (Ed.), (1990). *Going to School: The African-American Experience*. Albany: State University of New York Press.

Long, C. H. (1997). Perspectives for a study of African-American religion in the United States. In E. Fulop & A. Raboteau (Eds.), *African-American Religion: Interpretive Essays in History and Culture*. New York: Routledge.

Maluccio, A. (1995). Children: Direct practice. *Encyclopedia of Social Work*. Washington, D. C.: National Association of Social Workers Press.

Markus, G. B., Howard, J. P. F., & King, D. C. (1993). Integrating community service and classroom instruction enhances learning: Results from an experiment. *Educational Evaluation and Policy Analysis, 15*, 410–419.

Martinson, J. (1994). *Wesleyan Ways of Speaking: Transforming Experience through Sunday School Talk*. Unpublished doctoral dissertation, University of Illinois at Urbana-Champaign.

Maston, A. S., Best, K. M., & Garmezy, N. (1991). Resilience and development: Contributions from the study of children who overcome adversity. *Development and Psychopathology, 2*, 425–444.

Mathews, A., & Wright, L. (1994, March 20). Utah's people of color: The east-west wall hasn't fallen in racially divided S. L. Valley. *The Salt Lake Tribune.*

Matthew, P. (1997). *The Concise Dictionary of Linguistics.* Oxford: Oxford University Press.

Maynard, D. (1985). How children start arguments. *Language in Society, 14,* 1–30.

McAdoo, H., & Crawford, V. (1991). The Black church and family support programs. *Prevention in Human Services, 9,* 193–203.

McCabe, A. (1997). Developmental and cross-cultural aspects of children's narration. In M. Bamberg (Ed.), *Narrative Development: Six Approaches.* Hillsdale, NJ: Lawrence Erlbaum Associates.

McMahon, A., & Allen-Meares, P. (1992). Is social work racist? A content analysis of recent literature. *Social Work, 37,* 533–539.

Mehan, H., Lintz, A., Okamoto, D., & Willis, J. (1995). Ethnographic studies of multicultural education in classrooms and schools. In J. Banks & C. Banks (Eds.), *Handbook of Research on Multicultural Education.* New York: Simon and Schuster.

Michaels, S. (1981). "Sharing time": Children 's narrative styles and differential access to literacy. *Language in Society, 10,* 423–442.

Michaels, S. (1984). Listening and responding: Hearing the logic in children's classroom narratives. *Theory into Practice, 23,* 218–224.

Michaels, S. (1985). Hearing the connections in children's oral and written discourse. *Journal of Education, 167,* 36–56.

Michaels, S. (1991). The dismantling of narrative. In A. McCabe & C. Peterson (Eds.), *Developing Narrative Structure.* Hillsdale, NJ: Lawrence Erlbaum Associates.

Miller, P. (1982). *Amy, Wendy and Beth: Language Learning in South Baltimore.* Austin: University of Texas Press.

Miller, P. (1994). Narrative practices: Their role in socialization and self-construction. In U. Neisser & R. Fivush (Eds.), *The Remembering in Self: Construction and Accuracy in the Self-Narrative* (pp. 158–179). New York: Cambridge University Press.

Miller, P. (1999, April). Working-class children's experience in comparative perspective: Challenges and insights from research on personal storytelling. Paper presented at the biennial meeting of the Society for Research in Child Development, Albuquerque, New Mexico.

Miller, P., Fung, H., & Mintz, J. (1996). Self construction through narrative practices: A Chinese and American comparison. *Ethos, 24,* 1– 44.

Miller, P., & Moore. B. (1989). Narrative conjunctions of caregiver and child: A comparative perspective on socialization through stories. *Ethos, 17,* 428–449.

Miller, P., Potts, R., Fung, H., Hoogstra, L., & Mintz, J. (1990). Narrative practices and the social construction of self in childhood. *American Ethnologist, 17,* 292–311.

Miller, P. & Sperry, L. (1987). The socialization of anger and aggression. *Merrill-Palmer Quarterly, 33,* 1–31.

Miller, P., Wiley, A., Fung, H., & Liang, C. (1997). Personal storytelling as a medium of socialization in Chinese and American families, *Child Development, 68,* 557–568.

Mitchell, E. P. (1986). Oral tradition: Legacy of faith for the black church. *Religious Education, 81*, 93–112.

Moore, T. (1991). The African-American church: A source of empowerment, mutual help, and social change. *Prevention in Human Services, 10*, 147–167.

Morgan, K. L. (1989). Caddy Buffers: Legends of a middle-class black family in Philadelphia. In L. Goss & M. E. Barnes (Eds.), *Talk That Talk*. New York: Simon and Schuster/Touchstone.

Moskovitz, S. (1983). *Love Despite Hate: Child Survivors of the Holocaust and Their Adult Lives*. New York: Schocken Books.

Moss, B. (1988). *The Black Sermon as a Literacy Event*. Unpublished doctoral dissertation, University of Illinois, Chicago.

Myers-Lipton, S. (1996). Effect of service-learning on college students' attitudes toward international understanding. *Journal of College Student Development, 37*, 659–667.

Nakoryakov, M. (1994, April 22). Utah population, ethnic diversity to keep climbing through 2020. *The Salt Lake Tribune*.

Neighbors, H. W., Jackson, J. S., Bowman, P. J., & Gurin, G. (1983). Stress, coping, and black male health: Preliminary findings from a national study. *Prevention in Human Services, 2*, 5–29.

Neisser, U., & Fivush, R. (Eds.) (1994). *The Remembering Self: Construction and Accuracy in the Self-Narrative*. New York: Cambridge University Press.

Nelson, K. (Ed.), (1989). *Narratives from the Crib*. Cambridge, MA: Harvard University Press.

Neururer, J., & Rhoads, R. (1998). Community service: Panacea, paradox, or potentiation. *Journal of College Student Development, 39*, 321–330.

Nicolopoulou, A. (1997). Children and narratives: Toward an interpretive and sociocultural approach. In M. Bamberg (Ed.), *Narrative Development: Six Approaches*. Hillsdale, NJ: Lawrence Erlbaum Associates.

Oaks, E. (1988). *Culture and Language Development: Language Acquisition and Language Socialization in a Samoan Village*. New York: Cambridge University Press.

Ochs, E., & Capps, L. (1996). Narrating the self. *Annual Review of Anthropology, 25*, 19–43.

Ochs, E., & Schieffelin, B. (1984). Language acquisition and socialization: Three developmental stories and their implications. In R. Schweder & D. Levine (Eds.), *Culture Theory: Essays on Mind, Self and Emotion*. New York: Cambridge University Press.

Ochs, E., & Taylor, C. (1992). Family narrative as political activity. *Discourse and Society, 3*, 301–340.

O'Connell, B., & Bretherton, I. (1984). Todders' play, alone and with mother: The role of maternal guidance. In I. Bretherton (Ed.), *Symbolic Play: The Development of Social Understanding*. Orlando, FL: Academic Press.

Ogbu, J. U. (1974). *The Next Generation: An Ethnography of Education in an Urban Neighborhood*. New York: Academic Press.

Ogbu, J. U. (1985). A cultural ecology of competence among inner-city blacks. In M. B. Spencer, G. K. Brookins, & W. R. Allen (Eds.), *Beginnings: The Social and Affective Development of Black Children*. Hillsdale, NJ: Lawrence Erlbaum Associates.

Oser, F. (1991). The development of religious judgment. In G. Scarlett & F. Osler (Eds.), Religious Development in Childhood and Adolescence. *New Directions in Child Development, 52,* 5–26.

Patterson, G. R. (1982). *Coercive Family Processes.* Eugene, OR: Castilia.

Peshkin, A. (1986). *God's Choice: The Total World of a Fundamentalist Christian School.* Chicago: University of Chicago Press.

Peshkin, A. (1991). *The Color of Strangers the Color of Friends: The Play of Ethnicity in School and Community.* Chicago: University of Chicago Press.

Philips, S. (1983). *The Invisible Culture: Communication in Classroom and Community on the Warm Springs Indian Reservation.* New York: Longman.

Piaget, J. (1932). *The Moral Judgment of the Child.* London: Routledge & Kegan Paul.

Pinderhughes, E. (1989). *Understanding Race, Ethnicity, and Power: The Key to Efficacy in Clinical Practice.* New York: Free Press.

Polanyi, L. (1985). *Telling the American Story: A Structural and Cultural Analysis of Conversational Storytelling.* Norwood, NJ: Ablex Publishers.

Potts, R. (1989, April). West side stories: Children's conversational narratives in a black community. Paper presented at the biennial meeting of the Society for Research on Child Development, Kansas City, MO.

Potts, R. (1996). Spirituality and the experience of cancer in an African-American community: Implications for psychosocial oncology. *Journal of Psychosocial Oncology, 14,* 1–19.

Preece, A. (1987). The range of narrative forms conversationally produced by young children. *Journal of Child Language, 14,* 353–373.

Reid, W. (1995). Research overview. In R. L. Edwards (Editor-in-Chief), *Encyclopedia of Social Work* (19th ed.). Washington, D.C.: NASW Press.

Rhoads, R. A. (1998). In the service of citizenship. *The Journal of Higher Education, 69,* 277–297.

Rhodes, J. & Davis, A. (1996). Supportive ties between nonparent adults and urban adolescent girls. In B. Leadbeater & N. Way (Eds.), *Urban Girls: Resisting Stereotypes, Creating Identities.* New York: New York University Press.

Riggs, M. Y. (Ed.) (1997). *Can I Get a Witness? Prophetic Religious Voices of African American Women: An Anthology.* New York: Orbis Books.

Rogoff, B. (1990). *Apprenticeship in Thinking: Cognitive Development in Social Context.* New York: Oxford.

Rogoff, B., Mistry, J., Goncu, A., & Mosier, C. (1993). Guided participation in cultural activity by toddlers and caregivers. *Monographs of the Society for Research in Child Development, 51* (183).

Rosengren, K., Johnson, C., & Harris, P. (Eds.) (2000). *Imagining the Impossible: Magical, Scientific, and Religious Thinking in Children.* New York: Cambridge University Press.

Scarlet. P., Stack, P., & Sullivan, L. (1994, February 26). For Utah's Black Christians, there's no one religion. *The Salt Lake Tribune.*

Schiele, J. H. (1996). Afrocentricity: An emerging paradigm in social work practice. *Social Work, 41,* 284–293.

Seaborn-Thompson, M., & Ensminger, M. I. E. (1989). Psychological well-being among mothers with school age children: Evolving family structures. *Social Forces, 67,* 715–730.

Shantz, C. (1987). Conflicts between children. *Child Development, 57,* 283–305.

Sheridan, M. J., Bullis, R. K., Adcock, C. R., Berlin, S. D., & Miller, P. C. (1992). Practitioners' personal and professional attitudes and behaviors toward religion and spirituality: Issues for education and practice. *Journal of Social Work in Education, 28,* 190–203.

Shuman, A. (1986). *Storytelling Rights.* New York: Cambridge University Press.

Shweder, R. A. (1996). Quanta and qualia: What is the "object" of ethnographic method? In R. Jessor, A. Colby, & R. A. Shweder (Eds.), *Ethnography and Human Development: Context and Meaning in Social Inquiry.* Chicago: University of Chicago Press.

Sigel, S. (1998). Practice and research: A problem in developing communication and cooperation. In W. Damon, I. Sigel, & K. Renninger (Eds.), *Handbook of Child Psychology* (5th ed., vol. 4).

Slaughter, D. T., & McWorter, G. A. (1985). Social origins and early features of the scientific study of black American families and children. In M. B. Spencer, G. K. Brookins, & W. R. Allen (Eds.), *Beginnings: The Social and Affective Development of Black Children.* Hillsdale, NJ: Lawrence Erlbaum Associates.

Slesinger, D. (1981). *Mothercraft and Infant Health: A Sociodemographic and Sociocultural Approach.* Lexington, MA: Lexington Books.

Smetana, J., & Gaines, C. (1999). Adolescent-parent conflict in middle-class African American families. *Child Development, 70,* 1447–1463.

Smitherman, G. (1977). *Talkin and Testifyin: The Language of Black America.* Boston: Houghton Mifflin.

Sobel, M. (1988). *Trabelin' On: The Slave Journey to an Afro-Baptist Faith.* Princeton, NJ: Princeton University Press.

Spencer, M. B., Brookins, G. K., & Allen, W. R. (Eds.) (1985), *Beginnings: The Social and Affective Development of Black Children.* Hillsdale, NJ: Lawrence Erlbaum Associates.

Sperry, L. L. (1991). *The Emergence and Development of Narrative Competence in African-American Toddlers from a Rural Alabama Community.* Unpublished doctoral dissertation, University of Chicago, Illinois.

Sperry, L., & Smiley, P. (Eds.) (1995). Exploring young children's concepts of self and other through conversation. *New Directions for Child Development, 69,* San Francisco: Jossey-Bass.

Sperry, L., & Sperry, D. (1996). Early development of narrative skills. *Cognitive Development, 11,* 443–465.

Stack, C. B. (1974). *All Our Kin: Strategies for Survival in a Black Community.* New York: Harper & Row.

Stewart, M. W. (1935). Religion and the pure principles of morality: The sure foundation on which we must build. In H. Gates, Jr. (Ed.), *Spiritual Narratives* (1988). New York: Oxford University Press.

Sue, S., Fujino, D., Hu, L., Takeuchi, D., & Zane, N. (1991). Community mental health services for ethnic minority groups: A test of the cultural responsiveness hypothesis. *Journal of Consulting and Clinical Psychology, 59,* 533–540.

Sullivan, H. S. (1953). *The Interpersonal Theory of Psychiatry*. New York: Norton.

Tatum, B. D. (1992). Talking about race, learning about racism: The application of racial identity development theory in the classroom. *Harvard Educational Review, 62*, 1–24.

Tatum, B. D. (1994). Teaching white students about racism: The search for white allies and the restoration of hope. *Teachers College Record, 95*, 462–476.

Thompson, M., & Ensminger, M. (1989). Psychological well-being among mothers with school-age children: Evolving family structures. *Social Forces, 63*, 715–730.

Thornton, S., & Garrett, K. (1995). Ethnography as a bridge to multicultural practice. *Journal of Social Work Education, 31*, 67–74.

Tierney, J. P., Grossman, J. B., & Resch, N. L. (1995). *Making a Difference: An Impact Study of Big Brothers/Big Sisters*. Philadelphia: Public/Private Ventures.

Tizard, B., & Hughes, M. (1984). *Young Children Learning*. Cambridge, MA: Harvard University Press.

Vandenberg, B. R. (1986). Beyond the ethology of play. In A. W. Gottfried & C. C. Brown (Eds.), *Play Interactions: The Contribution of Play Materials and Parental Involvement to Children's Development*. Lexington, MA: Lexington Books.

Van Soest, D. (1995). Multiculturalism and social work education: The non-debate about competing perspectives. *Journal of Social Work Education, 31*, 55–66.

Vuchinich, S. (1987). Starting and stopping spontaneous family conflicts. *Journal of Marriage and the Family, 49*, 591–601.

Vygotsky, L. S. (1978). *Mind and Society: The Development of Higher Mental Processes*. Cambridge, MA: Harvard University Press.

Wang, X., Goldin-Meadow, S., & Mylander, C. (1995, April). A comparative study of Chinese and American mothers interacting with their deaf and hearing children. Paper presented at the biennial meeting of the Society for Research in Child Development, Indianapolis, IN.

Ward, M. C. (1971). *Them Children: A Study of Language Learning*. Prospect Heights, IL: Wavelength Press.

Wentworth, W. M. (1980). *Context and Understanding: An Inquiry into Socialization Theory*. New York: Elsevier.

Werner, E. E. (1989). High-risk children in young adulthood: A longitudinal study from birth to 32 years. *American Journal of Orthopsychiatry, 59*, 72–81.

White, O. K. (1972). Mormonism's anti-black policy and prospects for change. *Journal of Religious Thought*, Autumn-Winter.

Wiley, A., Rose, A., Burger, L., & Miller, P. (1998). Constructing autonomous selves through narrative practices: A comparative study of working-class and middle-class families, *Child Development, 69*, 833–847.

Williams, K. (1991). Storytelling as a bridge to literacy: An examination of personal storytelling among black middle-class mothers and children. *Journal of Negro Education, 60*, 399–410.

Williams, K. (1994). *The Socialization of Literacy in Black Middle-Class Families*. Unpublished doctoral dissertation, University of Chicago, Illinois.

Wills, D. W. (1997). The central themes of American religious history: Pluralism, puritanism, and the encounter of black and white. In T. Fulop & A. J. Raboteau

(Eds.), *African-American Religion: Interpretive Essays in History and Culture*. New York: Routledge.

Wilson, M. N., Cooke, D. Y., & Arlington, E. G. (1997). African American adolescents and academic achievement: Influences of parents and peers. In R. W. Taylor & M. C. Wang (Eds.), *Social and Emotional Adjustment and Family Relations in Ethnic Minority Families*. Mahwah, NJ: Lawrence Erlbaum Associates.

Wingfield, H. L. (1988). The Church and Blacks in America. *The Western Journal of Black Studies, 12*, 127–134.

Wright, L. (1994, March 27). African Americans: Utah's people of color. *The Salt Lake Tribune*.

Yeh, M., Eastman, K., & Cheung, M. K. (1994). Children and adolescents in community health centers: Does the ethnicity or the language of the therapist matter? *Journal of Community Psychology, 22*, 153–163.

Young, V. H. (1969). Family and childhood in a southern Negro community. *American Anthropologist, 72*, 269–288.

Zimmerman, M. A., & Maton, K. I. (1992). Life-style and substance use among male African-American urban adolescents: A cluster analytic approach. *American Journal of Community Psychology, 20*, 121–138.

Zinsser, C. (1986). For the Bible tells me so: Teaching children in a fundamentalist church. In B. B. Schiefflin & P. Gilmore (Eds.), *The Acquisition of Literacy: Ethnographic Perspectives*. Norwood, NJ: Ablex Publishers.

Index

facts, verifiable, 133, 135, 142
faith
  of Edith Hudley, 181–2
  versus science, 10
  and self-esteem, 26
  in stressful situations, 26
families
  and adversity, 11
  and spirituality, 9
  stories about, 102
famous African-Americans, 147–50
fantasy, 89, 117
figurative speech, 16, 114–16, 124,
  125, 200
First Baptist Church
  adult–child conflict at, 16–17
  author's introduction to, 4
  biblical stories at, 90–1
  as case study, 12
  children at, 13, 86, 200–1
  and Computer Club. *See* Computer
    Club
  and educational achievement, 17
  founded, 53
  general information, 34
  history of, 14
  interviews, 42–3
  as "mother church" of black Bap-
    tists in Utah, 53–4
  outreach program, 57
  personal experience stories at, 93–
    6
  relationship with community, 167
  as research site, 34, 40–3
  and sense of community, 54
  socialization goals of, 33
  use of hypothetical stories, 97–100
First Baptist Church Sunday School,
  34–42
  See also goals; Sunday School
Fitts, Leroy, 26
Foster, Michelle, 101, 106
freedom, 8, 9, 23, 24

Gaines, Cheryl, 142
Garvey, C., 135
Gary, Lawrence, 11, 28

Gates, Henry Louis, 29–30
generalizations used in teaching,
  113–14, 124–5
gifts, 19
goals
  for living, 8
  of Sunday School teachers at First
    Baptist Church, 90, 92, 97
  use of storytelling to accomplish,
    82
God
  equality in eyes of, 26
  and hate, 3, 9
  loves all, 79–80
  as master, 9
  obedience to, 98
  ultimate justice of, 23
Goodnow, Jacqueline, 10
greed, 145–6
guidance, 20

Hale-Benson, Janice, 25
Harris, Paul, 10
hatred, racial, 3, 78, 182
  coping with, 9, 15, 70, 78
Heath, Shirley Brice, 21, 92, 115,
  174, 179, 198
Hill-Lubin, Mildred, 27, 29
historical present, 16, 122–3, 127–8,
  199
Hudley, Edith, 3, 10, 181–2, 184,
  186
humanity, 20
hypothetical narratives, 15–16, 33,
  96–100, 124, 200
  and biblical text, 97
  use by children, 99–100
hypothetical questions, 111

identity, alternative, 22
Ima, Sister (teacher of 12–15-year
  olds), 36–7, 40, 66–8
  on application of biblical concepts
    to everyday life, 82
  on call-and-response sequences,
    108
  goals of, 81

Moskovitz, Sarah, 26
motivation, 8, 71, 74, 85
multicultural education, of European-
    Americans, 72, 85, 177, 189
music, 120, 126–7, 156
myths, childhood, 10

narratives, 15, 86–104, 200
    linking with everyday life, 111–23
    and music, 120
    participation in, 30, 106–11
    and socialization, 29, 105
    topics of, 88
    See also storytelling
National and Community Service,
    178
National Association for the Advance-
    ment of Colored People
    (NAACP), 53
National Baptist Congress of
    Christian Education, 57
National Baptist Convention, U.S.A.,
    Inc.
    and Christian education, 24
    Foreign Mission Preaching Team,
        57
    Intermountain General Baptist As-
        sociation, 58
    lesson commentaries, 68
    "Nationals" annual meeting, 64
    Sunday School Board, 38, 39
National Baptist Western Regional
    Youth Conference, 58
nonserious options, 136, 139

obedience, 23, 98
Ogbu, John, 11
Ogden, Utah, 52, 53
Okamoto, D., 105
oppositional speech, 130
oral tradition, 29, 30
    See also narratives; storytelling

parenting, effects of church involve-
    ment on, 28–9
participation
    active, 107–8

of children, 19, 20–1, 30, 33, 86,
    124, 198–200
definition of, 107–8
in narratives, 106–11
through storytelling, 105–28
pastors, roles of, 34
Patrice, Sister (teacher of 6–8-year
    olds), 36, 63–5
childhood, 76
on children's development as
    Christians, 78
on importance of listening, 75–6
teaching style of, 199
teaching techniques of, 64, 104,
    114
Patterson, Gerald, 136
personal experiences, 91–6, 200
    and biblical concepts, 15, 82–3,
        93
    in European-American com-
        munities, 92
    and fantasy stories, 89
    and research strategy, 33
    significance of to socialization, 92
playful conflict, 68, 135–41
Polanyi, Livia, 112
positive functioning, 28
poverty, 7, 54
prayer
    as coping strategy, 28
    example of use, 95
    and socialization, 7
prejudice, racial, 70, 78, 79–80,
    177
    by blacks toward whites, 72
prevention strategies, 30–1
pride
    in community, 63
    personal, 154
priesthood, in the Mormon com-
    munity, 56–7
privacy, 102
Prosser, Gabriel, 23
protagonists
    children as, 16, 102
    teachers as, 15
protective factors

centrality of, 33
and child development, 29–30
children's participation in, 7, 14,
    16, 200
as context for socialization, 82–4,
    85
frequency of, 103
identification with characters, 90
initiation of, 106–7
and resilience, 13
and socialization, 86, 105–28
and spiritual beliefs, 86
spiritual development through,
    29–30
and Sunday School goals, 15
See also narratives
strategies for living, 8
strength, community as source of, 67
stress, coping with, 7, 8–9, 26, 27–8
students (university), 172–91
    and cross-race relationships, 173–
        5
    and diversity, 175–7
    responses to service-learning, 182–
        3
submission, 23
Sunday School
    for adults, 125, 126
    and children's socialization, 7, 11–
        12
    and emergence of children's spir-
        itual belief systems, 7
    goals of, 15, 75, 77–8, 80–1
    importance of stories in, 88
    and literacy development, 21
    narrative practices in, 15
    practices and beliefs associated
        with, 13
    and resilience, 13
    role of, 80–2
    routine practices in, 16
    storytelling in, 33
support, 60, 195
survival, 24

Tatum, Beverly, 179, 183, 187, 190
teachers

African-American, 4–5
public school, 71–2
and storytelling, 13, 16, 83
Sunday School, 13, 14, 60–8 (*see
    also* names of individual
    teachers)
teasing, 17, 62, 66, 136, 141, 154
texts, Sunday School, 80–1
theology, 24–6, 128, 197
tithing, 150–2
tokenism, 54
touching, 60
traditions, 9
Trinity African Methodist Episcopal
    Church, 53
Turner, Nat, 23

Underground Railroad, 23
underground settings (for worship),
    24
unemployment, 54
Utah, 51–8
Utah, University of, service-learning
    at, 177–88

Vacation Bible School, 157–8
value, children's sense of, 63, 69
values, 27
verbal conflict, 16–17, 18, 129–43,
    199, 200
    children's participation in, 7, 14,
        200
    frequency of, 130–1
    initiation of, 17, 131–2, 141, 142
    playful, 68, 135–41
    regarding verifiable facts, 133,
        135, 142
    topics of, 132–5, 142
verbal play, 62, 64, 66, 68, 154
videos, 158
visionary experiences, 22
voting restrictions, 24
vulnerability, 31
Vygotsky, Lev, 115

Ward, Martha, 21
"War of Heaven," 56

Washington, Booker T., 57
Ways with Words, 179
Werner, Emmy, 26, 30–1
Wiley, Angela, 28
Williams, Kimberley, 21, 29
Willis, J., 105
women
    interest in children, 77

spirituality of, 9
written text, 64

Young, Brigham, 51
Youth Emphasis Day, 154
youth programs, 19

Zinsser, Caroline, 92, 123